T0386569

ROBERT KUOK

a memoir

First impression November 2017
Second impression December 2017
Third impression December 2017
Fourth impression February 2018
Fifth impression April 2018
Sixth impression August 2018

Published by
Landmark Books Pte Ltd
5001 Beach Road
#02-73/74
Singapore 199588

Landmark Books is an imprint of
Landmark Books Pte Ltd

ISBN 978-981-4189-73-6
Printed in Malaysia

ROBERT KUOK

a memoir

with
ANDREW TANZER

◇LANDM△RK◇BOOKS◇

To my late mother, Tang Kak Ji
The true founder of the Kuok Group of Companies

and

To my brother, William
A great human being who died too young

CONTENTS

FOREWORD

This is the story of a remarkable man with an extraordinary sense of time and place.

Robert Kuok is well known as a highly successful businessman, making his name in commodities before turning to shipping, logistics, property and hotels. In this deeply personal and revealing memoir, he tells us what made him the man he is.

Born into the minority Fuzhou community in colonial Malaya, experiencing the Japanese Occupation during his youth, promoting the economic transformation of a newly independent Malaysia as a young man, and throwing heart and soul into the rejuvenation of his ancestral homeland in the Deng Xiaoping era and beyond, Robert Kuok has moved seamlessly across cultures and through momentous change.

His upbringing brought him face to face with the very best and the very worst of human nature, and gave him an uncanny ability to draw from the best and shun the rest.

He is equally at home in the back streets of Johor Bahru and the high streets of London; the boardrooms of Hong Kong and the corridors of power in Beijing. He is at once a Confucian sage and an English gentleman; a canny trader and a hard-nosed negotiator. He is a strict taskmaster, yet generous to a fault.

His keen sense of identity and values come to him through his beloved mother. She sacrificed everything for her sons; he was devoted to her throughout her life.

Robert Kuok's memoir is at times inspirational, at times uproarious and at times heartbreaking. It is the story of a man whom I count among my very best and most loyal of friends.

David K P Li
Chairman and Chief Executive
The Bank of East Asia, Limited

PREFACE

This book, the memoir of Robert Kuok, is written first and foremost as a tribute to Robert's mother, Tang Kak Ji, and brother William, an idealist who perished young fighting for his beliefs. Robert tells the story of how he built the Kuok Group, an Asian-based global enterprise that employs hundreds of thousands of workers, but in a sense his mother is the true wellspring of the Kuok Group. A virtuous woman of high principles, she imbued Robert with a set of very fine values, including modesty, humility, integrity, loyalty, morality, discipline. The strong influence of his late mother shines through in Robert's telling of how he has conducted business and his own life.

This memoir can be read and enjoyed by anybody. It contains the colourful (but sometimes tragic) family history. Robert's parents emigrated from China to British Malaya, where Robert was born. His father seeded the family business but died suddenly without a will. The bulk of the book is a fascinating account, filled with business and management insights, of how Robert built the multi-industry and multinational Kuok Group from 1949 into what it is today.

Although Robert was born and bred in Malaysia, he never forgot his Chinese roots. He has conducted business with China since the 1950s, and when the country, emerging from the self-imposed isolation of the Cultural Revolution, opened its doors to foreign investors, Robert was one of the first Overseas Chinese to respond to China's call.

A student of history, culture, or sociology is also in for a treat. Robert's formal education in an elite British colonial college abruptly came to an end in December 1941 when Japanese bombs began raining down on Singapore. But he is blessed with a prodigious memory, keen powers of observation and analysis, acute instincts, broad interests and a powerful curiosity that enables him to soak up knowledge. As a result, the reader will learn much about living under British colonialism, the Chinese diaspora in Southeast Asia, life under the brutal boot of Japanese occupation during World War II, post-colonial Southeast Asia, and the rise of Asian economies and China.

Multilingual, multicultural and almost culturally like a chameleon, Robert has conducted business around the globe. This book is peppered with observations and insights into different cultures and peoples; and with experiences, some of them humorous and even comical, of conducting business with people of different nationalities.

If not in the shadows, Robert Kuok has at least stayed out of the limelight during his long and prolific business career. We feel privileged to have been able to work with him in preparing this memoir, thus sharing his fascinating life with the public. To us, Robert has lived up to the wisdom and fine principles passed on from his mother. Peering down from the heavens, she would be proud of her son.

Andrew Tanzer
McLean, Virginia

Kay Kuok
Singapore

September 2017

ACKNOWLEDGEMENTS

Writing and publishing my memoir has been a long journey on which I embarked in 2002 and finished in 2017. I needed help, and along the way I was greatly aided by a number of friends, staff, and family members.

I would first like to extend special thanks to Andrew Tanzer, my comrade-in-letters for this project. Shortly after meeting Andrew, then an American business-magazine journalist long-resident in Asia, I felt that he was just the man to record my reminiscences and help me to craft a book. Drawing on his knowledge and grasp of Asia, reportorial and interviewing skills, he teased out my stories over many months of sessions and did not disappoint in producing the manuscript.

For the Chinese edition, I am indebted to Maggie Tsai for her stellar work in translating the English manuscript into Chinese. My lovely niece, Kay Kuok, served as a kind of Chief of Staff on this project, liaising with Andrew over many years, pushing the manuscript forward and helping to publish this book.

I am extremely grateful for the painstaking help from my longtime, redoubtable assistant, Miranda Wong, who burned the midnight oil to transcribe Andrew's interview transcripts. Two of my able staff members, Stella Fung and Juliana Tsoi, assisted with the Chinese translation, as did a dear friend Chen Yu-Hwei (Mrs. Glen Cheng). Wong Siu Kong and Kwok Ping Leong both read and commented on the Chinese version.

To help update the memoir prior to publication, Andrew's brother Jeff Tanzer did some work on the manuscript; Andrew Burns, introduced by my good friend David Li, Chairman of Bank of East Asia, provided valuable editing; Helen Wong of Kerry Holdings transcribed yet more hours of taped interviews; and my third daughter, Ruth, helped me to edit some content added at the 11th hour.

Finally, I would like to express my gratitude to Goh Eck Kheng, the publisher of the English edition of this book, for taking on the project and guiding me in the unfamiliar world of book publishing.

CHRONOLOGY

HISTORICAL BACKGROUND		FAMILY & BUSINESS
	1893	Kuok Keng Kang (Father) born in Fuzhou, China
	1900	Tang Kak Ji (Mother) born in Fuzhou, China
	1909	Kuok Keng Kang immigrates to Singapore
Qing Dynasty ends; Republic of China born	1912	
	1920	Tang Kak Ji immigrates to Malaya; weds Kuok Keng Kang
	1921	Kuok Hock Khee (Philip) born in Johor Bahru, Malaya
	1922	Kuok Hock Ling (William) born in Johor Bahru, Malaya
	1923	Kuok Hock Nien (Robert) born in Johor Bahru, Malaya
Great Depression begins	1929	
Japan declares war on China	1937	
Japan attacks Pearl Harbour, invades Malaya	1941	
Japan surrenders, ending Pacific War	1945	

	1947	Robert Kuok marries Joyce Margaret Cheah
	1948	William Kuok, member of Malayan Communist Party, goes into jungle
		Kuok Keng Kang dies
Mao Zedong establishes People's Republic of China	1949	Robert Kuok and Kuok family members establish Kuok Brothers Ltd.
	1953	William Kuok killed in Malayan jungle by British forces
Malaysia gains independence	1957	
	1963	Robert Kuok makes first fortune on London sugar market
	1964	Malayan Sugar Manufacturing starts production in Prai, Malaysia
Singapore becomes independent from Malaysia	1965	
General Suharto takes power in Indonesia	1966	Federal Flour Mills begins milling in Port Klang, Malaysia
		Philip Kuok leaves Kuok Group to become Malaysian ambassador to the Benelux countries
Racial riots in Malaysia	1969	
	1971	Shangri-La Singapore opens
		Bogasari Flour Mill starts production in Indonesia
Deng Xiaoping takes power in China, launches Open-Door Policy	1978	

Mahathir Mohamad becomes Prime Minister of Malaysia	1981	
	1983	Joyce Kuok dies of cancer
	1984	Signing of China World Trade Center agreement in Beijing
	1993	Kerry Holdings buys controlling interest in *South China Morning Post*
	1995	Tang Kak Ji dies
Hong Kong returns to China	1997	Robert Kuok retires
Asian financial crisis begins		
	2003	Robert Kuok returns from retirement
Xi Jinping named new Chinese leader	2012	

PART I
–
JOHOR BAHRU

1
MOULDED BY MOTHER

MY EARLIEST MEMORY is of crying and feeling very heartbroken. I ran into the darkest corner and fell asleep. It was 1925. I was one and one-half years old. Mother had left my brother, William, and me and taken my eldest brother, Philip, with her to China. Instinctively, we felt she wasn't coming back.

Father had abused Mother virtually from the day they were married in 1920. After an arranged marriage, she learned all sorts of awful things about Father. He womanized even in the first few years of marriage. He smoked opium and gambled. Sometimes, he would disappear for two or three days. She had had enough of her husband. So she went back to Fuzhou and made up her mind never to return to Malaya again.

Mother left us in Johor Bahru with a governess from Fuzhou, whom I always called Ah Poh. I still have a picture in my mind of William and me crawling under tables and tall chairs, curling up into balls and falling asleep, as if those were the only places where we could find security. I felt forlorn, abandoned and miserable, though the presence and love of Ah Poh, who was particularly attached to me, managed to stabilize that dark period in my life.

Ah Poh was illiterate, so she asked people to write letters to Mother on her behalf. She wrote, "Madame, you must come back! Your two children are pining for you!" Then, one day, after an absence of one and a half years, Mother returned from China.

My father, Kuok Keng Kang, was born in Fuzhou in December 1893, the Year of the Snake. He was the youngest of six brothers and lost his parents when he was five or six years old. His father was a second son who, under the law of primogeniture, lost out to his eldest brother. The way it went in feudal China, the bulk of the rice fields and other family properties always passed to the eldest son. The others just got a pittance.

The brothers' families lived and ate communally. The eldest brother favoured his own sons and discriminated against my father very badly. When the harvest was bad and there was not enough food on the table, his eldest brother would make sure his own children had larger portions of food and extra bowls of rice. Father was bullied by his brother in other ways. So Father grew up abused and deprived.

Southeast Asia provided an escape. The first to go south was my fourth uncle. He sailed to Singapore in 1906 or 1907 at the age of 17 or so and soon landed a job as a clerk in a Chinese shop. Within two or three years, he became one of the favourite employees of the proprietor. This shop operated as a middleman that received produce from the hinterland, graded and packed it, and then supplied the local British hongs such as Boustead, Guthrie, and Harrison & Crosfield.

Letters were conveyed by boat, taking four or more weeks to travel from Fuzhou to Fourth Uncle in Singapore. Gradually, it came to his ears that his youngest brother, my father, was still being bullied. He arranged for Father to be put on a boat to Singapore. I think the year must have been about 1909. So Father was the second emigrant among his brothers. We think he was about 15 years old when he arrived, scrawny, underfed, and underweight.

Father had, at most, one or two years of middle school education. He could write simply, read newspapers and letters. He was not erudite, but he was good with numbers and very shrewd, with a tremendous personality and way with people. When Father arrived in Singapore, he worked together with his fourth elder brother in the Chinese businessman's shop. Father was even smarter and more precocious than his brother, obedient and hard-working. He soon became the boss's favourite.

I heard Father say that for the first several months he wasn't paid a salary. He was the first to serve, the last to eat; the first to wake up, the last to go to bed. (They all slept in the shop). Finally, the boss said to him, "Ahh, you have worked very hard. Here are three cents." Father had a haircut with one cent, bought himself a new pair of clogs with the second cent and a new singlet with the third.

After several years, the two brothers had saved enough money to strike out on their own. As natives of Fuzhou in central Fujian, the administrative centre of the province, they were regarded as rather timid and cautious people – not as adventurous or business-minded as the southern Fujianese of Quanzhou or Xiamen. Instead of trying to compete in Singapore, they decided to venture across the crocodile-infested Straits of Johor by sampan and set up shop in Johor Bahru. This was some time during the First World War. Malaya produced spices that were in great demand. Prices shot up, they made money, and, by 1919 or 1920, Father and his brother were wealthy.

My mother, Tang Kak Ji, was born in December 1900, the Year of the Rat. Mother's family was much better off than Father's. She came from a small landlord family of Fuzhou that also owned properties in Shandong in northern China. Mother was the favourite of her father, who was scholarly and dabbled in Chinese herbal medicine. He was a very kind and well-educated man, a wise father who showed his daughter a great deal of affection. So, unlike

Father, she grew up surrounded by warmth and love.

Fuzhou was a customs treaty port of the British, and Mother grew up very anti-imperialist and anti-colonialist. Four British firms were present in Fuzhou: British American Tobacco, Jardines, Butterfield & Swire, and Brockett – the last, a small firm owned by a Newcastle Englishman who was the maternal grandfather of Joyce Cheah, my late first wife, and Eileen Cheah, my eldest brother Philip's late wife.

One day, when Mother's father was away on one of his rent-collecting trips up north, her mother brought in foot-binders to bind her feet. Luckily, within a few days of this, her father returned. On seeing what had happened to his beloved daughter, he cuffed his wife and said, "You stupid woman!" He took a pair of scissors and cut off the binding. Mother's feet ached for quite a few weeks, but they were not deformed.

Tang Kak Ji had an incisive mind of her own, and applied herself as a student and enrolled in a women's college in Fuzhou – this in an era when very few women in China attended college. Her mother had a younger brother who befriended my father's second brother after a kungfu bout.

One day, my second uncle boasted to Mother's uncle, "I've just received a letter from my youngest brother. He is doing so well in the South Seas."

To which Mother's uncle replied, "Ahh, I have the most intelligent, beautiful niece, who is studying in college. Why not let's make a match?"

So, Mother was plucked out of school to marry a complete stranger who had made good in the South Seas. She did not like leaving China one bit, nor quitting college without completing her studies. But she had to obey orders. In those days, nearly all marriages in China were arranged. She was brought up traditionally, which meant that her father's word was law.

He just told his daughter: "I've found a suitor for you, your opposite number in life. I've checked up, and from all accounts he's the right man for you. Give up your studies and go out and marry him." Mother loved her father very dearly. So, in 1920, at age 19, she sailed from Fuzhou to Singapore to marry Father according to Chinese rites.

Father and Mother were not well-suited to each other. Like almost all successful Chinese businessmen of the day, her new husband smoked opium, gambled and kept mistresses. By about 1921, he had amassed a fortune of some 500,000 Malayan dollars. He seemed to feel that, as he had started from the lowest rung of society, he had conquered the world and was entitled to all the pleasures that life offered.

Born into a very traditional society, Father expected a docile and submissive wife whose role in life was to serve his needs. That he did not get. Mother had modern ideas. She was a highly refined and educated woman. So there was a clash of wills from the start. Yet, it was a very one-sided marriage, and Mother was the one who suffered.

I have many fond early memories of my mother and my governess, Ah Poh. But Father neglected his three boys. We hardly saw him and he barely spoke with us. Naturally, my two older brothers and I grew up loving Mother more.

As Philip and William were closer and shared more thoughts and had discussions with each other, I felt like the odd boy out. They had already established a strong bond when I came on the scene. We were each 14-15 months apart: Philip was born in May 1921, William in July 1922, and I in early October 1923. Because they were older and because I was built very slight and small, they could do things physically that I couldn't do. So I felt more and more isolated.

As a result, I clung to Mother. She noticed it and started taking me on virtually every outing to visit her friends or relatives. I became very close to her because of that. They would sit and natter for one or two hours, and I would lie in Mother's lap, with the drone of their talk lulling me to sleep. This happened quite often, hence my ability to recall those moments. Consciously and through my subconscious, I was listening to the conversations of the grown-ups. I think because of that, more than for any other reason, I became the most streetwise of the three Kuok boys as we grew up.

I always felt that Father was very prejudiced against me. He thought I was selfish and self-centred. A plate of chicken would be placed on the communal dining table. I'd spot a good piece of meat, pick up my chopsticks, reach out for it and Father would glare and bark, "Don't!" Once or twice I had to leave the table hungry.

From a young age, I had a calculating mind. I was precocious and an extrovert. I would sing and dance; I liked to perform. One day, at about the age of five, I was singing something very innocent about Father's company, Tong Seng & Co. Suddenly, he came charging from his bedroom and slapped me across the face. I felt very unfairly treated. What had I done wrong?

Growing up, I felt ignored by most of the people around me, especially by Father and his third brother. Philip, being the eldest, was the spoilt one, both by Father and by Third Uncle.

I remember Third Uncle would take a few coins from the wooden cash box, walk a few paces across a narrow lane to a tiny Indian stall, and buy a bar of Nestlé's chocolate. Then, he would take Philip by the hand to a corner, hand him the chocolate and say, "Have this, and don't share it with your brothers." This got me very angry. To this day, I resent that image of Third Uncle for being mean.

But such meanness can incite you to achieve great things. I take insults – insults to my physical being, to my mental being, to my pride

– very deeply. I can't shake them off! I bear these insults to my sense of fair play and justice to this day. It's almost an inextinguishable flame, which is why I make a very bad enemy. I just felt: "I want to show you. I will show you." From early on, I developed this strong anger which, in many ways, propelled me forward in life.

Even at a very young age, we could sometimes sense enormous tension at home. When Father and Mother came back from trips to Singapore together, they would go into their bedroom, slam the door, and quarrel.

I recall one harrowing episode recounted by Mother to us, her three sons. While she and Father were returning from Singapore to Johor Bahru in their chauffeur-driven car, they got into a fight. Along the winding road, Father opened the door and tried to push Mother out. The Malay driver, upon seeing what was happening through the rear mirror, shouted, "Towkay [boss], don't do it, don't do it! It's very dangerous, very dangerous!" Cars in those days were built with all kinds of things to hang onto, so Mother managed to cling on and prevented Father from throwing her out of the car. The men of those days regarded women as private chattels, like movable furniture that they could trade or throw away as they saw fit.

Father cared about no one except himself. Good years in business had brought decadence into his soul. He led a life of total escapism. A few times a month, he would disappear to Singapore and not return for several days and nights. He had mahjong chums there, and would gamble and what-not, and come home totally spent. As a good wife, Mother would make special double-boiled nutritious soups for him.

Father managed to kick his opium habit in 1928. He didn't set out to break it; his Malay friends broke it for him. They lured him onto a slow boat to England, and only after he had boarded the vessel did he realize that he had no access to his opium and pipe.

He later told Mother that on three or four occasions he considered throwing himself overboard because the withdrawal symptoms were so punishing.

But I should point out that Father had a good side too. He could endear himself to any new person he met. He had a very winning way about him. Ten out of ten Malays adored him. He saw the Malays as the gentlemen of the region, while to him the Johor Chinese were not so much gentlemen but a mercenary, calculating, treacherous crowd.

In business, he was shrewd and a cut above his peers. He had a naturally intuitive mind, and possessed a great deal of native wisdom and business sense – the DNA of the Han Chinese. By and large, most Chinese are good at reading people. So long as man lives on earth, he is basically an animal, and in the animal world you have to sniff out your opponent. Father had just that little edge over others. He could size people up very quickly. I remember him judging Indians, too, which is difficult for Chinese. He had come up in life the hard way and was very streetwise.

Odd as it may sound, he was in many ways a moral man. No doubt, he was unfaithful to his wife. But to the Chinese businessmen of his generation, that was not an act of immorality. In conducting business, he appeared to us to be very gentlemanly. He was generous to friends. He excelled at winning the hearts and friendship of the people he dealt with in government, especially the Malay civil servants. I don't recall Father ever engaging in any kind of mean talk or sinister plotting against competitors. I appreciated his business morals, but I couldn't reconcile this aspect of him with the way he treated me personally.

Father spoke good bazaar Malay, but he didn't speak English; neither did Mother. He felt greatly handicapped in business because of his lack of English. He saw that Malaya, particularly the economy, would remain very strongly British. You would not get very far unless you had a good command of the English language. So he sent his three sons to the same English school – the Convent Girls' School.

The school's Irish nuns asked us to acquire English names. Since father didn't know any English, he asked his only English-speaking clerk to select names for us. This man had studied some history. So the clerk said, "Okay, let's call Hock Khee 'Philip', after King Philip of Spain. Let's call Hock Ling 'William', after William the Conqueror. And let's call Hock Nien 'Robert', for Robert the Bruce of Scotland." So we were called by those names from early primary school.

I have unhappy memories of the aggressive Catholicism in Convent Girls' School. You weren't to be superstitious, yet, when there was thunder and lightning, the nuns shouted, "Quickly, get down on your knees and pray the 'Hail Mary'!" Is that not superstition? Then, the senior nun, in very strong language, had the nerve to berate the Chinese boys for being seen with their mothers worshipping idols in "ugly pagan temples".

I must put Father's behaviour towards his family in the context of his business. By about 1928, when I was only four, he had fallen on hard times. He then suffered about 10 years of difficult business conditions right through the Great Depression. His profits were poor in most years, and at times cash was extremely tight. He must have been a very frustrated man during the Depression; perhaps this partially explained his ugly behaviour towards Mother.

He had a good run in business from 1917 to 1922 and made close to $500,000, which was a sizeable fortune in those days. I would estimate that less than 1,000 Chinese families throughout the length and breadth of the Malay Peninsula and Singapore had that kind of money. So he was a wealthy man by any standard.

One of his best businesses was serving as a government contractor under the English colonial system. One of the contracts that his Tong Seng & Co held was to provide supplies to hospitals and prisons. He also produced charcoal in mangrove areas using slow-burning fires, and he started the first cold-storage business in Johor Bahru. He would start a business, lose money, close it and start another. That would make money for a while, and then the cycle would repeat.

Around the time that I was born in 1923, my fourth uncle, who was by then a very sick man, left to go home to China. Father was the main achiever in the business, but the two brothers ran Tong Seng & Co as partners. Fourth Uncle called Father and said, "I want to go home for treatment. If I'm cured, I'll of course come out again. Please reduce all our assets to cash and let me take it back. I'll buy properties and erect new homes in our joint names in China." He never came back and he did not keep his promises to his youngest brother.

Having all the cash suddenly siphoned out of a company is like draining all the blood from the body. Mother was never given sufficient money to run the home – and sometimes none at all. For years, she had to scrape by day-to-day. When business was particularly bad, Father would come back from the shop on Jalan Trus (there were two shops, one on Jalan Trus and the other on Jalan Ibrahim, where I was born) and have a long, evening talk with her. I recall times when she pawned her simple gold ornaments and handed the proceeds over to Father.

My two brothers and I could sense that there was never enough money, and that Mother had to be very careful in spending every cent to get the most mileage out of it. So we bathed and shampooed our hair with laundry soap and, as a result, broke out in sores from time to time. If a servant at home broke a dish, even Mother, who was so well educated and cultivated, would sometimes raise her voice in great anger.

As children, we often considered the food on the table wanting, and we sometimes clamoured for better. Mother would strongly admonish us and say, "You are lucky to have food to eat! There are many families, even in this town, who are going without three square meals a day." My physique suffered from the lack of meat, and I grew up very thin and scrawny. I remember, when I was 16 and studying in my O-level year, I weighed just 84 pounds (38 kilograms). I was the second smallest in the class of 30 students.

Mother was reduced to making our inner shorts from calico wheat-flour bags printed with brands like Anchor or Blue Key. I felt very ashamed to be seen by other students when I had to take off my outer pants in the locker room for sports day.

However, many of my Chinese classmates were much worse off. When I was 16 years old and about to matriculate to college, I learned from a classmate who had been with me for five years, who always looked neat and tidy, that he walked miles to and from school every day in the humidity of equatorial Malaya. He told me that a friend gave him an orange one day. He had never eaten one before, and he treasured it so much he ate it, rind and all.

Through the bad times, Father kept up the pretence of wealth by insisting on keeping a motorcar. Every time I got in the car to go to school, there would be a 20-30 percent chance of the tire going flat or the gasoline running out. So, we often had to walk the rest of the way. We were only acting like the sons of a rich towkay.

I have indelible memories of the Depression years. There were rubber plantations from Johor up to the Thai border. Rubber was the backbone of the Malayan economy. As a young man, I drove out of Johor Bahru to the villages of Skudai and Kulai, just 10 and 20 miles away, which depended on the rubber industry. They looked like ghost towns. The people were dehydrated and semi-starving. At eleven in the morning, the streets were deserted, the shops shuttered. The only creatures you saw on the streets were mangy dogs.

As a boy, I witnessed Indian moneylenders who came knocking at Father's door. From about 1926 to 1941, Father was almost always short of cash. He borrowed money to start new businesses, only to see them fail. The tide of the Depression was against him, but he didn't realize it. He did not have enough education to sense that the tide was coming to drown him, and that he should take evasive measures and run to high ground like some of the wealthier, better-educated businessmen of Singapore, Penang and Malacca.

So he resorted to borrowing from Chettiars, a money-lending class of southern Indians especially from the city of Madras in the province of Tamil Nadhu who operated the length and breadth of the Malay Peninsula. Their shops were unusual. While most shop fronts were built on ground level, the Chettiar's shop floor was raised about two feet (half a meter). When you entered, you removed your slippers or shoes and walked barefoot onto the platform. Clad in their typical dhoti, they all sat on the floor in front of little desks. The interest rate the Chettiars charged on unsecured loans was around 14 percent per annum, and if you borrowed $10,000 they would probably extend you only $9,500 due to front-end fees.

When I was ten or eleven, I remember the Chettiars sending their debt collectors to hound Father, but in a gentle way. It was almost funny to see. Our house had two doors. There was Jalan Ibrahim, the main street in front. The street behind was Jalan Tan Hiok Nee, named after an early wealthy Chinese merchant. The Chettiar's office was further down Jalan Tan Hiok Nee, so the collector would appear at our rear door, at about ten-thirty or eleven in the morning.

He'd knock. We had been trained by Father to say, "Father's not at home."

They would speak in Malay: "*Mana towkay, mana towkay?* (Where is the proprietor? Where is the proprietor?)."

So we would say "*Towkay* has gone out."

And the man would shake his head, "*Saya tahu, saya tahu* ('I know, I know')." He would smile to himself, but not budge an inch. He would hang around for two or three hours on the pavement outside our door. If Father had to leave the house he'd sneak out the front door. I thought to myself: how miserable that we had to lie.

By about 1936, Father had fallen in love with a young woman, so whatever cash he could squeeze out of his remaining few operations he would spend on his new love. By 1938, his first child by his second wife, my half-sister, was born. Then very quickly came other children, another daughter and three sons. He lived with his second wife.

One day, when I was around 14 years old, there was a big uproar in our house. In tidying up the home, Mother had opened Father's very smart cowhide briefcase, which he had bought on his 1928 trip to London. In it, she found letters in Chinese carelessly kept by Father – letters written in a woman's hand. She was shocked by what they said, "You promised to send your so-called wife and so-called children back to Fuzhou, because you claimed that you did not marry her officially. You promised that you would take me to a registry to solemnize our wedding. So why haven't you kept your promises?"

Mother was enraged. Big rows took place and from then on there was hardly any peace at home. Mother was heartbroken upon learning that father was keeping a second wife, who, by that time, was already pregnant. More and more, Mother's sufferings propelled her toward Buddhism. She began to lead a very ascetic life and eventually became a vegetarian.

My brothers and I owe our upbringing completely to Mother. She laid down key principles: Be faithful, have gratitude and — one of the most important ones — never boast. She was in my mind the epitome of a refined person. She believed that nobody should flaunt wisdom, success and wealth. She always said, "Don't boast. Never talk big." You never heard Mother saying one word of praise about herself or her children. Yet, she was not overly self-deprecating to the point of inverted snobbery either. She was just very, very refined. While some mothers coo like doves over their children, swooning over their children's little antics, Mother was exactly the opposite. She felt that any such behaviour by a parent would only result in the child growing up very spoilt.

As Mother had attended good schools in Fuzhou, she was steeped in what the Chinese call *rujiao* — the teachings of Confucius and Mencius. She imparted to us a very typical, Chinese cultured-family upbringing. *Rujiao* teaches a person the correct behaviour for life on earth. Mother, gently and sometimes not so gently, drummed into her three boys the values of honesty, and of never cheating, lying, stealing or envying other people their material wealth or physical attributes.

Through words and through example, she laid strong foundations in our minds and in our psyches of how to live our lives, how to differentiate between good and evil, and even how to comport ourselves during adulthood. She taught us humility, modesty and to seek the shadows, as opposed to a high profile and the strong glare of the limelight. Mother herself was a perfect example of everything she preached. And so it was, that minute-by-minute, hour-by-hour, day-by-day, we were imbued with the great strength of character of this wonderful human being. Her influence on me is very deep and lasting.

There was happiness with Mother although she had more than her fair share of worries. I have already described how Father was often so uncaring that he did not leave Mother enough money to buy fresh food for the family. On many occasions, he also didn't leave any for food for the workers in his two shops. Most of them were rough coolies who wore just short pants down to their knees. When a truckload of rice came, they would hump the 220-pound (100 kilograms) bags of rice on their shoulders, walk up a little gangplank to the shop and stack the bags 12-14 high. These were people who needed a lot of energy to do their work. So the shop manager would call and say to mother, "There's no cash in the shop to buy vegetables or meat for today. The cook is here, but there's no food." Then Mother would somehow scrounge, find the money and make sure they got it first, because she knew her priorities very well. These were hard-working people, paid almost slave wages, who needed the food.

With what little money was left behind, she would buy food for us. She would admonish us, "Please finish every grain of rice in your bowl. Do not forget that each grain represents one drop of a farmer's blood." And she would see to it that we did indeed finish every grain.

Even when she had those big rows with Father, she would always remind us that the quarrels were that of husband and wife, and that filial piety should on no account be impaired. In other words, your relationship is that of son to father, and filial piety is always filial piety. She was such an intelligent, caring person that Father's Jalan Trus shop employees always came running to her with business or personal problems. She displayed great leadership qualities right through to her death in 1995.

Mother made us do much of the housework. She would say, "Do you think you're going to grow up as squires, as a rich man's sons?

Even if your father were rich, I would not allow it. Don't expect the house to be run by the servants!" Once a week, we had to wipe the mahogany chairs and tables, some of which had carvings. In those days, there was no air-conditioning, so the dust from the street would come right into the house and almost blacken the furniture. We'd take an old towel, a pail of water, and scrub for two or three hours. Occasionally, we'd fall asleep from fatigue.

Mother was very strict and continually preached thrift. She humbled us. But we realized later in life that she was just making us strong. When I compare her with how I spoil my own grandchildren today, my only feeling is sadness. I am doing what comes naturally to me. I cannot simulate poverty. The conditions of her own poverty compelled her to treat us that way, although she also saw merit in that situation. It taught me thrift; and by being thrifty, through a parsimonious existence, you become streetwise very quickly.

From her daily housekeeping money, Mother would give us five cents a day. Of the three boys, William was the most careless with money. He wanted to be generous. He would spend it on himself or on anybody else who needed it. Philip was halfway in between William and me. I would spend one cent and save four. I was always the richest of the boys at home, but I remained very lean and hungry all the time.

Mother instructed each of us to drop our coins into cigarette tins with sealed lids in which we'd cut holes with a screwdriver. Within a few weeks, my tin would be full to the rim; then I would start another moneybox. Sometimes, I found my brothers trying to steal my money. They would wield a very thin knife or a fork and try to manoeuvre a coin upright inside the tin to slide it out. We used to have mini-rows over it. When I had more than one tin-full of change, they would come to me and, in pleading tones, ask to borrow money. Of course, when brothers borrow money off you,

you never get it back.

As a disciplinarian parent, there was no one fiercer or more demanding than Mother. She cracked the whip. If we were naughty, she'd make us take off our pants, and she'd wield a mean rattan on us, which of course left welts on our buttocks. Or she would purposely cane us on the exposed parts of our lower legs when we wore shorts to school, just to embarrass us and to remind us to refrain from doing naughty things.

I was probably caned 50-70 times in my life that I can remember – heavy caning to very light caning. William and Philip were caned more. I developed a very cunning knack. She would always cane my older brothers first. I would immediately start to cry, actually from fear, from sheer terror. The others didn't cry at all; they just took it very stoically. And so when it came to my turn, Mother would give it to me at half or one-third the force, and if she caned William seven or eight times, she would whack me just two or three times.

We felt outraged by the caning, but later we realized the wisdom in what she did. It was painful, but it was meted out of wisdom. Financial misery and deprivation drove me on in life. But the greatest single influence on me must have been my strict upbringing by Mother. She was always next to me.

If I had to describe Mother in one sentence, I would say that I have not come across a more highly principled person in my life. She would counsel me in very soft, calm words, "Never be greedy; never be greedy. Think of the poor people of China." She was always telling me to act fairly and justly and to eschew selfishness. She also was forever urging me not to be ungrateful in life.

I sometimes asked her, "Why do you keep on reminding me?"

She would answer, "I have detected in you a tendency to discard the bridge once you have crossed over it. I hope you'll never do that to your friends, in business or otherwise."

She had no improper thoughts in her mind. She lived a highly moral, correct and proper life, and yet she never lacked a sense of humour. She just wouldn't compromise with any form of evil or unfairness. Mother cared greatly for the poor and would pray and recite Buddhist scriptures every day.

Throughout my life in business, I always felt that Mother's pure life, her goodness, excellent faith and adherence to Buddhism protected my actions. An unseen hand, a bit of luck, seemed to attend me in many of my dealings or meetings with people. I put this down to Mother's constant presence and her prayers.

2
THE WUHAN SONGSTERS

THE MALAYA into which I was born was a British colony in all but name. The British used very benign terminology, claiming that their colony was the Malay Protectorate; the British were only there to protect the poor Malays. The state of Johor was known as an "unfederated" Malay state. It was under the "beneficial guidance" of a British advisor, not a British governor. These terms aside, Singapore, Malacca and Penang were 100 percent British colonies.

Between 1923 and 1928, my own guess is that my hometown of Johor Bahru must have had a population of 30,000-40,000. The town then had a radius of about two and one-half to three miles (4-5 kilometres). If you ventured beyond that, you might encounter wild tigers or leopards or panthers. The population of Johor Bahru was about 60 percent Malay, 35 percent Chinese and a tiny percentage of Indians, Eurasians and others. The British were civil servants, school teachers, military advisors, and plantation owners and managers.

The British were masters of divide-and-rule. Malays, Chinese and Indians each looked inward to their own communities. They never thought to unite as one people, which would have made it harder for the British to maintain control. Admittedly, when I was a boy, few among the local population were equipped for the modern world – the world of engineering, commerce, economics, and cunning politics was foreign to us.

Father felt that the land and resources rightly belonged to the Malays. However, he admired the British colonial administration for bringing law and order and creating the basic infrastructure in the town – electricity, piped clean water, and public water stands. He liked the clean, honest and methodical government the British brought to Johor State.

Johor Bahru was particularly good because we had the very strict and benevolent Sultan Ibrahim, great-grandfather of today's sultan. One of Sultan Ibrahim's military assistants, a Major Ahmad, had sons and daughters who went to our house to play, and invited us over to their bungalow in return.

Among the British overlords, there were some very decent, fine human beings. But overall, the British were racist, arrogant, and patronizing. They wore the mantle of the vastly superior race; their facial and body language was one of contempt, of utter disdain toward the natives. The majority of the English regarded it as a chore that they had to raise these poor monkeys on trees, and train them to walk on the ground. If the English passed you in a corridor, more often than not, you didn't exist to them.

From the time I was born, human rights and almost all aspects of decent society were absent in Malaya and Singapore because of colonialism and racism – more racism than colonialism – from the whites. The British set up their own social and sports clubs, which allowed in only white members. The Civil Service Club of Johor (what a misnomer!) was a white man's club.

The white man usually lived in exclusive areas, on choice pieces of land on little hillocks with the best views. Their homes were specially developed, with modern plumbing. The rest of Johor Bahru had frequent outbreaks of typhoid. Public health was generally very poor.

Many of our English teachers sent from England were fine,

decent people. Whilst they were teaching us you never felt the racism. But, at the end of the day, they lived in their own golden ghettoes, eating, drinking and playing apart from the locals. The locals just served them drinks when they were thirsty from playing tennis and laundered their sweaty clothes. Not a single Britisher was able to rebel against the system. One or two young British questioned these practices in their minds when they first arrived. But a year later, you never saw that same look on their faces. I remember thinking to myself that they had fallen into the vat of colonialism and become dyed the same colour.

Most of the Indian teachers in the English schools were very warm and excellent educators. Chinese teachers were by and large acceptable, but then you had the odd one whom I would term a colonial running dog.

One of the most important events affecting my entire life was the overt act of Japanese aggression on the Chinese nation and people. Japan had already occupied much of northeast China. After the infamous, trumped-up Marco Polo Bridge Incident, Japan openly declared war on China and invaded with all its military might on 7 July 1937, a date referred to by all Chinese alive at the time as the Double Seven. I was not quite 14 then.

The invasion aroused great anger in the hearts of the Overseas Chinese of Singapore and Malaya, who still identified very strongly with their homeland because the region was run as a colony. There was no such thing as a sense of nationhood. The way the British ruled, the Chinese were Chinese; the Malays were Malays; the Indians were Indians.

In Singapore, the leader of the Chinese community at the time was Tan Kah Kee. When the Sino-Japanese War broke out, he was 63 years old. He rallied the Chinese community and established the China Relief Fund. Ostensibly, he obtained the agreement of the

British authorities that ruled Malaya and Singapore. His purpose was to help the war victims in China – children who had become orphans, women who had become widows, and people who had been maimed or incapacitated by bombing or other acts of war by the Japanese.

Within a few months of launching the Relief Fund, Tan Kah Kee brought from China a large singing troupe called the Wuhan Songsters. The Songsters came to Singapore in the latter half of 1938 and were an instant hit. People flocked to see them perform. The Wuhan Songsters stayed for well over a year.

There must have been more than 100 people in that troupe: stage-prop managers, a band, and 70-80 singers. They were basically high school and early college students who had fled the coastal cities of China and moved into the interior after the Japanese invasion. They had assembled in Wuhan, living in very poor physical circumstances. They were highly patriotic young men and women.

The Wuhan Songsters sang in ensembles, with boys' and girls' voices coming through very harmoniously. They had excellent sopranos, baritones and tenors. The performances were held in school halls, church halls – wherever they could improvise. They sometimes gave matinee performances so that schoolchildren could come and listen. I saw the show a number of times and befriended the bandleader, Xia Jiqiu, who was a songwriter and composer.

The content of the songs tugged at your heart. Many of the tunes aroused great anger against the Japanese. One was called *Tongbaomen*, "Fellow Brethren." It was a deeply stirring song about how the Japanese, these wolves in sheep's clothing, quietly trained their armies to conquer the whole of East Asia.

The performances lasted two to three hours, because there was encore after encore after encore. Being enthusiastic and patriotic, the Songsters refused to leave the stage. The conductor might say, "Oh, you're all tired," and they would demur, "No, we'll sing some more."

The Wuhan Songsters galvanized the Chinese of Singapore and the Malay Peninsula. Singapore and Malaya were truly the centres of Overseas Chinese opposition to Japanese aggression. Hence, the Chinese in Malaya were targeted after the Japanese invasion of Southeast Asia in December 1941. The Japanese massacred about 50,000 Chinese in Malaya and maybe another 20,000-30,000 in Singapore.

Chinese would come to the Wuhan Songsters' performances and donate very generously. My rough recollection is that about $10 million in Malayan dollars was collected, which was a lot of money in those days. Mother was very active in the China Relief Fund, which had branches in every town and large village throughout the Malay Peninsula. She was elected chairwoman of the woman's wing of the Fund's Johor Bahru branch.

Tan Kah Kee was a great figure later honoured by Mao Zedong as the greatest of the Overseas Chinese. Even today, Tan is much revered in China. He did a lot for China, but Mother always said – and I agree – that the most patriotic Chinese were the hawkers and rickshaw-pullers who donated their hard-earned money, often their entire day's gross income, to the China Relief Fund.

Many of these labourers barely fed and clothed themselves through their daily earnings. Hawkers would announce during the show from the floor, "I will fry *kway teow* and donate my gross takings for the next two weeks to the China Relief Fund!" Rickshaw-pullers would give their proceeds for a week.

Our British colonial rulers tightly suppressed feelings about the Japanese. Those with the courage to express their anger and to write articles were usually Leftists. These were being watched by the so-called Chinese Protectorate.

"Chinese Protectorate" was a great misnomer. These so-called protectorates were really organs of physical and mental control over the Chinese. They were closely linked to the police and the Special Branch and were charged mainly with monitoring the left-wing activities of the Chinese community, never the right-wing activity.

And so, for the sake of the survival of their movement, the Leftists kept a very low profile, similar to Ho Chi Minh's activities under the French in Vietnam. Though the decent British would regard Japan's actions as reprehensible and condemnable, Britain and its overseas colonial governments played ball with the Japanese.

After Japan invaded China, many people grew to dislike Chiang Kai-shek's Kuomintang regime because it was repressive and tended to cooperate more with the Japanese than to fight them. Mother despised the Kuomintang, Chiang Kai-shek, and his coterie. She considered the Communist Party the true heroes of China. Only they were willing to stand up to Japanese aggression.

Mother had a strong love for China and a very deep understanding of her country and people. As a child, she had travelled widely in China when her father took her on his trips to collect rent in Shandong and other provinces.

As my two older brothers left me out of their games when I was a child, I stayed close to Mother. I became steeped in her Chinese values. I was always very proud of being Chinese. Then, the historical accident of listening to the Wuhan Songsters and meeting them stirred in my heart even stronger pro-China – and anti-Japan – feelings.

The stories about the awful Japanese atrocities and massacres in China kept mounting. The hearts of the Chinese people in Singapore and Malaya were filled with anger and passion. We felt that there were no obstacles we couldn't conquer; we would even destroy that hideous monster called the Japanese Army one day. A lot of Singapore and Malayan Chinese went to China to fight the Japanese. Many of them died. Some left without even obtaining their parents' agreement. They just left their homes with minimum clothing, almost the same way their parents had migrated south from China.

The Thais made peace with the Japanese from day one. We heard stories about a sudden upsurge of Japanese residents in Thailand, all dressed like Europeans, with hose, shoes and cork helmets.

Then came more ominous news. Near the northern boundary of Malaya, Japanese took a sudden interest in taking photos and setting up easels to paint. The same thing happened in Johor Bahru. A causeway crosses the Straits of Johor. If you're facing Singapore island, on the left side of the causeway was Seletar. The Japanese would set up easels and paint Seletar.

All of them were spies.

These were not like the Japanese who had come to Johor Bahru in the 1920s. A very nice Japanese man ran a professional camera shop right next door to us. Watanabe was his name. We had a common wall, and most nights we would hear his wife playing the *shamisen* and singing classical Japanese songs.

There was a Japanese dentist six or seven shops down from us. Then, on another street, a Japanese opened up a hairdressing salon. On Jalan Trus, between Father's shop and the Chinese school, were two or three shops with Japanese prostitutes plying their trade. Little lamps were lit inside the shops, behind wooden and rice paper *shoji*, and you saw shadows. Sometimes the women would venture out and sit in front of the curtains.

Soon after the Double Seven declaration of war on China in 1937, these shops began to disappear.

Even in school we could almost smell gunpowder. I remember a history teacher, an Oxford-graduated Englishman about 40 years of age, who, in a 1939 O-Levels class, talked about the war clouds gathering in the Pacific. He said the Japanese, having committed aggression on China, might have their eyes on the rest of East Asia. He said intelligence reported that the Japanese had laid the keel of the *Yamato*, the most powerfully built battleship known to man. But he told us not to worry about it, because as soon as *Yamato* opened up all of its big guns and fired its first salvo, it would just go belly up. British intelligence had mistakenly reported that the battleship was badly constructed and top-heavy.

The beastly, inhuman behaviour of the Japanese made me want to go and serve China, to join the army or whatever, to fight Japanese aggression. In 1939, when I graduated from school, I was 16 and all stoked up with that kind of feeling. I was going to China to fight, even if it meant getting killed on the first day. It doesn't matter when you're young. I didn't have much happiness at home anyway.

I studied in English up to O-Levels and graduated from English College in Johor Bahru in 1939. After completing Standard One at Convent Girls' School, I had entered the government English school, Bukit Zaharah. I studied there for three years from 1932 to 1934, and from Bukit Zaharah you automatically fed into English College.

With good O-Level results at English College, you could even get into the best universities in England, such as Oxford or Cambridge. In Singapore, there were two universities offering top-quality tertiary education – the King Edward VII College of Medicine and Raffles College, which taught arts and science. I was always within the top ten in the class in English College, even though William and I had almost a running battle with the colonialist teachers.

I don't have happy memories of English College. You were meant to sit and listen. The teachers almost treated questions as insubordination. Looking back on it now, I can see that they were probably not that well trained and were only covering up their own inadequacies. But it made me angry that we had to sit and listen, no matter what they said.

Then the coming of the Wuhan Songsters to Singapore in 1938 inflamed me further, feeding the indignities I had suffered at the hands of colonialist educators, and the sometimes mean behaviour of the Eurasians of Johor. This got me more and more spiteful of all the trappings of the English language.

Therefore, I decided to study Chinese at a Chinese school in Johor Bahru. My best memories of my school days come from those 17 months in the Chinese school. For the first time, I found happiness. There was no air of colonialism or patronizing behaviour.

The teachers were underpaid. The school hardware was pitifully sparse, almost unhygienic. These Chinese schools were not government supported; the Chinese community supported them. What could businessmen give to the schools when they themselves were on the verge of bankruptcy during the Great Depression?

The teachers came in cotton suits that were hardly laundered or pressed. I'd just come from a colonial school, whose headmaster came to work in a woven worsted wool suit and tie. The deputy principal of the Chinese school, who was very poor, wore a white twill jacket that had become semi-yellow. But he was a lovely human being. So I began to differentiate between form and essence. I realized that true human values and human worth have almost zero connection with money.

It was a bit humiliating when I started Chinese school in January 1940. I was 16 and had finished O-Levels. But I had to go back into primary three of Chinese school. Each desk, with two riveted chairs, seated two. The boy I shared a desk with was about nine years old.

In the first half of 1940, I really buried myself in books. I swotted and I swotted. I've never studied harder in my life. The teacher said to the whole class: tomorrow is *beishu* – you had to recite. I joined school as a real novice in Mandarin and in reading Chinese. I spoke Fuzhou dialect at home with Mother and Cantonese with the servants. I had learned some Mandarin interacting with the Wuhan Songsters. But I was really thrown in the deep end in school. Some of the teachers were strict and I saw them beat fellow students.

I think I mastered the language of elementary school. Within months of my joining the Chinese school, I began to be an avid fan of the Chinese cinema. When I graduated in May 1941, I was top of class, top of school. The headmaster, a fellow Fuzhou native, gave an oration, including a part about me.

By that time, the war clouds over Malaya were already getting very dark. On one of the rare occasions that Father showed concern for his first family, he said to Mother, "Go tell that stupid son, don't even dream of going to China! If he goes, he'll probably die there. So why not go to Raffles College?" Mother then got to work on me. Some of my classmates from English College were already enrolled in Raffles College, not having taken my detour to the Chinese school. So when Mother spoke to me, I saw the sense in her words.

I entered Raffles College in Singapore in May 1941. It was a very pleasant interlude. Did it do much for me? Maybe. I did throw myself into economics and English poetry for six months. And because of that short interlude at Raffles College, I got to know many of the future leaders of Malaysia and Singapore. I met Abdul Razak, who was to become the second Prime Minister of Malaysia. And I knew Lee Kuan Yew, the future Prime Minister of Singapore. Kuan Yew, who was one year ahead of me, was then known as

Harry Lee. I recall that he was very, very driven. I have not come across anyone more driven than Kuan Yew. He wanted to be the best informed, the one with the most cogent views, the views that would prevail. Even at Raffles College, Kuan Yew already had a strong fiduciary sense. He was born with it.

When I was a student at Raffles College, I leaned towards a professional career in law or politics. I wasn't interested in business. Due to Japan's aggression towards the rest of East Asia and my thorough disgust of colonialism, I thought politics was the only solution. So I was going to study law as a means of entering politics.

Then the war changed everything.

3

UNDER THE JAPANESE HEEL

IN EARLY DECEMBER 1941, we were sitting for second-term exams in Raffles College. The first day of exams was 8 December. I recall that it was a Monday. Our cubicles were very small, so, on Sunday night, we all paced the corridors to review for our history exam. I did that until about two in the morning. I went to bed and had barely fallen asleep when I heard a rumbling noise through my sleep at about 4 am. It was a sound none of us had ever heard before: bombs exploding. We all tumbled out of bed. Bombs were raining on Singapore. We knew it was war. We later learned that some watchmen sitting on the pavement not far from Raffles College had been killed in the bombing.

Word came to us: please go to the notice board for an important announcement. In a big notice signed by Mr Dyer, the school principal, we were told that the College was closed. All students, except those who were enlisted as air-raid wardens or St John Ambulance assistants, should immediately pack up and return to their homes. There was a fear that if we did not go back immediately, we might get cut off by the advancing Japanese troops. Japanese warships were assembling within a few hours of the Malay Peninsula. Raffles College to our house in Johor Bahru was about fifteen miles (24 kilometres), so I was home by eleven in the morning.

On the afternoon of 8 December, the Japanese landed their troops up in Kota Bahru and also crossed at the Kedah border.

Kedah was Malaya's border with southern Thailand, where the Japanese had been gathering from the last days of November. They poured across the land border, then came down into Kelantan in simple boats.

Japanese forces didn't arrive in Singapore until the early days of February 1942. But by late December, some of their shock troops were already infiltrating Johor Bahru. I am sure that some were disguised as Malays wearing sarongs. The British drew up their initial defences within just a few miles of the Thai border. And they would regularly make a 30-70 mile (50-110 kilometres) retreat. The British troops had badly underrated their enemy, who were battle-seasoned, having fought in China for many years. The British started off thinking they were the superior race. Suddenly, they found that people almost half their size were battering the life out of them.

As the Japanese moved down the Malay Peninsula, they behaved like Genghis Khan's troops in the modern age. They would enter a town, cut people's heads off and hang them on lampposts. The word would reach the next town, and the town was ready to surrender. The British troops were getting scared out of their wits. It was rape and pillage.

I stayed at home and went frequently to Father's shop to get the news. Father ordered us to evacuate to a pineapple plantation belonging to the richest Chinese businessman of the day, Lee Kong Chian, founder of the Lee Rubber Group. My cousin Hock Yao was then working for Lee Rubber. We left Johor Bahru at the end of December 1941 in open lorries.

Lee Pineapple Plantation was east-northeast of Johor Bahru in the direction of Kota Tinggi. At the 18th milestone (29th kilometre), you turned in and, not long after, reached the 10,000-acre plantation. There were about 100 of us: 60 from the Kuok clan, and four or five Cantonese families.

Our group comprised about 40 family members, and many were young children; the rest were maids, cooks, and other retainers. Each grown man would have a family of five to seven, so you didn't need all that many adults to reach a headcount of 40. In fact, at the time, it was just one uncle and Father in Malaya, but there were also the children of three other uncles from China. For example, my mother had raised Hock Kin and Hock Seng with my brothers and me after their father, Uncle Number Four, returned to China. Other cousins of mine had come to Malaya without their fathers.

Father said he would stay behind to mind the shop with my older cousins. When the Japanese were approaching Johor Bahru, he packed up with his second family. They moved to another camp a short distance away from us. From then on, Father stayed with them.

We slept in a freshly made labourers' dormitory built about four feet (1.2 metres) off the ground to keep out the damp. You could smell the sourness of the fresh timber. On top of the timber, we spread out straw mats, then bed sheets and blankets. We all slept like that, under mosquito nets, in a common room.

I had a good life in the plantation, although I came down with pineapple sores. When you walk through the rows of pineapple plants, very fluffy pollen with tiny thorns comes off the leaves, flies through the air and sticks in your pores. Luckily, we had brought some pharmaceutical products, one of them an ointment called Zambuk. I also remember bathing my legs in an antiseptic like Dettol, and then covering the sores with the ointment.

We stayed in the pineapple plantation for about ten weeks. You got used to the rustic, village life. We tended vegetable plots. Luckily, I had taken some of my best books with me. The book I liked most of all was Palgrave's *Golden Treasury of Poems*. William and I read the anthology from the front to the back, from the back to the front, and sometimes we'd compete with one another in reciting poems.

We were visited two or three times by squads of Japanese soldiers on bicycles, each group consisting of three to five soldiers. Mother had been appointed leader of our camp. She sat on the ground, smoothed out the sand and wrote Chinese characters. The Japanese wrote back.

Mother was very shrewd. She ordered all cosmetics to be destroyed and women – we had girls in their teens – to wear their drabbest clothes. There were one or two streams from which we drew our water supply. Streams always twist and bend, so she ordered all the young girls to go past two or three bends away from our dwelling area so that if the Japanese tried to look beyond one bend or two bends they would still not find them. And the girls were not to hide; they were just to pretend that they were there washing, and to stick together, never to be alone. The girls were never found nor molested.

There was tension one day when the soldiers said they were going to come back that night. We thought that couldn't spell anything good. The Cantonese friends of ours had brought three guns with them to the plantation, which they had buried on Mother's instructions. That afternoon, they had a meeting and Mother agreed that the weapons should be excavated and loaded. The men were posted as sentries on the little hillocks in the plantation waiting to see whether the Japanese approached. Nobody turned up, and at about 1 am the men came back to camp to rest. The second night the same thing happened.

Luck was with us. Only later did we learn that the Japanese troops had been called away to muster for the assault on Singapore. When the attack was launched, we heard a lot of shelling. The British shelled Johor from Singapore. The Japanese bombed Singapore from the air and shelled the island by cannons from Johor.

One day, Cousin Number Six – he was a tough chap, physically the biggest Kuok – announced that he was going to walk through the jungle to Johor Bahru. When he arrived in town, he saw heads on many lampposts, freshly severed, with blood still dripping. Then a Japanese on a bicycle rode past him. A hundred yards (91 metres) away, the Japanese put the bike against a wall and went inside a house. My cousin went up to the bike, took it, and cycled back to us through the jungle. I have no doubt that his head would have been on display if he had been caught.

My two brothers were also keen to find out news and, after many entreaties, they finally received special permission from Mother to follow Sixth Cousin back to town. Then, there was silence. Mother was worried sick that she had lost one or both of her sons. Then, two or three days later, word came back that William had been stricken ill with malaria.

The Japanese had posted notices on walls ordering all residents of Johor Bahru to return to town to register with the Japanese authorities. So, within 36 hours, we struck camp. Early one morning in mid-March 1942, on bicycles and on foot, we all retraced the distance to Johor Bahru. I took Mother on the crossbar of my bicycle. I put a woollen sweater around the crossbar to make it comfortable for her, and she perched sideways with her hand on the middle of the handlebar. We passed Japanese sentries on the way. We were told to get down and very politely bow with our heads almost knocking the ground.

On the way back to town, our party stopped at the small village of Ulu Tiram. There, we saw some crazed people sitting on the pavement. They had gone out of their minds, having witnessed a terrible massacre by the Japanese.

I heard the story second- or third-hand, but apparently what had happened was that, as the British forces were pushed down the Malay Peninsula towards Singapore, the Eurasians of southern Malaya decided to group together. They chose as their refuge a little Catholic church in Ulu Tiram. They came from many towns in the state of Johor. In total, they numbered about 80 souls: men, women, and children. They took with them all the things from their daily lives. The battles were raging a day's walk away, and of course there was nothing to do. They seemed to be unaware of the enormity of the tragedy and barbarity that was gripping Malaya.

To pass the time, these Eurasian families had evening gatherings, playing gramophone records, a little dancing, maybe a little alcohol – in normal times all very innocent behaviour. A small detachment of Japanese soldiers came by, attracted by the noise. The Japanese asked for drinks. Maybe one of the soldiers groped or tried to grope a girl. There were screams and a scuffle and a sudden stand-off when weapons were drawn on both sides. The Japanese were outnumbered. Then, the tension broke. The Japanese smiled apologetically and withdrew; pistols were holstered. The Eurasians breathed a sigh of relief.

One or two nights later, a truckload of Japanese soldiers came back, cordoned off the area, and an orgy of killing took place.

When I heard this story, I realized how each of the decisions made by Mother and the other community leaders were crucial to our survival. Lee Kong Chian was a rubber baron, but we didn't seek refuge in his rubber plantations; we went to his pineapple plantation. Rubber plantations are like deep forests while pineapple fields are only waist high, so one can see clear across them. To Japanese soldiers, we would just look like peasant workers, not fugitives in hiding. We were told to bury all our weapons. Mother ordered us to throw away all alcohol. Yet, she knew that when the soldiers came, we had to offer them something, so we offered them tea and cheap cigarettes. The girls were ordered to hide upriver, but always to be washing clothes so that they didn't look like they were hiding. Each of these decisions tilted the balance towards survival.

When we returned to Johor Bahru, we discovered that the roof and the entire middle part of our house were gone, blown apart by a shell. All of our trunks of clothing had been looted. Our family ancestral book had been thrown into a corner and was sodden with rainwater.

The Lee business empire included an ice factory outside Johor Bahru town, 300 yards (275 metres) from our house. My brothers went there and lived in the workers' quarters, sleeping on mattresses placed on the floor. Most of us joined them. Father continued to live with his second wife and younger family.

Mother tended to William, who was very weak and at times delirious from malaria. I also helped to look after him. I crossed through rubber estates, taking shortcuts, to go where I thought there would be an Indian who owned a few cows. In Johor, we used to get our milk from these very lean Indian cows, which were milked sometimes in front of your doorstep. So I went and bought a couple of bottles of milk and brought them back to the ice factory.

William recovered, but a week later, I, too, was stricken with malaria. Malaria is an awful illness. I remember that in my delirium I felt as if I had lost my head. They propped me up on high pillows, but I still felt as if my head was way below me. I had shivering spells when, even with four blankets on me, I felt cold. I swallowed liquid-quinine until I'd got fully deaf. It took me five or six weeks to knock the malaria out of my system. By then, I was just skin and bones.

From mid-1942 until the end of the war, Mother, my two brothers and I lived in a tiny house we rented directly opposite the Roman Catholic church on the narrow Jalan Greja (Church Street), which ran up and down a slope. The floor area of that house, including a central open-air courtyard, was less than 600 square feet (56 square metres). There were two small bedrooms and an entrance hall-cum-dining room. At night, we would unfold canvas beds and two of us would sleep in the hall.

Naturally, we were physically thrown very close together. There were no recreational activities, because if you went out too much you ran the risk of losing your life. The Japanese had put an iron-clad lock on the whole town and you couldn't travel.

The Japanese imposed a strict curfew in Johor Bahru from the day they arrived. We were under their heels until the day that we were "liberated". I must say, the Japanese soldiers came across as fairly stupid. Many of their actions made no sense. They really believed, like Hitler's Nazis, that they were a super race, and that it was their sacred duty to uplift the poor, colonized Asians and to liberate them!

In 1942, I already thought that the Japanese would be gone, blown away, within two years. I just didn't see that they could win the war. They could win many battles with their mad, frenzied acts, but I couldn't visualize them winning the war. Yet, I thought the dark clouds over our heads would never lift. The sky was bright, but I felt as if I never saw the sun. It was darkness! I used to get up at one or two in the morning and write poems about our misery. It all felt so depressing.

You've got to be a very clever people to win a big war and to rule half of the world – but the Japanese didn't behave as clever people. In the first few weeks of conquering any town, they would hold marching exercises as part of their campaign to terrorize residents. They marched six to eight to twelve abreast, chanting Japanese martial songs and stamping on the ground in an exaggerated manner.

The Japanese carried out extreme forms of torture on their

victims. For example, the Kempeitai administered the "water treatment," where they stuffed a hose down a prisoner's throat and pumped in water until the poor fellow's stomach had inflated like a football. Then they'd kick the victim's belly. The Japanese converted a few places in Johor Bahru into torture chambers. The Kempeitai headquarters was in the building next to the railway station. (By coincidence, Kuok Group built a big complex on that site in the mid-1990s).

The Japanese treated the Chinese worst of all. With the exception of those who had completely gone over to the Japanese side and become their informers and spies, all Chinese were suspect in their eyes. The Japanese had fought the Chinese in China for over four years and knew the calibre of the Chinese. Later, in 1944 and 1945, I saw "comfort women," young Chinese girls who'd been brought from southern China and Taiwan to function as sex slaves.

The informers wore hoods with two slits for their eyes. In Johor Bahru and in Singapore, whole streets were blocked and all males between 18 and 50 years old were ordered to report to such-and-such a street corner for the Sook Ching, or "purge through cleansing" exercise. The hooded Chinese sat beside ugly-looking Japanese soldiers and interrogators. As the local men filed past, every time the informer pointed at one of them, the man would be pushed aside and taken to join another group. These who were singled out were later taken to remote places and summarily executed.

Several of my classmates from my Chinese school in 1940 were from a lovely Chaozhou family. They had three or four sisters and their father was a kind and generous man. Other Chinese schoolmates told me that this family was rounded up and taken to a field outside Johor Bahru town. The women were raped and killed, the men butchered, and all were buried in shallow graves. Many other Chinese families were likewise massacred, slaughtered.

The Japanese went to towns where there were lots of Malays. The soldiers blocked off streets and then, at a certain hour, they rounded up all the Malays on the streets. They took them back to their camps, shaved their heads, and turned them into camp cleaners to do all the menial work. This happened to a young, Malay man whom I employed after the war. If the forced labourers were obedient and good, the Japanese would give them wooden swords and make them so-called local officers.

There was a kind of green-uniformed military police who rode around on bicycles. These were more disciplined than the others, as it was their duty to be on the lookout for misbehaving Japanese soldiers. When the MPs saw drunken Japanese soldiers on the streets, they would jump off their bicycles, rush across and harangue them. You usually saw terrified looks on the soldiers because obviously the MPs were armed with big powers. The misbehaving soldiers would get slapped – the slaps were so loud that you could hear them: left and right and left and right. The MPs would administer twenty slaps if they were being kind to the guy.

One day, there was a knock on the door. We didn't know who it was. We opened the door and a man dressed in a Japanese uniform, cap, and with a long sword barged into our house. He turned around and spoke to Mother in the Minnan dialect of southern Fujian province. He asked us to please close the door.

He told Mother, "I'm Taiwanese, but I got inducted into the Japanese army. I'm almost of officer rank. I have a real sword. In Taiwan, they only give us wooden swords." He seemed to miss home, and took the opportunity to befriend us. From then on, he would occasionally visit us and sometimes stay for lunch or dinner.

One day he said, "Your three boys are strong, young men. If they don't volunteer for work, the Japanese will suspect that you're very anti-Japanese, and you could be lugged in for questioning." He added, "I know someone in Mitsubishi Trading, the biggest Japanese corporation in Singapore. I have heard that they're going to open up a small office in Johor Bahru and send a Japanese manager in to run it. One of your sons should volunteer as his assistant."

I glanced around. My brothers kept quiet, so I volunteered.

Within a few days, the Taiwanese made an appointment for the Japanese to see me. He came with an official car and took me down to Singapore. We arrived in Raffles Place, Meyer's Chambers. Mitsubishi occupied the whole block. He took me upstairs and instructed me to wait outside an office. Half an hour, forty minutes later, he ushered me in to meet the Japanese, who looked me over. Then he introduced me to a youngish Japanese man who wore thick-rim glasses and was almost bald-headed. He said, "This is Uemura Goro-*san*, and he is going to Johor Bahru to start the office. You'll be the first employee serving him."

The next day, Uemura came to Johor Bahru, met up with me and we started the office together. That was July 1942. I worked with Mitsubishi all the way until the Japanese surrender was announced in mid-September 1945.

I justified working for Mitsubishi very easily. I detested the Japanese, but what alternative was there for me? There was nothing else to do. You either took a job as a clerk or you stayed at home and were suspected of being anti-Japanese. The only other option was to go into the jungle to fight.

But we could not take Mother with us into the jungle. All three of us brothers knew we had to put Mother's well-being first of all. We had seen her suffer so much in her lifetime. We had to protect her. William later admitted that were it not for Mother's safety, he would long ago have gone into the jungle to join the Communist Party to fight the Japanese. But we all knew, as soon as one of us did that, the rest of the family would be in danger and would not live to see the end of the war.

The Japanese Military Administration gave Mitsubishi a monopoly on importing and supplying rice and cigarettes to Malaya. Mitsui was given sugar and salt. From that you saw the pecking order; you knew who were the biggest supporters and financiers of Japan's aggression: Mitsubishi, followed by Mitsui.

Almost all the rice was imported from Thailand. Malaya only grew, at best in those days, 30 - 40 percent of its rice requirement. I was the clerk put in charge of rice and, later, cigarettes. The exporters at the other end would deliver and consign the rice to Mitsubishi in Singapore. Mitsubishi would unload the rice and transfer it into lighters, which are non-motorized barges. A tugboat would lead three lighters around the southern end of Singapore into the Straits of Malacca, then into the Straits of Johor up to Johor Bahru.

I bicycled to work, a distance of about a mile (1.6 kilometres). Four or five times a week, the lighters brought rice from Singapore. I got up very early in the morning and bicycled down to the jetty to make sure that the lighters were there and that all the Chinese labourers were ready to uplift the rice. The supervisor in charge was a Malay gentleman whom I got to know well.

I had to make sure the rice was received in good order and that there had not been much pilferage. Every lighter carried about two or three Indian workers, who sometimes poked in hollow metal rods with sharp ends to funnel some rice out. I inspected all the edges. Sometimes I'd say, "Why, why is this?" I'd tell my assistants to go and search the Indians' bunks, and then we'd find two or three bags of rice.

Once the rice was in Johor, it was delivered to the warehouses in the middle of town, to which wholesalers and shopkeepers would come to purchase the staple. Father became one of those rice wholesalers. His very good friend, Onn bin Jaafar, was appointed by the Japanese Military Administration to be Food Controller of the State of Johor. Years later, Dato Onn led the movement that formed the Malayan Union, and it was he who founded United Malays National Organization (UMNO), which to this day is the ruling party of Malaysia.

Dato Onn told Father, "There's no other business you can do today. I'll give you a rice license. If you're a rice merchant, at least your family will be well fed. Take it Kang." Father listened to him and, in 1942, took up a rice wholesaler-cum-retailer license.

The irony was that as I had become the head of Mitsubishi's rice department, Father bought rice from me. That said, I hardly saw him during the Japanese Occupation, as he was living with his second wife and family. I made out the invoices. He sent his nephew, my number five cousin, Hock Chin, to buy the rice from me. Hock Chin brought an allocation sheet signed by the Food Controller of Johor or one of his assistants. I knew the prices each day for the different grades of rice.

I was only 17 when I began working for Mitsubishi. I found work to be highly therapeutic. You can't just sit at home reading books all day. No matter whether it is Shakespeare or Dickens, there is a limit to the length of time you can read books.

Eventually, eight Japanese worked in the Mitsubishi office. They were, by and large, college students whose studies had been interrupted by war, or university graduates. They were real civilians with no military bearing at all. The one closest to having a military bearing was my immediate boss, Uemura.

As head of a section, I had a desk and my assistants sat on both sides of me. Uemura quite often weighed into my Malay assistants and slapped them. Later, I found that Uemura had a good heart. He was just short-tempered. One day, he told me in his guttural, ungrammatical English, "Get me six young Malays to help you run rice department." So I recruited six of my old schoolmates. I think he slapped five out of six over the three years they worked there.

Uemura was quite close to me, although we had a kind of love-hate relationship. Every time he slapped my Malay colleagues, I would show him my temper and refuse to talk to him for two or three days.

He'd come up to me and ask, "Why, why?"

I'd say, "Because you behave like that. How can you behave like that?" I always stood up to him.

I saw what made the Japanese tick. I admired their discipline. That's what made Japan what it is today: discipline – not brilliance, but discipline. You obeyed orders, even if the orders were wrong.

My job also allowed me to make some money on the side, a bit of black-marketeering, you might call it. One rice trader came to me and said, "Hey, you're in charge of rice. If you favour me in buying all the sweepings, I'll share my profit with you." I thought this was pretty good, so I began to make money.

In addition, some of the rice at the bottom of the lighters would inevitably get damaged by water. We had a system of putting this damaged rice out for auction. Sometimes, rice merchants came to me and said, "Why don't we form a small consortium and you take a 25 or 30 percent share?" I had money. My salary was quite good and I hardly spent anything. So I parked cash with them and they'd sometimes win at the auction. Because I'd become a partner, I received a portion of the profits.

The Allied bombing started from the end of 1944. With each passing month, the bombing became more frequent until it was almost daily by the spring of 1945. The Allied B-29s flew over from bases in Ceylon and dropped their bombs on Sembawang, the former British naval base in Singapore, which, as the crow flies, is some four miles (6.5 kilometres) from Johor Bahru.

One day, I saw a B-29 shot down by a Japanese fighter aircraft. We had dug air-raid shelters on the little lawn in front of the office near the sea. Every time the sirens came on, we all rushed down into the shelter. Sometimes, I would not go in, because, being a senior clerk, I had lots of things to wind up. I would stand under a tree and watch these B-29s come over in formation. I saw these tiny, mosquito-like Japanese "Zero" fighters darting in and out.

Then, suddenly, I saw a plane take a hit and explode in flames. I saw some airmen bail out and white parachutes float down. That evening, as I went to fetch my bicycle, a truck drove past. Inside it was a white, blindfolded figure. He was at the head of the truck, hanging on to the rails, and there were three or four Japanese soldiers around him. They were taking him to the Kempeitai station to be grilled.

The little light we would see above our heads got darker and darker by the day. We wondered whether, in the Allied attempts to retake Malaya, we would die in the crossfire, or bombing, or in a Japanese massacre. But, thank God, when you're young, you shake off these worries and take your life in your own hands. Why should I worry so much; why should I be so self-centred? If everybody thinks in this way, then you have an air of bravery and courage.

Ironically, while Malaya was suffering so much, I was getting relatively wealthy, if a man can truly be wealthy under the Japanese heels. Through my private trading, I had amassed quite a few hundred thousand dollars – maybe even a million or two – of "banana money" (they were so called because the notes had bananas trees printed on them). But from late 1944 until the end of the war in September 1945, the value of this Japanese-issued currency declined precipitously. From November 1944, prices of goods escalated 100 percent every three or four weeks; from

January to August 1945 prices spun completely out of control. The economy was collapsing.

In 1944, Mitsubishi sent the chief from their office in Muar, north of Johor Bahru, to Johor Bahru to head the entire Johor State operation. He was a civilian named Nagaoka Koichi, a very fatherly man perhaps in his early 40s. There were no walls in our office and Nagaoka would walk around. He was a very democratic man, whereas all the other Japanese held an attitude of "I'm superior; you're inferior." For Nagaoka there was no pecking order.

One day, Nagaoka sauntered, sauntered and sauntered about the office, casting the odd glance in my direction. Then he came over to me.

When I first went to see Mitsubishi in July 1942, they got my Chinese name confused with my brother Philip's. So Philip changed his name to Pen I – he became known as Kuok Pen I – and I became known as Kuok Ho Kee in the Mitsubishi office.

Nagaoka came over to me and asked, "You are Ho Kee-*san*?"

I answered, "Yes, sir," and stood up since he was the big boss.

He said, "I'm the general manager here. My name is Nagaoka. May I sit down?" So he sat down, chatted and got me relaxed. He said – in good English – "By the way, the coffee served in this office is not so nice to drink. I hear there are good Chinese coffee shops in Johor Bahru. Do you think you could take me out to drink some good coffee?"

I replied, "Yes, any time."

He said, "Are you very busy now? What do you say we go now?"

So I took him to a Chinese coffee shop, just the two of us. I think at that time coffee was about $50 a cup in banana dollars.

The Japanese Imperial Army had, by then, attacked Imphal and Kohima at the Burma-India border. Every day, there was propaganda claiming Japanese successes and saying that India would soon fall. What Nagaoka said to me that day shocked me.

"We are losing the battle, the war, in Imphal and Kohima. Our troops are being destroyed. They are fleeing in all directions. The retreat is a rout. Don't believe what you hear from the Japanese propaganda machine. They are feeding all of you and even me packs of lies."

You have to understand that there was an information gap in my life during the nearly four years under Japanese occupation. Many people secretly listened to BBC or Voice of America, but if you were caught, you would be tortured by the Kempeitai and one out of two would be killed. You could listen to the Voice of Syonan (as Singapore was called by the Japanese), but it was all naked propaganda.

Nagaoka continued, "You know, the Japanese are a good people. But greed spoiled them. In staying out of the First World War, we supplied materials to the war machines of both sides. So we got rich. Japanese military might started with the defeat of the Russian Navy in 1905. After that, the military machine expanded and began to dominate our society. All liberal-minded Japanese were either assassinated or terrorized." He added, "The root of evil is companies like my company. The merchants of Japan are greedy. They wanted to get richer, but Japan is without raw materials; so they looked across the seas to China. As they grew richer they wanted more. The greed became unstoppable and now we are waging this terrible war, killing hundreds of thousands of innocent people.

"I served my time in the army. We all have to. I was sent to Manchuria. I told my troops that the world has a bright future. This is a mad war. My orders to them were, 'Stay alive! Whatever you do, don't get killed.' My mission to my troops was to save them."

I have telescoped several coffee sessions into one. There were about four or five such sessions in 1944 and 1945, during which he unburdened himself to me. At the first session, I feared it was a trap to lure things out of me, so I just listened and didn't say a word. But he trusted me that much. He talked so positively and openly to me that I grew to trust him fully. It was always me alone with Nagaoka in the coffee shop.

Once, he denounced the Japanese military, government and even his company managers for stupidity. "The Malays are a wonderful people, but they don't have enough to eat. Do you know that rice is rotting in southern Thailand because there's no means of transporting it to Malaya? Mitsubishi operates 50-60 trucks. What are we doing with them? We are fulfilling army contracts to go into the jungles to haul logs for the army. The army builds stockades around every village to prepare for the day when the jungle rats, the Malayan Communist Party, come out to attack the Japanese.

"The trucks could have gone to southern Thailand to bring rice down to feed the people. Why can't we understand that before we go we should leave some goodwill behind and make the people understand that we are not purely evil?"

Nagaoka was a wonderful man. I felt as though the two of us had formed a bond. When my brother Philip married Eileen Cheah in August 1945, Mother cooked a wedding feast in our tiny Jalan Greja house. We invited two Japanese guests: my immediate boss, Uemura, and Nagaoka.

After the war was over, I said goodbye to my Japanese colleagues. They had to surrender themselves to a civilian internment camp.

One evening, some weeks later, I took a nostalgic bicycle ride back to the Mitsubishi office along the seafront. As I was riding, I saw truckload after truckload of Japanese prisoners being ferried down to Singapore to board ships. They were all huddled standing up, slumped or slouched, in these open trucks. At first I didn't pay much attention. Then, at the moment I lifted my head, there was

Nagaoka in the front of a truck, his head held high, gripping the bar. His fellow compatriots were all bowed in shame. Here was this man who rightly felt proud of being a Japanese. I'll never forget that scene.

The best thing to come out of the war years for me was my relationship with Nagaoka, whom I continued to communicate with after the war. In fact, when I made my first visit to Japan in 1958, Nagaoka met me at the dock in Yokohama. On every subsequent trip, I would be in touch with him, and, as he was not in very good health and not well off, I would slip him a little packet of Japanese money. It was very sad when I received a note saying that he had passed away. In my eyes, Nagaoka was more human than any of my fellow compatriots, Malays, Chinese or Indians.

4
WILLIAM

EVERY MORNING, I light a joss stick and bow before the family altar and Buddha's altar. On the left side is the ancestral tablet, where I pray to my ancestors and to the memory of my departed loved ones. First, I bow in memory of Mother, a second time in memory of my brother William, and a third time in memory of my late first wife, Joyce.

I consider William to be one of the great men of his time, a wonderful human being. He was a man who only cared for the underdog, someone who wanted society to be retooled so that the scales were not weighted entirely in favour of the establishment.

William's influence on me was always like Mother's; it became part of my being. The backdrop on the stage of my life is 70-90 percent Mother, 10-30 percent William. Frankly, no one else had a share in that backdrop: not Father, nor Philip, nor any of my friends or teachers.

William read voraciously. By the age of 13, he had already read very deeply, in English, all the books by the great philosophers of the world: Greek, German, French, Russian and British. He was so keen on languages, philosophy and eventually politics.

William was a dreamer, and I mean "dreamer" in the highest sense of the word. He had dreams of a wonderful, Utopian world. By contrast, from childhood until today, I've had my feet securely anchored to the ground.

From very early on in life, William showed extraordinary courage and strength. He engaged in friendly wrestling matches at the edge of an embankment. The loser would be pushed into the water. Quite often, he would be the victor, pushing people much heavier than him into the sea.

William always stood for fair play and what is right. He couldn't bear anything unjust. He was born with that streak in him, and it must have been strengthened by seeing and hearing his father's behaviour towards his mother. He was an extremely filial son. I think he loved Father greatly, but there was this black aspect to the picture which he, I suppose, couldn't rationalize.

Father used to like to have one of us thump on his legs, thighs and calves with two clenched fists shortly after he had lunch. He would lie down in bed, have a siesta and send for one of his sons. He found William to be the one who could give him the most satisfying massage. So, poor William was very often the one to be summoned by him, although Philip and I were sometimes also called upon. The massage could last an hour or even more, cutting into our school-book revision hours and our free time to go out and play.

Yet, William had more sympathy for Father than any of us. He saw the old man's problems, how handicapped he was with a very elementary level of Chinese education. William was more willing than me to look at the picture from Father's side. I could see he was very torn. He felt it was not right for him to judge Father's actions, yet, at the same time, he saw Mother being abused mentally and physically and put short of money to run the home.

In school, William always made friends with classmates who tended to be more withdrawn, rather than the bubbling, effervescent types. He saw in these youngsters something that the rest of us failed to see. It was amazing how he got on with them.

William only kept a few friends. One was James Puthucheary.

Then, later, he befriended my eldest brother Philip's Agricultural College classmate, Jacko Thumboo, the son of an Indian medical practitioner in Singapore.

From about 1936, William began to write a growing stream of letters to the editor of *The Straits Times* in Singapore. He used different pseudonyms, such as Democrat, Cosmos and Rationalist. He was anti-fascist through and through. In his letters, he came right out and said: no matter that British rule was clamped over our heads – that the fascism of Hitler, Mussolini and Hirohito was in a way parroting what the British, French, Dutch, Italian and other colonial oppressors had practised in their empires.

On one public holiday morning in early 1939, William, James Puthucheary and I rode our rickety bicycles to the English College tennis court. Not long after we started our game, a car approached. It was one of the Eurasian teachers. He stopped his car and asked, "Do you boys have permission to play?"

Now, as we were senior Cambridge students, the teachers knew all of us. We were the elite of the school. We said, "No sir, but we couldn't reach a teacher for permission."

William, who was very forthright, said, "Can you give us permission, if I ask you now?"

The teacher responded, "No. After all, you have already breached the rules."

William said, "But isn't that unreasonable? You are not using the court, so why are you withholding the right for us to play?"

The teacher took this to be insubordination. He retorted sharply, "I shall report you to the headmaster," and drove off. Of course the spirit had gone out of the game, so we soon packed up and went home.

The following morning before assembly, the headmaster sent for William. The teacher had made the report, identifying William as the ringleader. The headmaster said, "You were caught outright. Do you admit that you played without permission?"

William replied, "Yes."

"In that case, I have to give you punishment by six strokes of the rattan on your backside."

William answered, "I don't mind the six strokes of the rattan, sir, but I cannot accept the fact that I've done wrong."

William refused to give in, and the headmaster became more and more irate. "You either take this punishment or you are instantly expelled."

William responded, "You can do what you like to me, sir. I've already told you I cannot accept the accusation because I think it's an act of gross unfairness. It's unjust and improper." William was expelled on the spot.

The headmaster came into the assembly hall, still very angry. He said, "I have an announcement. I have expelled senior Cambridge student William Kuok Hock Ling for gross insubordination." Then he read out my name and James Puthucheary's name and said, "The two of you are hereby warned that if anything similar happens again, you will also be expelled."

I really felt very, very churned up about William being expelled from school, and for nothing, which I regarded as just another brutal, imperialist, colonialist act.

After cooling his heels for a few weeks, William joined a privately run school, where the educational standards were lower. He sat for exams as an external student and passed. After finishing school, William joined *Singapore Free Press* as a reporter and within his second year was made a sub-editor.

William wanted to see the world become a better world, and human beings treated as human beings. All those genes must have come from Mother's side. Father was in many ways a decent man, but I must concede that the Kuok genes are merchant and mercenary genes. Mother's side never cared for money. My maternal grandfather wasn't a man who cared for money; he cared for human values.

Mother always said that she loved her three sons equally. But in my heart, I always felt that she had a deeper love for William, who was in her eyes the perfect human being, a man who hated oppression in any form. She sensed in William qualities that were absent in Philip and in me. William was a selfless person. He cared for the well-being of his classmates, then of his fellow townsmen, and then he cared for the people of Singapore, the major city adjoining Johor Bahru.

He was for the underdog. It was just in his DNA. We had a few awful rows during our years at Mitsubishi, where he worked too, because of the way I disciplined some of my staff. He thought it was inhumane for any human being to behave like that. But that was my way, and I built the whole Kuok Brothers' Group displaying those same tendencies, whereas William gave his entire life to the poor and to the underdog.

I believe William joined the Malayan Communist Party (MCP) in late 1945 or in 1946. He never let on. I think his reason for keeping it close to his chest was not to implicate his family, because the British were hounding and persecuting the Communists who were literally driven into the jungle.

As the Communists had played a significant role in the resistance movement against the Japanese occupation forces, the Allied commanders couldn't be seen to be suddenly against the resistance movement right after the War. So, they kept up the pretence, but in their heart of hearts they wanted to eliminate the Communists. I believe that Ho Chi Minh and the Vietnam arm of Comintern were involved with the MCP.

In 1946, William moved to Kuala Lumpur and, with two or three assistants – one of them his friend Jacko Thumboo, he ran a tabloid newspaper as the mouthpiece of the left wing. To the British, left wing was Communist, and they had to be ostracized and stamped out.

William ran the paper from Klyne Street, in the same building that was the Kuala Lumpur office of the Malayan People's Anti-Japanese Army. In early 1946, when I went to Kuala Lumpur, I saw Chinese soldiers in the same battle fatigues that they had worn in the jungle.

The Malayan Communist Party was mainly Chinese – a lot of Fujianese, Hakkas and Hainanese. Many of the early founders of the movement in Malaya had come up through the Chinese-language school system. William was a rare exception since he was educated in English.

The British trumped up an excuse and closed down the paper in 1946. William came back home, but we often didn't see him for weeks. He became active in the Singapore Harbour Board Union, a militant union. He was advisor and, being good with a pen, wrote pamphlets for them. He spent days and nights at the union, sleeping on office desks and wearing the same clothes for days without washing. He never cared for his physical well-being.

I married Joyce Cheah, the youngest sister of Philip's wife Eileen, on 4 October 1947. William was a wonderful brother to me and a wonderful brother-in-law to Joy at the wedding and the wedding feast that followed. Joy was extremely fond of William. The irony was that in our young school days, William had taken a great liking to Eileen, but as soon as he saw that Philip had a crush on her, he immediately withdrew. I was not as close to William as Philip. William was really the spiritual strength to which Philip, who went through some very rough patches in his life, clung.

William saw that Joy was noble and honest, and that her brother and sisters looked up to her. He envied me that I was marrying her and wished me the best of luck. I think he saw in me a tendency to stray from my own married life, so on the day of my wedding he took me aside and said some strong but very fine words to me. He enjoined upon me to respect my marriage to Joy and never to betray Joy's trust in me.

I was never derisive about William's activities of helping the poor and championing the cause of the labour unions. However, I didn't think that business and politics needed to go together. He, on the other hand, felt that I was only keen on making money. One day in 1948, he sat me down and told me I was wrong, and that sooner or later I would recognize the worth of his advice – that politics and economics, and politics and business were intertwined.

William said, "Nien, I know you'll not listen to me because you have your own views on life and you are heading to become a successful capitalist. There's nothing wrong with that. I'm different. But you have to get interested in politics. If you get big in the business world, politics will not leave you alone. So, the sooner you start to take an interest in politics, the better."

William was of course correct. Politics and economics are indivisible; politics and life are inseparable.

I believe William rose to become the propaganda chief and one of the top ten in the Malayan Communist Party. As he was an English-educated Chinese, he would have been important to them. To the British, they were all terrorists.

When the British made their move to round up and imprison them all, William and Jacko Thumboo went into the jungle. I believe the Communist Party's headquarters had issued an order for Party members to retreat to their jungle bases in order to escape the British net.

I remember talking to William before he left. I said, "William, why go? Let them arrest you. Let them banish you to China. One day, we can plead with the future government of Malaya (I could already see that Malaya would one day win independence), and we'll bring you back here to the country of your birth.

"Do you know what the British will do to all of you? If they are losing the battle, they will even use the atom bomb on the jungles of Pahang to kill every one of you. They will not care whether they kill a few thousand innocent aboriginal tribesmen or precious wild tigers. Their whole purpose will be to wipe out every one of you. Your chances of surviving are very slight."

When William went into the jungle in July 1948, I realized that life is not only about making money. Here was my own brother, one of the finest human beings I have known, risking his own life to help the downtrodden. When Mother learned about William, she never uttered a word; but I think she must have felt the terrible sacrifice of her own flesh and blood.

After William went into the jungle, I missed him in the same acute way a lover misses an absent lover. I loved William very deeply.

Joy and I lived in a nice house in Johor. Our bedroom had a through breeze, so most nights we just opened the windows and slept under a mosquito net. There were evenings in tropical Malaya when there would be huge downpours, like waterfalls cascading onto the earth. Those rainstorms brought to mind that William was also experiencing similar rainstorms, and that no amount of dense forest can really shelter you from such heavy rain. The Communists were being chased by the British troops. I doubted that they enjoyed the safety of solid camps; I knew their life was harsh.

I recall often sobbing bitterly in bed, worrying about William in the jungle. Joy would console me and say, "He will be all right. He is a brave man."

I thought: "what a terrible life for my poor brother."

I recall the letters William wrote from the jungle, always to Philip, which Philip showed to me. But if he wrote seven to ten letters, Philip only showed me four or five. I think some of them were very personal. In resolve and in mental fibre, Philip was probably the weakest of us three, so he needed William.

After William disappeared into the jungle, a British Special Branch officer in Johor Bahru by the name of Leon Comber came to my newly set up Kuok Brothers Ltd office a few times. I had met Comber at cocktail receptions and at the Royal Johor International Club. Kuok Brothers had a small office on the ground floor.

Comber would suddenly pop in and say, "Hello, Robert. May I sit down?"

I'd answer, "Oh yes, please. There is a chair in front here. Do sit."

Then he'd say, "Aren't you going to buy me a cup of coffee?"

So I sent for a cup of coffee and he would just seem to be observing the office, looking around for signs. You know how they operate. He never once asked me a single question about William. He'd say, "How are things? How's business? Is your family well?" Kid gloves: You've got to admire that.

Comber married a famous Eurasian author, Han Suyin. She wrote a book called *And the Rain My Drink*, featuring characters apparently based on William, me and other people. Her husband perhaps furnished her with internal information. She talks about a family, middle class and fairly wealthy, where one brother went into the jungle and one was an arch capitalist.

In August 1953, the British forces ambushed William and his two bodyguards and killed all three of them in the jungle on the border of Negeri Sembilan and Pahang. One day, James Puthucheary came to see me and showed me a photo of William, lying with jungle leaves on his body.

I was, of course, deeply saddened, but my first thought was how to break the news to Mother. She loved William dearly. She knew he was suffering in the jungle, but she only asked about him once every few months. I decided that I would go with James that very moment to Mother's room to break the tragic news.

I told James to wait outside. I decided to keep the photo from her because that would have been too harsh a blow. I went in and said, "Mother, I have some bad news." I could instantly see that she knew what had happened. She was so telepathic. Her face suddenly turned as white as a sheet. I should have stopped then, but what other story could I tell?

So I said, "William has been killed." It was like a knife to her chest. She fainted and fell backwards with a thump onto the wooden floor. She was of light frame, so mercifully she wasn't badly injured. We managed to bring her around, but in the weeks and months that followed, there was deep sorrow in the house.

After that, Mother repeatedly exhorted us never to go into politics. She said, "I sacrificed one. That is more than enough. Please don't go into politics." After William's tragic death, her devotion to Buddhism intensified tenfold.

William devoted his life to justice. He saw bigotry and the awful, ugly aspects of British colonialism. He was expelled from school on unjust grounds. He saw the stupid ways of the Japanese conquerors. In a final straw, the British and Indian troops returned in 1945 as a re-occupation force.

It is a great and lasting tragedy that this remarkable human being was lost at the young age of 30, and so needlessly.

5
WORKING FOR FATHER

JAPAN SURRENDERED on 15 August 1945, but the British did not return to Malaya until the middle of September. When they did return, they were pitifully incompetent. Their intelligence had told them that the Japanese would not surrender, that the commander of the Japanese army in the Malay Peninsula and Singapore would dig in, fight and kill them and then commit hara-kiri. So the British held back and held back.

Then, some four weeks after the Japanese surrender, they sent a naval armada down the Straits of Malacca from southern India and Ceylon. On the coast outside Port Klang, the ships disgorged amphibious landing craft. The British hadn't even sent their spies to find out that it was all swamp and mud. They all got bogged down and would have been annihilated if the Japanese were still there to fight them. The whole scene was farcical.

The Allied forces never had to come back and fight. The Japanese just obediently laid down their arms. There was a ceremonial handing over of their swords, which was mere pageantry. But to make it seem that they were heroic victors, the Allies came with tanks and trucks, armed to the teeth. They rode through towns triumphantly. All the Chinese massacred were just forgotten.

Having suffered under the oppressive Japanese army of occupation, the peoples of Malaya – men and women, from the richest to the poorest, were praying for liberation by British or

Allied troops. What they got was a second army of occupation. Unfortunately, it seemed that the decent British had either died on the Death Railway in Thailand and Burma, or had become living skeletons in prisoner-of-war or civilian internee camps and had been quickly shipped back by troop ships to hospitals and convalescent homes in England and elsewhere. They were not around to advise and to make the reoccupation more humane.

When Charles de Gaulle went back to France, he was returning to his own country. The liberating forces hugged and kissed their countrymen. There was sheer joy and happiness. But these British and Indian troops had no feelings. They had disdain, amounting to contempt, for the local population. They had no thought of assuaging the hurt and suffering of the people of Malaya who had been under the Japanese heel for three and a half years. None at all! The British had come back to regain their colony, and that was how they behaved. It was shameful! There was no happiness in the eyes of these reoccupation forces. For them, it was another chore; it was an attempt to see where they could make some money or do some looting.

In August 1945, before the British had returned, they announced that the Japanese currency was from that moment no longer legal tender. The "banana dollar" was instantly valueless. The Japanese had passed a law when they came in 1942 saying that anyone caught with any other currency could be punished by execution. So now people had no currency of value. A bit of bartering went on, and gradually trade started, but from ground zero.

I worked in Mitsubishi up until early October 1945. Towards the end of August, the bosses at Mitsubishi told the staff, "Your jobs are terminated. All go home."

I went to my departmental boss, Uemura, and said, "I am prepared to carry on. You don't have to pay me. I just want to wind up my work." I knew there were still stocks of rice and cigarettes, and who would look after them? I felt a sense of responsibility. I didn't want to stay at home either.

I remember going to the office and being the only non-Japanese there. All the other Chinese had left and the office was virtually deserted. Before, there would be about 50 people at work. Now there were 15 at the most. I just turned up – with no ulterior motive – and for that the Japanese unexpectedly rewarded me.

Uemura came to me one day and said, "How much money do you and your father have?"

I asked "Why?"

He replied, "We have stocks of 200 or 300 bales of cigarette paper from Japan. I'll sell it to you for all this useless banana currency. You make an invoice; I'll sign it. You keep the receipt. Your property."

So I bought the very big reams of cigarette paper and gave them to Father. He eventually sold that cigarette paper for up to $400,000, legal tender, at a time when nobody had capital.

Then Cousin Number Twelve, Hock Seng, received a similar gift. He had been working in a Japanese cooperative society, a *kumiai*, which was the sole distributor of textiles. This *kumiai* ended the war with a big stock of cheap, Japanese floral cloth. The manager had taken a liking to my cousin and did the same thing for him. He said, "Give me some money and I'll sell all the remaining bales of textiles to you." So Hock Seng bought huge lorry loads of textiles with a valueless currency. He handed the goods to my father too. So Father, who continued with his rice trade, suddenly had capital in cash of some $700,000.

During my last week or so of working for the Japanese, Father's oldest nephew in Johor Bahru, my Cousin Number Five, Hock Chin, came by bicycle to see me at the office. He said, "Your father wants you to please go and help him. Please join the family firm."

Father wanted me, so I joined his Tong Seng & Co, though I regarded myself as only his employee. There was nothing else to do anyway. Raffles College didn't reopen until October 1946. All my life, I've believed in the therapy of being occupied. Man must work; work is therapeutic, it binds your mind and body together. When you work, you wake up earlier than everybody; you go to bed earlier than everybody because you need to recharge your batteries. You're not wasting your life away. Thank God, we didn't have television or stupid electronic games and all these awful magazines that sit on the newsstands nowadays, pandering to the base and vulgar instincts of man.

Within days of my joining Father in October 1945, he landed a contract with the British Military Administration (BMA). It was a contract to collect fresh vegetables and fruit every day from the countryside to be supplied to Japanese prisoners of war. These Japanese soldiers were brought from all over the Malay Peninsula and sent to a camp in a rubber estate near Renggam, about 40 miles north of Johor Bahru. To my recollection, at its height, the camp held about 80,000 Japanese prisoners of war.

I was put in charge of this fresh-produce contract. Tong Seng didn't have trucks at the time, so the British Army assigned me a detail of six Indian soldiers and six army trucks. I left home and set up a base in Segamat about 160 kilometres north of Johor Bahru. Every morning, the guards and I would drive to collect cheap vegetables and fruit such as bananas and pineapples from tilled lands on the borders of the jungle. Then we delivered the food to the Japanese POW camp at Renggam.

I remember staying in some awful Chinese-run hotels and inns. Downstairs would be a coffee shop where everybody, including beggars, would congregate. Upstairs would be two or three rooms to let. I would get a room and often see cockroaches and rats. It was like a cowboy town.

I could see the arrogance of the British officers. But as I spoke good English, I managed to charm some of them. One day, four or five months after I had started the job, Father said, "Send these gifts to the British officer's mess in Singapore." So, I went and met a Captain Paul and a Captain Leggett of the Second Division Cross Keys, both about three to four years older than me. They smoked pipes and acted very superior. Obviously, they were public-school types, the ruling class of Britain.

They said, "Robert, we like you a lot. Come to our mess."

Later that morning they said, "We're going out to the Japanese prisoner-of-war camp in Renggam. We'd like to take you along." They jumped into an open jeep, told me to climb in at the back and then raced from Singapore to Renggam at top speed on roads which lacked maintenance, and over Bailey bridges. I clung on, suffering all the way as my seat was not well cushioned.

When we got there, Paul and Leggett literally went in to loot the camp. The Japanese had been told anything of value had to be stripped. They surrendered air-force helmets, fur coats, long swords, watches, boots, etc – and these were piled into a huge heap in a circus-like tent. The two captains took whatever they liked, and said, "Help yourself, Robert." I did not touch a thing.

Just as the Japanese camp contract was winding down in September 1946, Father had another lucky break. Lt-Colonel Hugh Beadles, Food Controller of the BMA in Kuala Lumpur, appointed him as the South Johor essential-foodstuffs – rice, sugar and wheat flour – distributor. I became the manager of the food depot.

One day in September 1946, a Major Carter and a Captain Pritchard went from shop to shop in our neighbourhood. Pritchard was a public-school type who was a spitting image of the actor Rex

Harrison. Carter was more tubby, a nice Australian. Finally, they came to Father's shop.

They must have liked what they saw. Father and Hock Chin, both a lot older than these two soldiers, were present. The soldiers asked if my father would like to take on the government rice, sugar and flour agency and distributorship for southern Johor State. Just like that.

The BMA in Kuala Lumpur had devised its own essential foodstuffs distribution scheme after the war. There was no more Mitsubishi or Mitsui. In the big cities like Kuala Lumpur and Singapore, the British firms were given the monopoly. Boustead was handed rice; Guthrie got sugar; Sime Darby was given wheat flour. But in Johor there were no British shops. So we were appointed government rice, sugar and flour agents and distributors for Johor Bahru and the surrounding region.

Prior to awarding this contract, the BMA was distributing the rice itself as a government operation. I was ordered to go up and take over the government supply depot, which consisted of three or four big warehouses in the tiny village of Tampoi near Johor Bahru.

Father asked me to take charge of these operations. The chief of the godowns was Captain Norman Callan. Captain Pritchard arranged for me, with a letter in my hand, to meet Callan in Tampoi. I was 23. I remember Callan was one or two years my junior – at that time, the BMA was giving out fairly senior military appointments to very young people. At first he was a little bullying, but I soon got on well with him. We overlapped for about three or four days. At the end, I had to sign for all the stocks handed to me – many thousands of bags of rice, sugar and wheat flour. He saluted me and handed over the depot. Since that day, I have been associated with warehouses my entire life!

Before Captain Callan left, he said to me, "I want to draw your attention to a very wonderful young Malay whom I've been using as an errand boy. I think he deserves better. His name is Othman bin Samad, with a nickname of Kadir." Kadir was very winning; very alert. He was of Javanese stock, but born in Tampoi. He became one of the key people in the important, early years of the development of my own business.

Kadir, who was 17 or 18 then, told me a hair-raising story of how he was one of the Malays who was arbitrarily rounded up by Japanese troops in early 1945. He was in his village when the Japanese military came, blocked both ends of the street and grabbed the Malay men. They took them to a military camp and turned them into virtual army slave labour. They shaved their heads and didn't allow them out of the camp.

Kadir continued to work with me at Kuok Brothers, and, in some 12 years, had risen to become a full manager. He eventually joined the Board of Directors, and remained with us until he retired.

Because Father had many large buyers of rice, demand was greater than supply. He decided that one way to obtain more rice was to send a senior member of his staff on the two-day train journey up to Kedah, the main rice-growing area of Malaya which grew more than enough for its own consumption. I took part in some of those trips.

People not only needed rice; they also needed protein. In early 1947, Johor was very short of meat. Before the outbreak of the war, Father had operated two fresh red-meat stalls in the wet market of Johor Bahru, which was where almost everyone in town went to buy their meat.

The man who usually journeyed up to Kedah to buy rice came back and said, "Hey, people are now trading surplus water buffaloes there for their meat."

So father said, "Okay, buy three or four and bring them down."

These poor members of his staff would herd the live water buffaloes onto goods trains and stay with the animals during the entire journey south. Sometimes, the workers would get driven off the trains, hitchhike or ride on open trucks to the next station, and then bribe the stationmaster to let them get back on the next goods train. It took them a week or more to complete the journey to Johor. Then they dragged the water buffaloes to the nearest abattoir.

In the three years after the war, Father made $4 million in Malayan dollars. But he didn't know how to invest it. He just sat on his pile of money; he didn't make it work for him.

It was only after I joined his business that I realised how poorly the business was run. He was disorganized, vacillating and lacking in leadership skills. He did not reward good performance. He was afraid that if he gave one nephew a bigger appointment he would offend the others. His lack of action fostered a festering disunity in the shop. That was his nature. The worst were my Cousins Number Two and Five, who had taken up opium smoking and constantly displayed petty jealousy. Number Ten wasn't very bright over business. The company was really in quite a mess.

When I saw that, I realized that if I ever started a company, there would be no nepotism, no weakness. We are relatives – fine. But in the company, discipline matters. Whoever can produce the profits gets the reward. Simple. And I later cracked the whip over all my cousins, every one of them older than me.

I worked very hard for Father. I must have personally contributed at least 30 percent of his new fortune. I drove the shop, yet he didn't pay me properly. I received a salary of only $600 a month. He also paid Philip, who looked after the transport side, the same – and Philip already had one child and a second on the way.

Father's greatest strength in business was his shrewdness; he was a clever judge of the situation and the people involved. In this regard, he was cleverer than Mother, who was more principled and dogmatic. Father was willing to listen; he was pragmatic, a born businessman.

I was indispensable to him from 1945-1948. I did everything for my job. I gave it my all. But there was no love lost. The way Father treated me became rocket fuel inside me that drove me on. I was a truculent young man. He was a poor father to my brothers and me, and I showed my resentment of such treatment.

As my wedding drew near in 1947, Mother said, "Nien, I made plans long ago to return to China. I cannot postpone it any longer. I have many sorrows in my heart and I feel I have to go back. I wish you and Joy every happiness; but son, I am not going to be present at your wedding." She had made up her mind never to return. She wanted to sever with Father; not to divorce, but never to see him again. In June 1947, she said goodbye to her three sons and left for Fuzhou.

In October 1947, Joyce and I sailed from Singapore to Hong Kong aboard a Dutch passenger ship for our honeymoon. We stayed with Joyce's maternal cousin, Iris Prew, a widow whose Eurasian husband, a schoolteacher, had been killed by the Japanese in the war.

I showed the anger that I felt from bearing so much of the burden of the work at Tong Seng by spending ten weeks in Hong Kong on my honeymoon, despite entreaties from Father.

In late November or early December 1948, Philip received a letter from Mother. It was written in Chinese. As I could read Chinese, Philip showed it to me. Mother was bemoaning Father's selfishness. She had visited his relatives, and everyone was desperately poor. They knew how well he was doing, and she felt under enormous pressure to assist. She had asked for money and Father was withholding it. Mother felt helpless. Her letter was not meant to provoke, but Philip got into a tearing rage. My brother said that he was going to have it out with Father. By that time, I was seeing Father more often than Philip was because I was deeply involved in running Tong Seng. Father would come every evening to review the day's business with me.

I said, "Philip, you have lost your temper. Let me go down and ask Father to send the money."

The scene is still very vivid in my memory. I went after lunch, a little agitated because the letter had provoked me, too. I went in and, as bad luck would have it, Father was in a foul mood. I parked the car, walked into the shop and I didn't like what I saw. He wore a very nasty look on his face. I was rude. I said, "Eh, look at this letter from Mother." I don't think I even addressed him. He just glanced at the letter and pushed it aside, equally rudely.

Within seconds I was a volcano. I screamed at him, just short of hitting him. I was a young man of 25, full of vigour. I said, "Damn you! You treated Mother badly all along and you still treat her like that! You scum!" He stared daggers at me. He tried to cut me down with his glare. Two or three cousins in the shop tried to calm me. I stormed off.

A week later, Father was admitted to hospital after suffering a heart attack. He never came out. He had a second attack about three weeks later and died of coronary thrombosis on 26 December 1948.

I didn't know his health was so bad, but apparently it went into a downward spiral after that huge row. From time to time, I have felt that I had hastened his death.

PART II
–
BUILDING
THE BUSINESS

6
MY FIRST LOAN

FATHER DIED without a will.

Following the Japanese surrender, Father had re-registered Tong Seng & Co as a sole proprietorship. We went to court to get an appointment as managers, to permit us to continue to run the firm. The judge ruled that, as there were two widows, the firm and the estate should be wound up. He quoted as a precedent the ruling of the very famous Six Widows' Case of Singapore in 1908.

The judge said that as Father had died intestate, the law was very simple. One third of his nett estate after death duties was to be shared equally between the two widows, Mother getting one-sixth and the second widow also one-sixth. The remaining two-thirds would be shared among his children. Mother had three sons; second widow had three sons and two daughters. The eight children shared the remaining two-thirds, each receiving one-twelfth.

Mother came back from China shortly after the funeral. William's money was handed over to the official assignee. By that time, he had been in the jungle for about five months. When he finally heard that Father had died, he wrote to us in semi-parables – he didn't want to incriminate Philip – saying he'd been told an old businessman we knew had passed away and that he was sorry to hear about it.

I remember my inheritance was around $130,000 in Malayan currency. After the war, Father started from scratch and made about four million dollars. I believe that about three-quarters of a million went to pay off debts. After settling taxes and matters like funeral expenses and lawyers' bills, there was only about one and a half million left.

Then we formed Kuok Brothers Limited. In mid-January 1949, five of us met around a small table in our home in Johor Bahru. Apart from me, also present were Mother, Philip, Hock Chin (Number Five Cousin) and Hock Seng (Number Twelve Cousin). The latter had grown up in our household. We sat down and Mother said, "Nien, would you like to start?"

I said, "First, I'd like to assure all of you I've made up my mind to work flat out. I'm very confident that I will raise this new company of ours, Kuok Brothers, to great heights. Before any one of us at this table is dead, that person will be worth more, hopefully much more, than Father was at the time of his death." They probably thought I was braying to the moon!

I continued, "Let's talk about shareholding. Let's start with $100,000 at first as paid-up capital (the exchange rate then was $3.06 to the US dollar)." I didn't want more than 25 percent. I wasn't being humble, but neither was I arrogant. I just stated fact: 25 percent was fully sufficient for my family and me.

I noted that Hock Chin had been brought over by Father at a young age, trained to assist Father in his business and, at the time of Father's death, was general manager. If Father was CEO, Hock Chin was deputy. And Hock Chin had seven grown-up children. (I didn't have any children yet. Joy was expecting our first child within the next two months.) So I proposed 25 percent for Hock Chin too.

Immediately, Hock Seng, whom I adored and was like another brother to me, drew himself up, not taking my proposal very well. Before I could go any further, he blurted out, "Nien, I disagree. Your 25 percent I support because you deserve it. But Hock Chin, no!" I tried to persuade him.

Then Mother wisely said, "Can we put aside this problem of Hock Chin's share?"

Hock Chin sat very quietly. Philip joined Mother and said that he would talk with Hock Seng later.

I continued, "Hock Seng, you take 15; Philip take 15; Mother take 10." That left another 10. Now, Third Uncle had two sons. One was Hock Yao, Cousin Number Eleven. I said Hock Yao had always been rather disdainful of our family company and had preferred to work for Lee Kong Chian of Lee Rubber. So I suggested nothing for Hock Yao. I said, let's allot five percent to his younger brother, Hock Ming, who was Cousin Number Twenty-one. That left five percent, which I suggested we keep in reserve.

Then Mother said, "Nien, may I say a few words? Why don't we let the second widow have it?" So everybody agreed and somebody was sent over to talk to her. She paid in $5,000 and became a five percent shareholder. (She sold her shares a few years later after habitually gambling and losing money playing mahjong.)

Then we came to appointments. I said, "I'd like to propose that Philip, being my eldest brother, become Chairman. Hock Chin, as he was Father's general manager, should take the title of Managing Director. Hock Seng will be an Executive Director. I will also be an Executive Director, but at the same time Company Secretary." (I'd been reading up on the Companies Act.) So that's how we started. Kuok Brothers Limited was registered on 23 February 1949, and started business on 1 April 1949.

I drove the business right from the beginning. I'm not denigrating the others. I'm just stating a fact. Philip was less pragmatic than I was, but it was he who eventually persuaded Hock Seng to accept the idea of giving Hock Chin a 25 percent share.

Hock Chin, 17 years my senior, was a kindly man, but he had

been hooked on drugs for over 20 years and therefore a spent force. Hock Seng was a fine human being, but he was very shy by nature, didn't mix easily with others, and wasn't in extremely good health. Yet, during the difficult early years when we were trying to establish our fledgling company, he was always the stoutest and most dependable pillar. He was a man of few words, but clear-minded, and he always spoke straight to the point. Unfortunately, he died very young.

So it fell to me to run the business. I knew that I had what was needed to be a businessman, like a duck taking to water. I am a very focused person. When I do something, I want to do it well. But I must stress, Mother became the symbol for the business and the clan; she was the backbone.

At the time of his passing, Father was rice agent and distributor for the southern one-third of Johor State. Within a few weeks of his death, Hock Chin and I made a trip to Kuala Lumpur to see Lt-Col Hugh Beadles, Controller of Supplies, Ministry of Trade and Industry under the British Military Administration.

Beadles, who was portly and quite tall, wore rimless glasses. He was a very fine man. He was friendly to Hock Chin and me, and said that he had read in the papers of my father's death, and he understood why Tong Seng's business had to be dissolved. "I trust both of you," he said. "The two of you have already been running the rice distribution business. Therefore, I am prepared to pass the agency to your new company." But, he added, since we had formed a newly incorporated business, we needed to come up with a banker's guarantee of $100,000.

I had already been playing golf for two or three years at that time, and was a member of a fairly exclusive golf club, the Royal Johor International Club. I had met the local manager of the Hongkong & Shanghai Bank, Mr Fawcett, and had had one or two games of golf with him. Fawcett was a nice, straightforward, and serious English bank manager. So I went to the Hongkong Bank. This was one or two months after Father's death.

I explained the situation to Fawcett – what happened to Father, how Father had been awarded this business and how the Government's Controller of Supplies wanted me to furnish a banker's guarantee from a reputable bank for the new company. Fawcett said, "I know, but we have to put friendship aside. You deposit $100,000 in a fixed account with the Bank, which you cannot take back, and I'll issue the $100,000 guarantee."

I wasn't happy, of course. It doesn't take a fool to realize that I would be guaranteeing myself. How does he guarantee me? My deposit would sit there for many years without interest, and this was 1949 when $100,000 was big money.

The British banks practiced blatant racial discrimination. They would lend to any white beachcomber before they would lend to decent local businessmen. You were trusted by the colour of your skin.

I would come up against that colonial attitude time and time again. In 1952, I began buying and selling Japanese toys supplied by a company in Singapore called Rickwood & Co Ltd. The sole owner was Rickwood, who was either Australian or British. I was 28 years old and Rickwood was about six to ten years older than me.

One day, Rickwood tried to woo me to buy into his company as a senior partner. He showed me what I later found out was a doctored set of accounts, even though he said they were audited. That's when I noticed that he owed the Hongkong Bank Singapore about $300,000. This man had been nothing but a sergeant in the Australian or British army, yet after demobilization, he was able to get that kind of financing to run a business. To live the life of a so-called successful British trader, he had bought a beautiful house on Andrew Road, close to the Royal Singapore Golf Club. It showed me that colonialism meant that the banks practiced blatant racism.

Rickwood wanted me to come in and buy 70 percent of Rickwood & Co's shares. I thought, well, I need an autonomous company in Singapore, a sort of Kuok Brothers Singapore branch. It would be useful in case one day Singapore and Malaya divide – as they eventually did – and adopt different sets of laws and different tax regimes. However, after I had paid a fairly substantial deposit, I began to smell a rat. We did our due diligence and found that his company was nothing but a can of worms. The man was trying to lure me into the firm to soak up his bad debts.

When I announced that I wasn't going to proceed with the deal, Rickwood suggested we talk over lunch. "We can discuss everything. I'll put everything right and you'll come in." When I confronted him, his face changed colour. He would not let me go. "Come back to the office with me afterwards. Come; come to my room."

We went upstairs to his office. In the wall was a safe. "Let me show you something." I thought it was very odd; why should I walk with him to the safe? Then he beckoned. He opened the safe in front of me and in the middle was a revolver.

"What are you showing me?"

"Oh, nothing, nothing; never mind." He was trying to intimidate me. He closed the safe. I just took it in stride. I didn't even remark upon it.

One of the greatest challenges I faced when I was coming up in business was obtaining credit from banks. I hated dealing with any bank after I suffered that mental bruising from the Hongkong Bank. I worked hard, but I didn't know how to project myself to bankers. My temperament, character and sensitivities are such that I could never humble myself before them, and that has been true to this very day.

But we needed bank financing to conduct business. We were not

My mother, Tang Kak Ji, before her marriage, c 1917.

My father, Kuok Keng Kang, c 1920s.

My mother and her family in China, c 1924. From left: my aunt, grandmother, grandfather, my brother Philip, mother, and my uncle.

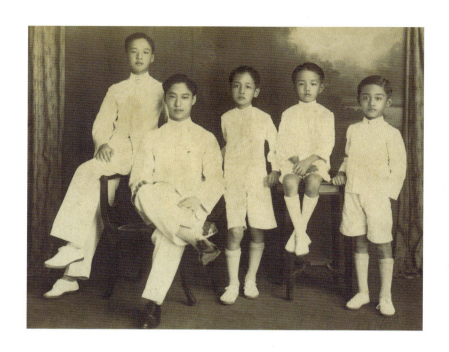

Top Kuok cousins, c 1927. From left: Hock Seng (12th cousin), Hock Kin (10th), Philip (17th), myself (20th), and William (18th).

Right Mother and, from left, William, Philip and myself, c 1935.

Left Father, c 1937.

Below With Ah Kow, my father's very trustworthy assistant and his son, November 1989.

Right My brother William, aged 25, with his niece, Philip's daughter, Kay Kuok Oon Kwong, end 1947.

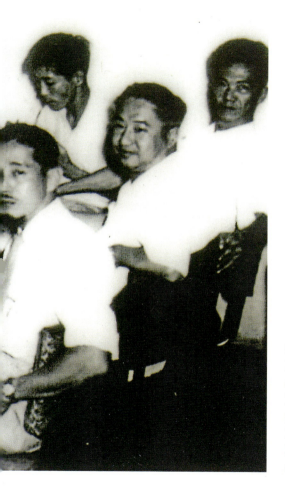

Some Kuok cousins, c 1950. From left are Hock Swee (14th cousin), Hock Seng (12th), Hock Chin (5th), myself (20th), Hock Toh (13th), Hock Kee (15th), Philip (17th), Hock Ming (21st), Hock Kin (10th), and Hock Yao (11th).

Top My mother's prayer room
in her house in Johor Bahru.

Right Mother in her Buddhist
robes, c 1970.

Left My late wife, Joyce,
c 1980.

Top Mother and my children
from Joyce, c 1959. From left:
Ruth, mother, Beau, Sue, Jill
and Ean.

Left My wife, Poh Lin, 2013.

Top My wife Poh Lin and I with our children, Hua, Yen and Hui, c 2003.

Standing from left: My sons Hua, Ean, Beau, and my nephews Edward and Chye. Seated from left: myself, Ean's son Meng Xiong and my brother Philip, c 1984.

Singapore-born; we came from Johor. We swam out of a tributary of the main river, but Singapore only trusted the fish in its own river. Who was this funny-looking fish?

That's where Bangkok Bank aided me. Most banks didn't talk to us until Chin Sophonpanich of Bangkok Bank came along. As soon as Bangkok Bank trusted us, we could also go to other banks.

One afternoon in Singapore, a Teochew rice-trader friend said to me, "Aren't you going to the airport this evening?" I was then commuting daily by car from Johor Bahru to my Kuok (Singapore) Ltd office.

"What for?" I asked.

He replied, "The founder and big boss of Bangkok Bank is arriving tonight. The plane is due in from Bangkok about 7.30 pm. We're all going to meet him."

"Who is all?"

"Every rice merchant in Singapore."

So I thought, well, I'm a rice merchant, too. Can I afford not to go?

I was at the airport 45 minutes early. When Chin's plane landed, the rice merchants formed a long line of about 50 people. They squeezed and pushed me, and I got shoved down to be letter "Z" in the queue. I didn't mind. I was the new boy on the block amongst all those rice traders. About six out of ten were Teochews (Chin Sophonpanich was a Teochew); four out of ten were Southern Hokkiens. I was from Fuzhou – we had no clout anywhere.

Chin walked all the way down the line and shook each hand, as someone introduced him to the traders. I was the last to shake hands with him, and, of course, he was curious to know who I was. We exchanged cards. His aide said, "Oh, Big Boss Piak, this is Kuek Hock Nee (my Chinese name in the Teochew dialect). His company is called Kuok Brothers." Chin was very courteous, a fine gentleman, but a stern-looking man. In stature, he was a little shorter than me, but stockier.

Chin said, "One day, I will make arrangements to see you in your office."

I assumed this was just a pleasantry but, sure enough, three or four days later, my office in Singapore received a phone call to say Chairman Chin of Bangkok Bank would like to see me. So I replied, "Fine, I'm free," and waited. Chin came over with two aides, and we sat and chatted.

I later realized why Chin made that effort. Instead of waiting for people to visit him in the splendour of his office, he was actually checking out every shop. He wanted to see and feel how you operated, how you placed your desk, the sense of drive in the office, the atmosphere – and he had to do this personally.

It's not just the physical appointment of the shop. When you enter a man's office or shop, you can get a feel, a psychic feel, of how well that firm is doing or may one day be doing. It's an abstract thing. Can you feel something in the air? Is the firm charged with good electricity, or is it dull, fading, or dying?

Chin seemed very pleased with what he saw. Straight away he said, "What kind of business are you doing?"

And after I replied, he said, "Now look here. I'll give you ten million for letters of credit. And I'll give you banker's acceptances up to one half of that, five million. These trust-receipt facilities will enable you to draw the goods. Sell them first, and then repay me the money."

Bang, bang, bang. He did it just like that. I will never forget that act. A fantastic banker showed confidence in me. These are the helping hands a young businessman needs when he is setting out in life. I gained a lot of confidence about the possibility of getting more credit, more facilities to help my business grow. Here was a banker with whom I could interact.

Chin Sophonpanich was a real breath of fresh air. In colonial British Malaya, the British banks were extremely cautious about lending to Chinese businessmen. Nor did the equally dour, dowdy overseas-Chinese banks have much time for you. How is a man ever to get up in life when he can't even borrow one cent? Most of the Chinese businessmen of Singapore and Malaysia owe a lot to Bangkok Bank and Chin.

Bankers live by a simple creed: Lend money to those who do not need to borrow. When you're penniless, your banks will desert you as if you're a leper. That is one irony of the world. I don't entirely blame the bankers. I just think it's a heartless trade. I have often said, "Bankers are not my friends. Among my friends, some happen to be bankers."

One of the first things that drove me to make money in business was the humiliation I suffered at the hands of the banks. Until you get on to the top ledge, you are always in danger of drowning. Damn it, I thought! So that is the business world; that is capitalism? Now, if that doesn't drive you forward in life to make as much money as possible so you can thumb your nose at those bankers, then what will?

7

THE SUN SETS ON
THE BRITISH EMPIRE

I WAS TERRIBLY FORTUNATE to come of age at a time when
Malaya was undergoing dramatic change. My parents emigrated
from China to colonial Malaya, and that was the world into which
I was born and grew up. Then, the Japanese came and overran
Malaya – and the British. In turn, the Japanese were themselves
humiliated.

After the war, the sun set on the great British Empire. The
former colonies began to break away, starting with India. European
empires that had survived for four centuries or more were being
dismantled. It was the dawn of a new era.

I was old enough to understand events, and possessed the
enormous vitality and vigour of youth. As colonialism entered its
death throes, I was determined to capitalize on the opportunities.
I worked with Father for three years and three months, which gave
me a good grounding in business. When he died, I started a new
firm, and eight years later Malaysia became independent. Those
eight years were critical years of preparation for me.

There were a great many decadent Chinese and Europeans
around me. I made a few simple resolutions: I would not become
a member of the decadent world; I would work hard; and I would
take advantage of the loosened political straitjacket to succeed.

When we started Kuok Brothers on 1 April 1949, we were
ill equipped to face the world around us. The inside track of

colonialism still prevailed, under which the British and their Asian compradors, cronies, hangers-on, lackeys and boot-polishers all enjoyed favoured treatment.

Other businesses were dominated by the Chinese from southern Fujian and, from further south, the Teochews and Hakkas. These are strong Chinese dialect groups with their own cultures and practices. They ran the businesses of every town and city of Malaya and Singapore. Fuzhou, where my parents came from, was the administrative centre of the Province of Fujian. It was a place of learning, populated by mandarins and petty tradesmen. Where it came to ruthlessness, we were not half as ruthless; where it came to unscrupulous behaviour, we were not half as unscrupulous; where it came to dash and speed and determination, we were not half as quick as our Chinese competitors.

Colonialism gave rise to many of the problems that the world faces to this day. In every colony, the purported master race was given special favours. When I saw that the British colonial empire would not survive, I sensed two things. One: there would be opportunities for me to flex my muscles and spread my wings. I would no longer be hemmed in by the colonial rulers. Two: the British firms, like Guthrie, Boustead and Sime Darby, would not give up without a struggle. Independent Malaysia would need strong-minded businessmen, well equipped mentally to compete and challenge the old firms on a level playing field – something we never had in colonial times.

I was full-blooded and confident, and I despised the racism of the colonial rulers in Malaya and Singapore. I remember one firm – Harper Gilfillan – printed the words: "No receipt is valid unless signed by a European member of the staff" on its invoices. I thought that if they openly, without compunction, dared to insult 95 percent of their staff, then they were either fully mad or bent on self-destruction. If I were one of their local staff, I would want to sabotage them from the inside. Can you imagine? You are not telling your people, "Work hard and you shall be rewarded." You are saying that the white man is forever superior to you, just because he was born with another type of pigmentation.

I focused from the beginning on commodities with very ready markets: basic foodstuffs such as rice, sugar and wheat flour. Business revolved around the simple trading of these three commodities for the first ten years of Kuok Brothers.

I first concentrated on rice. Everyone in Asia must eat rice. We contacted the trading firms in Singapore and bought rice from them. We were honourable, so they trusted us, which was important since trade was seldom done on a cash-over-the-counter basis prior to delivery. We typically paid within two weeks. Occasionally, we'd seek two or three days' grace, whereas the norm in the trade was that two weeks became extended to four or six weeks. We therefore developed a good reputation in the trade. Because of this, if you met with a good seller, he would even give you a silent discount not known to the rest of the trade because he knew his money and goods were safe with you. It's just common-sense business, and we managed to make a bit of money.

We also received a wheat-flour allocation from Sime Darby for the Johor market. I indented from them 100, 200, 300 tons, and sent the flour to Johor Bahru for distribution to the same customers who were buying rice and sugar from us. These were dealers or retailers who sold the goods in their villages.

One day, while playing golf in Singapore, I met with one of Philip's schoolmates from Serdang Agricultural College. This man's father was fairly big in the rubber trade. I said, "Hock Soon, where can I get some office space? I want to branch out to Singapore. The basin in which I'm swimming is too small for me. I've got to swim out into the lake."

Hock Soon answered, "Well, I've got spare space. I'll let you have 600 square feet." He charged me quite a lot of money. I think it was $6,000. When I went down, all we got was about 250 square feet of space. When I'm diddled by people, I don't make a fuss; I just bear it in my heart. I have made a mistake; I have put my foot into a hole, twisted or fractured my ankle. So what! Let it heal and get on with it.

With our feet on the ground in Singapore, we began to look around. One day, at the end of 1952, I saw an advertisement in *The Straits Times* calling for tenders for the government rice agency which was up for renewal. This was a Federation of Malaya Government appointment for an agent in the port of Singapore to receive rice from overseas cargo ships, store it in warehouses rented or built by the Malayan Government in Singapore, and eventually to transport the rice to the southern half of the Malay Peninsula.

I checked around and learned that East Asiatic Company, a Danish firm, had been the agent for four or five years. White men's firms had held the agency since the reoccupation of Malaya and Singapore by British forces. Everybody warned me that we had no hope of getting it. No non-white-man's company had ever put in a tender. The local firms all went under the illusion that they would stand no chance whatsoever. But I did not subscribe to that theory. So I put in a tender, a very low bid, and lo and behold we were awarded the business. We even recruited some staff for the operation from East Asiatic Company.

So, from early 1953, we were the government rice agents of the Malayan Government in Singapore. All the shipments of rice came from Bangkok. Kuok (Singapore) Ltd was the consignee. As a little minnow, Singapore felt like a lake to me. Here was my vehicle, a government rice agency, which would pay me my bread and butter, cover our overheads, while I continued to look around. As soon as I could, I moved to 44 Cecil Street, the site of a rubber warehouse that I converted into an office with a shop front. We traded from there.

I sometimes travelled up to Kuala Lumpur, where college schoolmates invited me to dinners. At these parties, I met senior officers in the government, mainly locals who had been inducted into government service or who had been promoted through the ranks. Kuala Lumpur was always the centre of Malaya. It was where the British based their High Commissioner for the entire Malay Peninsula. He was on an equal footing with the officially designated governor of the Straits Settlements that comprised Singapore, Malacca, and Penang.

On those visits to Kuala Lumpur, I noticed that some of the Chinese businessmen in the city were stepping up the tempo of their "public relations" work. I purposely use the term public relations in quotes, because there was a very thin – and sometimes invisible – line between public relations and corrupt practices. Businessmen crossed easily from one to the other and back again. It was all pretty crude in those days.

A few messes had sprung up in Kuala Lumpur. "Mess" was a very common term used by the British. In the army, all the officers of each regiment, division, company or battalion had a mess. Uniformed officers of different ranks congregated in their respective messes. That was where they had their social life. When there were dances, they came in their ceremonial dress while their wives wore flowing gowns.

But these new messes were different. They were developed by the Chinese of Kuala Lumpur, together with some of their Malay friends, and were run as private clubs. It would be too glaring – too obvious – if the messes were purely owned and operated by Chinese, so you would usually find two, three or four Chinese and one, two or three Malays in control. The most famous one was Koko's Mess, which was the nickname of a famous Malay orthopaedic surgeon who was a member.

You often heard that rather than doing business in government offices, most real business was conducted in these clubs during cocktail hour. You'd buttonhole and lobby a man by grabbing him by the lapels of his coat, so to speak, and whisper into his ear. Then little things would be granted. A lot of white men – planters and civil servants – congregated at the Railway Station Bar in Kuala Lumpur.

At the messes, you would park your car and walk in very quickly, passing through a pair of swinging doors similar to those of a cowboy saloon. On one side would be civil servants, including one or two important ones whom the people running the clubs or messes would cultivate. In most of them, you saw a number of pretty young women about.

I was taken to these messes. There would be games of mahjong going on, and a bar area with chairs and sofas. Men lounged around, and the girls sat with them – a lot of apparently good, clean fun. But, of course, what transpired beyond that was seldom seen.

It was a decadent culture, and many of the Chinese businessmen in Kuala Lumpur would be in these clubs every night. It was almost as if they had to show off that they could down a bottle of brandy. People were drinking themselves stupid.

So I thought: good for me. While these people play on their banjos, I can plan, plot and drive my business plans forward. And with the waning of British colonial rule, fewer favours were being granted to British or other white firms.

As a young man, I believed that there was no substitute for hard work. I spent my time thinking up good, honest business plans and pushing them along without respite. This meant you had to work a minimum of 12 solid hours a day. I never had a day's rest, except for my 1947 honeymoon to Hong Kong with Joy, and a six-month trip to Europe with Mother in 1951. I worked every day of my life, including Sundays. I weighed about 100 pounds (45 kilograms) and was like a walking skeleton, working hard and driving myself all the time.

Post-war, the colonial British brought in quite a lot of unsavoury men – incompetent administrators, some even corrupt. But there were also some very good people. I met one in particular, a lovely, saintly man called Richard Kelly. If there was one Britisher who never played ball with or subscribed to what I call the ugly colonial ruler's ways, immortalized in the books of Somerset Maugham, it was Richard Kelly. Kelly was a man of the highest integrity who never handed out favours. He ran his job as Controller, Trade Division, of the Ministry of Trade and Industry in Kuala Lumpur impartially and very correctly, and he ran it well.

Kelly was a highly intellectual, scholarly graduate of Cambridge University. He had read Classics, and had the eyes of a poet. He was kind, soft-spoken and very balanced – in many ways a wise man. He didn't look down on any fellow being, regardless of colour or station in life. I never saw Kelly lose his temper; he was a real English gentleman. If I were forced to pick two of the loveliest people I have met in my lifetime, I would immediately name Nagaoka Koichi and Richard Kelly.

You could see in Kelly a man who was disturbed by many of the things that went on around him. Like the Buddha, Kelly was troubled by the inequalities in human society. And like the Buddha, he began to experiment with different forms of human belief and practice.

The colonial administrators were given about three months'

annual leave every two years. On several occasions, Kelly spent three to four weeks of his leave in a monastery in Burma. He sat in monastery rooms without walls, with no protection from the mosquitoes, eating one very light meal a day and meditating for three solid weeks. He was that type of man, a man with deep beliefs in the goodness of mankind.

I asked him to describe his experiences to me. It was really quite enlightening to hear him speak. When you were with Richard Kelly, you never sensed condescension or arrogance or pride. He was your equal as a human being; he was about the most learned Britisher I have met.

Then there was another man. I will not name him. This other man was very garrulous, with a good gift of the gab. He was always at the officers' messes of Kuala Lumpur, hobnobbing with his superiors. He was Richard Kelly's boss. One day, I was directed to him on a business matter. By then, he was well known to have two or three Chinese cronies. You knew from gossip that he was almost too close to these businessmen and business touts.

So I went to his office. He was a cordial enough person, sort of a slap-you-on-the-back, hail-fellow-well-met type, but you never knew whether his intentions were good or bad. As I was about to discuss my problem with him, his phone rang. The call was obviously from a very senior man because he was very deferential.

Now, all my life, I have tried to listen carefully. I was born that way. When I go into a room, I've seen everyone before they've seen me. I hear every sound, including those that others may have missed. Most of the time, I'm playing a game of poker and pretending I've seen nothing. I have always relied on my senses to guide me.

So, he underestimated me, because he didn't ask me to leave before he took the call. He kept on talking and, just listening to his words, I understood that the superior was asking him what he thought of Richard Kelly. I heard words like, "He's not one of us. Could be a dangerous man." By the drift of the conversation, I knew that he wanted to get rid of Kelly. Since Kelly did not share the values of the unified civil service, he was considered a potential traitor. I was truly aghast when I heard all these things.

Sure enough, before too long, Kelly's contract ended and it was not renewed. I had a very clear-cut confirmation of how the colonial administration of the post-war years worked and networked.

I have always regarded colonialism as one of the great curses of mankind, both for the perpetrator and for the colonized.

I would say that nine out of ten individual British civil servants were probably very fine people, model human beings. Often, when they were in school teaching us, or when we met them in the street, they were as nice as any other person. But when they went to their own clubs or started to talk business, they seemed to turn into different people.

When I was growing up, British manufactured goods enjoyed substantial preferential tariffs. Malaya and other colonies of Britain produced basic raw materials that were shipped back to England and processed – adding value and creating the real wealth. Then Britain shipped the finished goods back to Malaya, where they were protected from all competition by the preferential duty system.

The cars that plied the roads of Malaya and Singapore were of brands like Austin, Morris, Hillman and Singer. There were a dozen British makes that entered the market at preferential rates of duty. When the British Empire was dismantled, those cocooned manufacturers went belly up one by one.

In the 1960s, I was invited to meet the chairmen and CEOs of a number of companies in London. I went along and had lunch in their boardrooms. I recall observing that this was where the wealth of the former colonies reposed. You could smell the air of decay.

And it goes without saying that the burden carried by the colonized is far worse – sometimes even crippling. The world is still suffering from the long-lasting after-effects of colonialism: many of the problems in the Middle East, in Asia, and in Africa have their roots in the colonial era.

Colonialists like to think they are bringing civilization to the natives. They always play the same gramophone record: "Were it not for us, you would all still be ignorant people running around in bare feet." Such arguments are puerile. If the West had not come to interfere with China, would the clock have stopped ticking? Even if you could do some good, you have no right to go into people's homes and say, "You don't know how to run your home," turf them out and make "improvements".

In fact, colonialism stunts a country's development. The colonies never experienced legitimate economic development because the colonizers didn't harness the true energy of the people. It was one-sided development, as in King Solomon's mines, where those in charge cracked whips on the backs of Nubian slaves.

The Han Chinese know what it is to be colonized, by the Manchus and, before them, by the Mongols. We didn't invite these people to come and be our overlords! You can't understand the resentment of a colonized subject until you are colonized. If you think I'm talking a lot of nonsense, then I can only wish for you to be colonized one day. Then you can understand the indignities suffered by a colonized people. The worst thing in life is not shortage of food; it's human indignity.

Trade in rice was not terribly lucrative, but the volumes were large. Every now and again, there would be a disruption in the market, and prices would shoot up. If you weren't spending your time in the nightclubs drinking your mind into an alcohol-sodden state and you were the first to wake up in the morning, you could quickly run to the phone, call Bangkok and buy rice before the price rose.

There was no trade in rice futures in those days, only in physicals. So how could you get on the inside track? You had to make trips to Bangkok to develop strong personal ties with the exporters who had a very good feel for the market. Once we had reliable information, we would beg the Thai traders: "Come on, give me 500 tons."

They would say, "Oh no, Mr Kuok. You know the price is going up." They would always make an excuse: "All my stocks have been spoken for. You've got to buy at today's price, which is already £3 a ton higher. If you want, I can let you have 100 or 200 hundred tons, but there are eight people in front of you in the queue."

So you kept on haggling. Normally, he's willing to give you 400 tons, but he's now thinking 200 tons. If, after much back and forth, you can squeeze another 100 tons out of him, you think you've won. But he also thinks he has won, because he placated you with 300.

From 1953-1958 I made numerous trips to Bangkok to meet rice traders and to learn first-hand how the Chinese did their business there. I was broadening my horizon, almost like sharpening my weaponry. I started every morning between seven-thirty and eight, and usually ended at ten or twelve at night. I watched their ways, observing their faults and mistakes, and vowed to myself never to commit the same errors.

I was importing rice from Thailand to Peninsular Malaya and Singapore. I opened a branch in Malacca, and then later I bought into a firm in Kuala Lumpur. Eventually, we had a presence in all the major cities: Kuala Lumpur, Malacca, Johor Bahru and Singapore.

Before I made my first trip to Bangkok in August 1953, I communicated with a major Bangkok-based rice exporter named Ang Toon Chew. Ang formerly lived in Pontian Kechil, a small town 35 miles from Johor Bahru, and had bought rice from Father. He was very fond of Father, and he missed his old friend. After Father's death in 1948, Ang went to Bangkok and prospered. By 1953, he had become one of the largest exporters of Thai rice. I sent word to him, and Ang came to the Bangkok airport to greet me.

Ang Toon Chew was one of the finest Chinese businessmen I have ever come across. He was born in about 1913 and migrated as a very young boy from the Xiamen region in southern Fujian Province to Singapore. Through relatives, he ended up in southern Johor. He started his working life tapping rubber as a boy – this at a time when wild tigers still roamed and terrorized Johor. He later became a truck driver before entering the rice trade. Ang eventually became the single largest exporter of Thai rice, which I think is an amazing feat.

My early visits to Bangkok followed a similar routine. By seven-thirty every morning, most of the rice merchants were already attending to business. They would come to see me, as I was a fairly important rice buyer from Southeast Asia. Each one would take turns: Tomorrow morning you have breakfast with me, they'd say. They'd take me for Teochew congee, and of course we'd chat over breakfast. Then by 9 am I'd be in Ang's shop. I would just sit there and observe how he bought rice. People came with rice samples. Ang would put his hand through the grains, and then he would bargain. Sometimes, he would break off the bargaining if it grew too heated. He would relax over a cup of tea, and start again.

Deals were all done through brokers – the Thai rice millers and farmers never travelled from the rural areas to Bangkok except on holiday – and the brokers received a commission of one baht and nine satangs for each bag of rice sold. Ten bags made one metric ton.

I learned much about human behaviour and resilience from my Bangkok experience. Physical tiredness was simply not in their vocabulary. Ang's shop was two stories high. He conducted business downstairs but he didn't sleep upstairs. He stayed in a lodging house half a kilometer away on Songwad Road in the Chinese quarter. Rent was cheap and he could get masseuses to massage him any time he liked.

From Ang, who didn't flaunt his wealth, I learned humility. He worked hard; not intensively, but for long hours. Then he would have a very nice dinner and, of course, I would look forward to dinner with him every night. I wanted to observe what made the man tick.

If I had a business mentor in life, it was Ang. I can't say that I learned much from Father, except that I observed how shrewd and gentlemanly he was in dealing with his customers.

I was a young, new businessman coming up in the business world, so I had to learn everything from scratch. I didn't have anyone to teach me. But everything I do in life, every bit of action, is part of the learning process. If I hadn't been occupied doing those things, my very fertile mind and highly-strung, energetic body would have pushed me in other directions.

I have always felt that wisdom is in the air. Structured learning is fine. But you can pick, you can distil, wisdom by yourself. However, to do that, you have to hone your senses, listen more carefully, smell more deeply, see more sharply, and through that try to distil the wisdom from the air.

Now, there is only so much time in any given day. When you're awake, you must focus on what you really want in life. Many young men go in for the loveliest sports cars and other material things. I saw very early on that these symbols of luxury and pleasure are not the real things in life, and that they tend to distract you from focusing on what is important. For me, I was focussed on making money – not for the money itself, but to rise in the business world and ascend to the clouds, where the kingmakers and decision makers gather every day.

Thailand was like a land of milk and honey, blessed with an abundance of wonderful soil and hardworking people. The farmers in the fields were Thais, but the managers and organizers of commerce were Chinese. From banking to rice, Teochew traders dominated Bangkok, which is the political and economic nerve centre of Thailand. Teochew (Chaozhou) is a small district of Guangdong Province on the coast near Guangdong's border with Fujian. The people of Chaozhou are the best businessmen of China to this day. They have business rhythm and are good with their sums. And many of them are also ruthless and go for the jugular.

In those days, the rice trade was conducted in written Chinese and Chinese dialects. The two most common dialects heard were Teochew and Minnan from the southern part of Fujian. That situation prevailed even into Cambodia, Vietnam and Burma, which were then the other main rice-exporting countries. My experience in Thailand gave me a good grounding in Teochew and Minnan, so I became rather proficient in both.

After Bangkok, the next foreign business trip I took was to Rangoon, Burma, in 1955. I travelled there with six or seven Chinese rice merchants on an unofficial rice mission. Then Ang invited me to travel alone with him to Cambodia and Vietnam. We flew from Bangkok to Phnom Penh, which was very strongly Teochew, and stayed for two or three days. Then we flew from Phnom Penh to Saigon and stayed in Cholon, the Chinese quarter, spending most of our time dining with Chinese rice merchants. In Saigon, some were Teochew, others Cantonese, with the odd Fujianese.

I was in Saigon during the reign of President Ngo Dinh Diem and his younger brother, Ngo Dinh Nhu. The younger brother's wife was widely known as the Dragon Lady. President Diem ruled the country like the conquering Japanese army had run Malaya. I'll never forget what I saw.

One day, I was on the street with Ang when suddenly truckloads of soldiers appeared. The soldiers jumped off the trucks along an avenue. Every thirty metres there was a soldier. All the shophouses had to shutter their doors and everybody had to turn and face away from the street as Diem's motorcade passed. That only happened to us in Malaya when a Japanese general passed. I thought to myself, "My God, what a brutal dictator to treat his own people this way." He wasn't even a Japanese in Saigon, he was a Vietnamese in his own country. In my heart, I was cheering on Ho Chi Minh.

At my peak, I ranked within the top six or seven rice traders in Malaysia. Because margins on this trade were small, if we made $80,000 to $100,00 in Malaysian dollars a year, nett of all expenses, we considered ourselves lucky. The largest single market in terms of volume of trading was Singapore. But we traded up and down the Malay Peninsula, from Johor Bahru to Malacca to Kuala Lumpur. We even sent salesmen to Ipoh, Penang, and the smaller east coast towns.

When Kuok Brothers secured the government rice agency in Malacca at an open tender, we met with enormous opposition when we set up an office there. My twelfth cousin, Hock Seng, was the vanguard and he took all the arrows. But although he was vilified, he kept his cool. By the time he returned to Johor Bahru about seven years later, he had earned the respect and friendship of most of the businessmen of Malacca.

As our business grew in the 1950s, I was closest to Hock Seng, who was one of the five co-founders of the Group. He loved me, and he had a great dignity about him – a lovely, lovely man. He was, along with William, one of the two closest relatives to me of my generation.

I had lost William in August 1948 when he vanished into the jungle and Hock Seng also died very young in 1964. The poor man was born with webbed toes that never ventilated properly in the damp climate. He suffered repeated attacks of Singapore foot, and then the poison from the condition affected his kidneys. He went on dialysis toward the end of his life, but one day his kidneys packed up and he died a very painful death.

I have a vivid last recollection of this dear cousin of mine. He came to see me in my office in Singapore after we had moved from Cecil Street to Carpenter Street. I was shocked at the sight of him. He was literally grey, absolutely ashen, and had lost about one-third of his size. I tried very hard to hide my shock so as not to hurt him. We sat and chatted. From the moment he saw me to the moment he left, he wore a faint smile on his face. I saw him down the lift, to the car, and then he went back to Johor Bahru. In my heart I knew he had come to say goodbye. He died within days of that visit.

One of the larger companies supplying rice to Kuala Lumpur in the 1950s was a firm called Sino-Thai Corporation, whose prime backer was a friend of mine from Penang named Tan Kim Yeow. There were already about six or seven strong competitors in Kuala Lumpur, and one day Tan sent word to me, "Let's join forces?" So I went with Ang Toon Chew, my friend, erstwhile partner and competitor, to Kuala Lumpur to meet with Kim Yeow.

I said, "Let's not compete. Let's form a triumvirate of Tan, Ang and the Kuoks."

All my life, I have sought partners, because I know that there must always be teamwork in a society. If we cut each other's throats, the fourth or fifth dog gets the bone. I knew these two gentlemen would be worthy and honourable partners. They were decent people, and Ang, in particular, was a man of great integrity. We agreed, and Min Tien – a company that I had formed earlier in

Johor Bahru – took control of Sino-Thai.

By the mid-1950s, I could see that there really wasn't much margin or profit to be made in rice. Even a 14- or 15-year-old could set up a shop to buy and sell rice, so the competition was horrendous. It struck me as the least skilled of all trades. As a result, you couldn't grow very big. Every farmer looks after his own little plot; at best, a number of farmers might form a cooperative if they have enough sense among themselves to set up a jointly owned mill. Rice mills require very small capital and don't lend themselves to economies of scale, so the barriers to entry in the trade are very low.

Rice did not normally experience wild price swings. Imagine: if rice were a volatile commodity, there would often be widespread famine. Did the price of rice double during the year? If the price of rice was £40 a ton (in those days the trade with Thailand was still in sterling, not in US dollars), could it go up to £80? Could it drop from £40 a ton to £20? The chances were not that great.

As I also traded in sugar, I began to see that sugar was a far more volatile commodity than rice. Sugar prices moved up and down like a yo-yo. As a trader, you can only make windfall profits if a commodity is volatile.

Sugar prices could multiply from three cents a pound to 60 cents a pound because sugar is not a basic foodstuff. On the other hand, sugar is a vital ingredient in many products. I call sugar the cheapest luxury-cum-necessity in life. Sugar is a kind of pacifier. If you put a sweet in a crying child's mouth, he will turn to laughter. When there is no supply of sugar, the commodity can rise to almost any price short of the value of gold and diamonds.

Until about 1956, sugar was a tightly controlled commodity in Malaya. Only the European hongs in Singapore could import it. The sources of refined sugar for the British colonies were Taikoo Sugar (Swire) in Hong Kong, Tate & Lyle in England, and Taiwan

Sugar, which had been established by the Japanese when Taiwan was a Japanese colony. Taiwan Sugar, then under Chiang Kai-shek's Kuomintang Government in Taipei, believed that the white man was always the better trader, so they preferred to extend their offers to Guthrie, Sime Darby or Rotterdam Trading. Chinese firms cabling Taiwan Sugar wouldn't even get their cables answered, or would receive a terse response: "Regret. Unable Offer."

The only Chinese firm that was able to get offers out of Taiwan Sugar was a pseudo-white man's firm called Kian Gwan. Oei Tiong Ham, Kian Gwan's founder, had risen to become the sugar king of Asia under Dutch rule in Indonesia. There was a very famous saying in the 1930s and early 1940s that if you travelled by train from one end of the island of Java to the other, you never lost sight of Kian Gwan's sugar plantations. Oei sent his sons to be educated in Dutch universities, and also employed other Chinese Indonesians who had trained in British or Dutch colleges. So Kian Gwan was run more like a white man's firm.

I started to trade seriously in sugar in 1953 or 1954, first by buying from the British hongs in Singapore. I got to know one or two British managers in Guthrie, and I would personally go to their office to talk to them. They said, "Okay, we'll make you the sugar distributor for Taikoo Sugar in Johor Bahru. Your allocation is 80 tons a month." We sent our trucks to Singapore to take delivery from warehouses along Boat Quay on the Singapore River.

There wasn't much cost involved. We operated low-cost warehouses, and employed three to five sturdy men on low salaries who would hump the bags of sugar. Even with an allocation of just 80 tons monthly, in good times you could make $2,500 to $3,000 a month, or more than $30,000 a year, which was very, very good money in those days. So it quickly became obvious that sugar was much more profitable than rice. Profits in flour, which carried brands such as Sime Darby's Blue Key or Guthrie's Blue Anchor, were somewhere in between rice and sugar.

Therefore, from about 1955, I shifted my focus from rice to sugar. Then, Nasser of Egypt thumbed his nose at France and Britain by nationalising the Suez Canal Company.

The ensuing Suez Canal Crisis, in the fall of 1956, sent sugar prices soaring from £23 a ton to £55 a ton almost within a week. Suddenly, Guthrie's said they could no longer supply us our monthly quota. We had no real contract; it was just a gentleman's agreement. Guthrie probably had stocks; they were just denying me what was really an insignificant amount of money.

I was shocked that people could act like this. The whole affair struck me as sordid. But all that simply added liquid fuel to my ambition, and made me think and plan how to turn this lesson to my advantage the next time round.

8
MELTING SUGAR

MY FIRST DEALINGS with Mitsui & Co came through the flour trade. Mitsui heard that we were one of the companies that bought flour from Sime Darby, so they came to us. We placed orders with them, and through this trade I got to know Mike Horie, the Deputy General Manager in Mitsui's Singapore office. Horie, who had trained in Mitsui's London office before the war, took a liking to me.

My first big break in the sugar trade came in 1958. Mitsui wanted to sell chemical fertilizers – urea and ammonium sulphate – to India. India lacked foreign exchange, so it sought to barter 30,000 tons of surplus white sugar for the fertilizer. Since Japan would only import raw sugar, the missing leg in Mitsui's deal was somebody to buy the white sugar off them. Through their Singapore office, Mitsui's sugar department in Tokyo heard that a crazy young man called Robert Kuok was willing to trade in sugar.

So, one day in 1958, Horie came to see me with S Sumii, the deputy manager of the sugar department of their Tokyo head office, along with a Mitsui fertilizer man. One of the key elements of the deal was the tariff arrangement. Singapore, being a free port, did not have a preferential duty for sugar. But Malaysia extended a preferential duty of two Malaysian cents per pound to sugar from any British Commonwealth country, including India. This worked out to a duty advantage of $44.09 per metric ton, or almost 20 percent based on the price I eventually paid.

In those days, 30,000 tons of sugar was a very big deal. Nobody had done such a large deal in the history of Malaysia and Singapore. We had been buying Indian sugar from British brokers, but in small quantities – 100 tons, 500 tons.

Tate & Lyle of England was still a large supplier of white sugar to Asia. But British sugar had to travel a long way. When the bags of sugar moved from the cold air of England into the humid, hot steel holds of cargo ships, they became damp and therefore very unattractive to dealers. When sugar soaked into a gunnysack, it turns syrupy and can add more than ten pounds of weight to the sack. And who wants to buy sugar that is wet and almost turned into syrup?

When I signified that we were willing to participate in the Indian barter deal, Horie informed me that we needed to fly to Calcutta. Sumii, the senior Mitsui man in charge of sugar, flew from Tokyo to meet us. Mr Honda, a manager in Mitsui's large New Delhi office, also joined us. We stayed at the Grand Hotel, which was the best hotel in Calcutta at the time.

We met with the President of the Indian Sugar Mills Association, a man by the name of SS Kanoria. When we went into his office, we saw photos of him with the President of India, with Nehru, with all the leaders of India everywhere – all meant to impress his visitors. But, of course, in this case, I was really only a bystander. I was the beneficiary buyer of sugar at the end of the line. The barter arrangement was between the Indians and Mitsui.

The deal was done and then – crash – I collided with Chinese sugar in Malaysia. By complete coincidence, China suddenly made up its mind to earn foreign exchange by exporting as much sugar as it could squeeze out of domestic consumption. When I did my deal with Mitsui, I had assumed that there would be no competition in the Malaysian sugar market. I didn't know that a man named

Lim Kai, a Chinese sugar agent, had discussed plans with China to hit the Malaysian market. Our ships arrived at port, and a 3,000-ton shipload of Chinese sugar came in. The whole market quickly became oversupplied. All of the wholesalers who bought from us were losing money. Lim Kai and I were both bleeding.

So Lim Kai rushed to China to ask for a break and I turned to Mitsui for relief. I told Mitsui that I could not honour the rest of the deal because the banks, which noticed the massacre taking place, would no longer honour the letters of credit for me. The Japanese at first tried to pressure me, but I said, well, there's nothing I can do. Finally, they cut the sugar price by about £2 a ton, which put me in a stronger position to compete against Lim Kai.

Around that time, when I was returning to my shophouse on Cecil Street in Singapore, I bumped into a sugar-trading friend named Ho Yeow Koon, who was with another Chinese gentleman. Yeow Koon said to me, "Oh, meet Lim Kai. He wants to say hello to you, Robert." So I shook hands with Lim Kai, who I knew was my arch competitor. I was astounded to see such a big-built southern Chinese. He was about 1.8 metres in height, with a heavy frame.

Some weeks later, out of the blue, I received a cable from China, all in a numbers code. My clerks deciphered the message. The cable read: "*Guo Henian, qing ni lai Xianggang shangliang tangde shengyi. Wufenghang*" (Kuok Hock Nien, Please come to Hong Kong to discuss sugar business. Wufenghang.) Wufenghang was The Five Bountifuls Company, a wholly owned subsidiary of China Cereals, Oils and Foodstuffs Corp (COFCO), which in turn was a wholly owned subsidiary of the Ministry of Foreign Trade (MOFTEC).

My plane landed in Hong Kong at about 2 pm. After passing through immigration, I spotted Lim Kai, who pointed me out to a shorter man. That man was Lin Zhongming, who was then a junior officer at Wufenghang. He would later become the Chairman and

CEO of COFCO.

Lim Kai and a few Wufenghang managers came to collect me that evening for dinner. They toasted me with four or five different Chinese liquors, plying me with drinks until I got very drunk.

When I left the restaurant, another businessman present, a Fujianese who was their rice agent and who owned a large Packard car, offered to send me back to my Kowloon hotel. The last thing I remember was this man, Ng Tai Ek, driving his Packard onto the ferryboat. I then passed out. When I awoke the next morning in the hotel, I was fully dressed without my shoes.

What transpired during this 1959 trip was this: The Chinese realized that they could not compete against the sugar that I was importing from India as long as I enjoyed a preferential tariff. So they suggested that Lim Kai and I join hands. They were willing to forgive the existing contract and give us a new contract. And, eventually, after several trips, that is what happened.

At that time, mainland Chinese traders were not allowed to visit Malaysia or Singapore. The Lim Kai agency remained in name, but I became the real buyer from the early 1960s. The Chinese negotiated contracts with me for each block sale of 30,000 tons or 50,000 tons, and then the deals would formally pass through Lim Kai, who earned a commission.

Lim Kai was one of the most interesting and selfless people I have met in my life. He was born and brought up in China. He was an idealistic young man who loved China and believed in the Communist Party. He admired what the Party did to purge the evils of the Kuomintang Government and Chiang Kai-shek's coterie.

Part of Lim Kai's family emigrated to Singapore, where his grandfather, Lim Loh, was a very famous building contractor who built Victoria Memorial Hall and the old Parliament House. Lim Kai's uncle was Maj-Gen Lim Bo Seng, Singapore's war hero.

The sugar-for-fertilizer swap led me to a deeper involvement in Indian sugar. I found that I could compete with Guthrie and the other British hongs by importing directly from India, which enjoyed the $44-a-ton Commonwealth preferential import duty in the Malaysian market.

India asked you to buy in large 10,000- and 20,000-ton lots, whereas Guthrie could place an order for just 1,000 tons of Taikoo Sugar from Hong Kong. The Indian trade was more speculative, and the British hongs were not quite prepared to take on the risk. We were trying to pick up the crumbs from the tables of those barons. As our tables were quite barren, we were prepared to enter areas where the risk was relatively great.

One day, I received a call from Calcutta. A young Indian sugar agent, Narendra Wadhwana, was on the phone. He said, "Please come immediately. My father and I need to speak with you."

In those days, the telephone lines were not as clear as they are today, and lines were very easily cut, so you learned the art of talking quickly. Narendra put his father on the phone. "Mr Kuok," his father said, "If you can, get on a plane immediately and come over. We need to talk face to face."

I put the phone down, called my secretary and said, "Get me on the first flight to Calcutta." Then I called the house and asked my wife to pack some clothes for me and meet me at the airport. Two hours later I was airborne for Calcutta.

Narendra met me at the airport, called his father and the three of us chatted at the hotel until early in the morning. They had arranged for me to meet with the Indian Sugar Mills Association (ISMA) chairman the next day. That is how we did our first major business directly with ISMA, bypassing the London sugar brokers.

This experience drove home to me the importance of speed and trust. You must be super-quick in driving towards your goal, since you are not working in isolation and competitors will come at you from all angles. You must also develop resilience, and be able to bounce back after the inevitable reverses.

After my lightning trip to Calcutta, I discovered that I could also go myself and buy sugar from the State Trading Corporation (STC), a wholly government-owned body based in New Delhi and manned by top civil servants. A very decent senior official I often dealt with was Govind Narain, Chairman of the STC. From 1960-1962, I made two or three trips to India each year – until those business visits started to affect my health.

During the summer months, the heat in New Delhi is truly unbearable. A temperature of 38°C is low. I could not get into top hotels like Ashoka – they were always fully booked – and, on one trip in 1962, Narendra booked me into a hotel called the Jan Path (People's Road). Jan Path Hotel was a five-storey building. During the summer months, the power stations suffered breakdowns, so the lifts stopped working. I was given a room on the top floor because I was Chinese and not a favoured Indian or white man. The only water that came out of the taps was hot; there was no functioning refrigerator.

The Indian system of doing business involves giving you the run-around. In that heat, I would put on a suit and necktie, and go to an office. You were told to wait for one and then two hours. Then they'd say, "Please come back at seven-thirty in the evening." That is just their way. Or they held one Dutch auction after another, causing each one of you to cut each other's throat until you were almost dead from bleeding.

On one trip, I had to stay six weeks at a stretch in the middle of summer. Upon returning to Jan Path Hotel each day, I walked up flights of stairs and drank awful-tasting hot water. I could feel my energy draining away. There was nothing to read and no TV in the room. One day, when I lay in bed and shut my eyes, the whole world began to spin. It was the most awful illness I have ever had in my life. Even as I relate this experience, I feel dizzy. I quickly called Narendra who rushed over and asked the hotel management to summon a doctor.

I will never forget Major Chawla, a Kashmiri Indian doctor. He examined me, asked some questions, and said, "Young man, you are suffering a nervous breakdown. You are overtired; your whole system is in revolt. My advice, young man, is to get out of Delhi as fast as possible."

I said to Narendra: "Can you go and see Govind Narain and tell him I am not in a good state. I am prepared to stay one more day, but I don't think I can last much longer."

Narain said there was no way STC could come to a decision about my offer so quickly, but that they would cable me a reply within three or four days. So, I flew back to Singapore.

They responded favourably. They accepted my offer and sold me 30,000 tons of Indian sugar. Can you imagine? I nearly gave up my life struggling to buy those 30,000 tons! Within two days of receiving their response, I left with Joy for a much-needed vacation in Nasu, Japan, the Emperor's summer retreat.

I travelled regularly to India up until 1963. Then I stopped and started sending my managers. I can tell you, every time I sent a manager, my heart was full of sympathy for the man. I coined a phrase, "Who should we send to Siberia in the next trip?" For me, India was Siberia.

In the autumn of 1958, I took my entire family to Penang for a vacation. We stayed in a hotel next to the beach. We were sitting in wet swimming garb on the sand when a Hainanese hotel boy came down and said I was wanted on the phone – a long-distance call. I wrapped a towel around my damp body and ran up the stairs to the guest telephone on the third-floor landing.

On the line was my cousin Hock Yao, who, in my absence, was standing in for me at my desk in the Singapore office. Hock Yao said, "Nien, your friend Mike Horie of Mitsui came looking for you. I told him you're having a holiday in Penang. He wants me to pass you this message: 'Are you interested in building a sugar refinery in Malaysia? If so, please come down to Singapore immediately to discuss the subject.'" So I ran downstairs, informed the family, dried myself, called up for air tickets and flew to Singapore that evening.

Horie brought his manager, Matsumoto, from Mitsui Singapore to the meeting. Matsumoto sized me up and down – this was a big project – and did most of the talking. He carried instructions from Mitsui's sugar department in Tokyo. Mitsui and Nissin Seito (Nissin Sugar Manufacturing Co) had attended an economic seminar in Tokyo at which Tan Siew Sin, the Malaysian Minister of Finance, had invited the Japanese to set up factories in newly independent Malaysia. One of the Japanese companies had asked whether this included sugar refining with tariff protection, and Siew Sin had responded affirmatively. The Japanese had taken copious notes.

Mitsui asked if I would like to become their partner in such a project. I thought this was a godsend opportunity, and agreed immediately. They cabled Tokyo and, within two weeks, three more Japanese gentlemen appeared in Singapore. One was Mizuno Tadao of Mitsui; the others were Tsuchiya and Hama of Nissin. We had lunches and dinners together, during which the five of them sized me up.

The Japanese said they would return to Tokyo and draft a letter of application, but we should form that very day the spirit of *sansha* (three companies) and agree on a *sansha* spirit of unity. The three companies were Kuok Brothers, Mitsui and Nissin. They proposed that Mitsui and Nissin each take 20 percent and Kuok Brothers 26 percent, leaving 34 percent for other investors.

Then Mitsui sent me a poorly crafted draft of a letter of application to the Malaysian Government. It was written in incomprehensible English. With Matsumoto's permission, I rewrote the entire letter in language that the Malaysian British officers could read and appreciate (most of the key economic officials in the Government were still from Britain, Australia or New Zealand). We agreed that the joint-venture company would be called Malayan Sugar Manufacturing Co Ltd (MSM). In the letter, I introduced a final paragraph asserting that for this industry to find its feet, it was essential that it be accorded full tariff protection. The three parties signed the letter and submitted it to the Ministry of Economic Affairs (later renamed the Ministry of Commerce and Industry) in early 1959.

In July 1959, we received an official letter on government letterhead signed by the Deputy Director of the Industrial Development Division. It confirmed that licences had been approved for us and for another refinery, with tariff protection. However, we still needed to obtain formal tariff protection approval from the Tariff Advisory Committee.

Then the Japanese quickly invited us to Tokyo. I remember going to Mother and saying I wanted to bring Hock Chin, who was in name Managing Director of Kuok Brothers. Mother remonstrated. She said, "Hock Chin is unfit to go. You know, son, every few hours he needs to recharge himself with drugs." Hock Chin was popping opium pills. In the middle of meetings his eyes would stop focusing. He would excuse himself, as if to go to the toilet, step outside and swallow raw opium. Mother advised me to take Philip instead.

Philip and I stayed in bad rooms in Tokyo's Imperial Hotel. I remember all too well that every time the trains passed nearby we were wakened; we really only had peace between 1 and 5 am when the trains stopped running.

The first morning, we went to a meeting in Mitsui's office. Philip and I sat on one side of a long table. Ranged against us on the other side were about ten Japanese: Lawyers, accountants, a managing director from Nissin, a few from Mitsui and so on. They presented us with a very lopsided pro-forma agreement. It said, Nissin is to receive a technical guidance fee for ten years, at one percent of the selling price, renewable for another ten years, and to send 100 staff from Japan based on Japanese salaries; Mitsui was to be the sole raw-sugar buying agent, one percent commission on purchase price; Kuoks, we appoint you sole selling agents of the refined sugar in Malaysia, one percent commission.

I thought, they're keeping all the plums, conferring lush franchises on themselves and handing us zero. We naturally were going to be the ones to sell the sugar in the Malaysian market, as I was already a major sugar trader there. So now Kuoks, equal partners in the *sansha*, would be no more than the selling agent in our own country! If they didn't give the agency to us, MSM would have had to give it to someone else in Malaysia. Therefore, they were only offering me something that they could not handle themselves.

The seller of raw sugar always pays a commission, but here Mitsui even wanted another one percent commission from the buyer. Nissin was in essence saying: sugar refining is a very complex, intricate industry. I laughed to myself. I didn't have to study chemistry to know that this was nonsense.

Almost from day one, I spotted decency in two men: Mizuno Tadao of Mitsui and Tsuchiya of Nissin. Hama, the production manager sent by Nissin, was square. He was a good man, but because he was square, when his boss said, "Do this," he would do it, regardless whether it was the decent thing to do.

I argued a bit with the Japanese as a formality. Within minutes,

I had my strategy all worked out. That evening, I told Philip, "Phil, we're being clobbered. It's a case of, if we don't like it they won't go with us. Without them coming with us we don't know how to do sugar refining." So I said, "Let's go with them. We'll just massage a bit of the vileness out of it, but I don't think we'll get many concessions. We'll just go through the motions."

There were about three or four days of the typical Japanese tactics and techniques of wearing you down. For instance, if there was a real issue which was blatantly wrong it might take us two-thirds of a day for them to make a concession that they could have made in two minutes. I could see that the going was very rough, but I thought: how far can they get? They're coming to my country to start an industry.

I said to the Japanese, "How are you going to proceed in Malaysia? Frankly, without me, you will fail because the business-engineering part is going to be the most difficult."

They said, "What do you mean by business engineering?"

I replied, "How do we get tariff protection from a newly independent nation that has no concept of tariff protection and where the British are still in control of the economy?" When they questioned how I could achieve such a difficult task, I said, "I am confident I can achieve it. For one thing, some of the Malaysian leaders are my old schoolmates and friends. I have an entree to them, and the rest is my persuasive power." I had obtained the minutes of the session in Tokyo at which Tan Siew Sin, the Malaysian Minister of Finance, had promised full tariff protection, and felt certain the promises would be kept.

All of my arguments fell on deaf ears in Tokyo. They only trumped up their side of the picture and even hinted that, after all, they had chosen me. Neither Philip nor I were happy, but we felt that we had to keep quiet at this stage. We signed the agreement and returned home.

Then Philip and I developed the local strategy. I said to him, "Phil, the local sugar market is very fragmented. There are 50-70 traders of some significance. I think we'll need friends to neutralize their opposition. Let me approach them."

One such friend was Ang Toon Chew, the gentleman who had shown me the rice trade in Bangkok in the 1950s. His company in Malaysia was called Nai Seng. Another was Tan Kim Yeow, who ran Wah Seong Ltd of Penang. Both traders agreed to come in as outside partners on the same terms as I entered. They each purchased about ten percent of MSM's shares.

MSM's initial capital was MYR6 million. When I invested $1,560,000 for my 26 percent stake, I remember my accountant (Cousin Number Thirteen) came to my room and said we didn't have enough money, that we shouldn't enter this business. I shouted at him, "Don't be foolish! Now we have a strong incentive to work harder to find that money!"

We signed the *sansha* agreement in the summer of 1959, but then ran into a brick wall in the shape of the British and other white civil servants who still manned the Malaysian Government after independence. The civil servants understood that for Malaysia to industrialise, the new industries would need tariff protection. The government set up a Tariff Advisory Committee (TAC), chaired by Oscar Spencer, the Secretary for Economic Affairs. But our application for tariff protection met with months of silence. They were not going to convene the TAC. We were blocked and blocked and blocked.

The British gave independence to Malaysia on 31 August, 1957, without a fight. Independence was handed on a gilt-edged, filigree plate to a government led by Tunku Abdul Rahman, Tun Razak and Tun Dr Ismail. But the dismantling of English colonialism took a lot longer than it took to win independence. The British cleverly persuaded Tunku Abdul Rahman and his leading ministers that the native population (comprising Malays, Chinese and Indians) was not sufficiently equipped to run the economy.

I yearned for meaningful economic independence for Malaysia. I remember discussing my views in frequent letters to and conversations with Ismail Ali, a wonderful Malay friend of mine in the government. We agreed that all the Malay political leaders at the top, including Tunku, were concentrating too much on the trappings of freedom or independence – what uniform to wear, what national anthem, etc. – and not enough on true economic independence from the British.

Our fears were well-founded. The British remained in strong charge of the economy for a good five to seven years after 1957. British civil servants, and some Australians and New Zealanders, maintained control over the main economic branches of government – the commanding heights – such as the Finance Ministry, the Central Bank, the Tax Department, the Commerce and Industry Ministry, and even customs, railways and the ports. The scales of colonialism fell off in stages, accelerating from about 1962.

So, when I applied for tariff protection in 1959, the British and other white civil servants blocked me for over two years. Sugar, being an agricultural crop, is subject to the vagaries of nature. In disastrous crop years, the volatility of sugar is such that prices can easily escalate as much as five times. Most sugar-producing countries grow sugar mainly for domestic consumption and then dump any surplus on the international market. If you have a refinery, you can be blown to bits in years of surplus, which occur 80-90 percent of the time. It was obvious that tariff protection would ultimately be given. The British civil servants, however, were simply trying to delay us, hoping that we would give up and go away.

The white civil servants were protecting the interests of Taikoo (Swire) of Hong Kong and Tate & Lyle, the sugar kings of England. Tate & Lyle had enjoyed strong tariff protection in the British market for over 200 years. And yet Tate & Lyle had the audacity to send a cable to the Tariff Advisory Committee in Malaysia strongly opposing tariff protection for MSM. A number of the TAC members were British, but an Indian clerk told us all these stories.

So, Philip and I would drive the 386 kilometers from Johor Bahru to Kuala Lumpur and ask to see Tan Siew Sin, the Minister of Commerce and Industry in connection with our MSM licence application. At first Siew Sin wouldn't even see us, and we came back empty-handed. I said to Philip, "Don't worry, water can wear down a stone."

The British director-generals needed clerks and secretaries to do the donkey work for them. Many of these were either Chinese or Indians who had a sense of fairness and who sympathized with our lot. They observed that we were being bullied and vilified behind our backs. They encouraged us to continue the struggle, because they could see light at the end of the tunnel for us.

Then, in November 1959, Khir Johari, a young, energetic Kedah Malay, was appointed Minister of Commerce and Industry. I complained to him about what the British were doing to me. He said, "Is that so?"

It was Khir Johari who helped me to break the logjam, the stranglehold of the white civil servants. Finally, in 1962, the TAC agreed to hold the tariff protection hearing and soon granted full protection by banning imports of refined sugar, a policy that continues to this day.

When I got word that we were winning our case, I went again to see Khir Johari. I said to him, "The Japanese foisted a very unfair agreement onto me."

He said, "Send me a copy." He had his civil servants go through it. Then, in his letter granting tariff protection to MSM, he incorporated a few paragraphs stating, "Before the plant can be built, all agreements signed with foreign partners must be vetted and approved by this Ministry." In other words, his Ministry had the right to suggest amendments if it felt the agreement was too one sided.

The Japanese got very alarmed. They saw my hand, so they sent Mizuno to see me in Singapore. He came alone. I said, "Mizuno-san, my office is very small and dingy. This is going to be a very important talk. We are friends, but we are going to talk as businessmen. Come to my house."

Mizuno Tadao was born into a farming family in Gifu Prefecture in Japan, known traditionally for cormorant fishing, and went to the elite Hitotsubashi University in Tokyo. Then he joined Mitsui, which put him into its sugar department and dispatched him to work in Taiwan Sugar (Taiwan was a Japanese colony at the time). After the Japanese conquered Southeast Asia, Mizuno was sent to Java to work in the Javanese sugar industry.

So Mizuno and I chatted alone on the patio of my house that day. He was very tense, but friendly, and quickly came to the bone of contention. He said, "Kuok-san, if you will not give way and persuade your government to change its stance toward the Japanese partners in this venture, the Japanese are going to withdraw from the project."

I replied, "Mizuno-san, if that is the final attitude of the Japanese, it is something I cannot prevent. But listen to me. After two and half years of stupendous work by my brother Philip and me, we have moved the mountain and achieved protection. You know that there are many potential partners on the horizon, such as Tate & Lyle, just waiting for you to get out. It would be such a shame."

That rocked him. He asked, "Then what is the solution?"

I said, "Look here. You know how unfair the original agreement was. For an agreement to work, there must be fairness."

He asked, "Then what is fair?"

I answered, "What is sugar refining, Mizuno-san? Is it so complicated? Nissin: at the most, five years' technical guidance fee, half a percent. If it's true it is difficult, we will ask for a renewal." As events proved, we could have let all of the Japanese technicians go home after three years.

Then he said Mitsui had a problem with the procurement of raw-sugar. I said, "It has to be joint buying by Mitsui and Kuoks. Kuoks have always been traders, so why should you be the sole buyers? The commission should be half a percent, not one percent." He returned to Japan and the agreement was revised, but they were no longer happy with me.

When the news hit the sugar world that Kuok Brothers had signed an agreement with Nissin Sugar and Mitsui to start a sugar refinery, the British looked down their noses at the deal. Some of them said, "This thing will never get off the ground." They were still out to sabotage the infant Malaysian sugar-refining industry. I was told as much to my face when I visited the offices of C Czarnikow, which at the time was the most blue-blooded of the British sugar traders. Czarnikow was the sole sugar-export agent for Queensland Sugar of Australia (through CSR – Colonial Sugar Refining Company), which was becoming the leading supplier of raw sugar to Malaysia.

I was in London in 1962 or 1963 on one of my early sugar trips. One of Czarnikow's senior directors, Vincent Beckett, asked me to call on him at his office. Czarnikow was already the broker for

Mitsui, and I had just succeeded in breaking Mitsui's stranglehold on the raw sugar-buying rights for MSM. I thought that since Czarnikow was Mitsui's broker, it would be churlish for me not to see them. So that afternoon, after lunch, I went across.

Beckett was a very severe-looking man. We sat down and exchanged one or two simple pleasantries. Then he started to lecture me quite rudely. He said their relationship with Mitsui went back almost to the time of the founding of Czarnikow. His message was, "Who are you? We are such old friends. Nobody can break our friendship."

I interposed at one stage and said, "Who is suggesting breaking your friendship?"

Then Beckett said, "Why should you start a sugar refinery in Malaysia? Your country is importing white sugar from Tate & Lyle and Taikoo of Hong Kong nicely. Why do you want to set up the refinery?"

I was furious. I replied, "It is none of your business!"

He started to try and browbeat me, by which time I literally saw red. I shouted at the man, "Who do you think you are? You are uncivilized and rude! Don't ever dare call me again!" I stalked out of Czarnikow's London office.

This goes to show to what extent British colonial and monopolistic thinking still lingered even into the early 1960s.

I had an almost identical experience with Mitsui. I was in my London hotel room when I received a call from the London office of Mitsui & Co. The President of Mitsui London, Ikeda, invited me to lunch.

We sat down at a City restaurant. Japanese are a little more polite, and Ikeda spoke a few pleasantries. Then a similar lecture began. "Mr Kuok," he said, "I want you to know that where Mitsui is concerned, our best friend in London is Czarnikow. Mitsui will never source sugar through anybody else in the world except Czarnikow."

I could sense the drift of conversation. I said, "That is, of course, every right of Mitsui."

He didn't like what I said, so he went on to bully me: "Where this refinery is concerned, we will make every effort to see that all the raw sugar is bought through Czarnikow."

I almost screamed at him, "Do you think you won the War? Do you think Malaysia is a colony of Japan? Did you invite me to lunch to insult me?" I threw my napkin on the table and walked out.

The writing was on the wall: The dominant player on the Malaysian sugar scene would be MSM, which started production on 8 August 1964. Already, by 1961, 80 percent of Malaysia's 250,000 tons a year of refined sugar passed through my hands. Until 1964, China sold 50,000-80,000 tons a year to Malaysia through me. Even Tate & Lyle and Taikoo appointed me their sugar agents in 1963. They knew that, in a year or two, I would stop all business with them since my tariff-protected refinery would supply all the white sugar. MSM dominated the sugar market of Malaysia from about the mid-1960s, knocking out the competition.

We built the MSM refinery in Prai, near Penang. Tunku Abdul Rahman, the Malaysian Prime Minister, officially inaugurated the plant on 12 December, 1964. When the refinery opened, I was living in Singapore and travelling quite often to London for sugar trading. I was Chairman of the board of MSM, my brother Philip was Managing Director and CEO, and Geh Ik Cheong was Executive Director. Philip and Geh ran the refinery from 1962 (during construction) until Philip left for his ambassadorship in Europe at the end of 1966. I then assumed Philip's titles and even moved into his house near Prai.

MSM was the first standalone sugar refinery in Southeast

Asia (Thailand and Indonesia had sugar mills with small adjunct refineries). Our initial volume was 400 tons a day melt, or some 140,000 tons a year, which quickly expanded. Refineries in Europe and America barely work more than 270 days a year. We pushed our refineries to work about 330 days a year. The demand for refined sugar in Malaysia kept escalating, so we kept escalating. By comparison, Taikoo's volume was 80,000 tons a year.

Today, MSM refines 3,000 tons a day in Malaysia. By the time I sold it to a Malaysian government entity, we were selling sugar more cheaply in Malaysia than the price of sugar in Thailand. We owned the refinery for over 45 years. I would say that we made in all about three billion Malaysian dollars, which is a very satisfying reward for our hard work.

PART III
–
THE FRENETIC YEARS

9
VINTAGE 1963

I WENT TO ENGLAND on the spur of the moment a few days after the Chinese New Year in February 1963. Europe was suffering from its worst winter in over 80 years. I felt the sugar market was about to move. It was just a hunch; I could have been completely wrong.

I flew in a Boeing 707 together with my good friend Tan Kim Yeow. The two of us shared three seats in economy class. Kim Yeow was always very kind to me. He gave me the window seat; he took the aisle seat. He said, "Robert, you're the bright trader. When we arrive in London, I know you're going to work hard." He made me sleep most of the time stretched out over the empty middle seat, with my legs on his lap. Kim Yeow really mothered me.

In those days, there were stops between Singapore and London. Looking out the window within a few hours of departing Bombay, I could see snow everywhere. Teheran Airport was grey, and the snow continued as we passed over Europe. At Heathrow, the tarmac was swept clean, but the banks of snow were piled some ten feet high.

Kim Yeow, who held the Rothman's cigarette distribution rights for northern Malaysia, had befriended one of the top men in Rothman's, an Irishman by the name of Patrick O'Neill-Dunn.

When we arrived in London, we were met at the airport by a liveried chauffeur with a Rolls-Royce. He drove us to Dunn's house in Cambridge. When we got there at about five in the evening, it was already dark. I stepped out of the car, and my slip-on shoes were covered by the snow. We struggled into the house and were warmly welcomed by the whole Dunn family. "Please get ready," Dunn said. "Wash up. We are going to have an early dinner and then put you off to bed."

The head of Rothman's then was Anton Rupert, a South African. Rothman's maintained a permanent two-bedroom apartment in London's Grosvenor House Hotel, which had about 500 rooms and a wing of apartments. Dunn offered Kim Yeow the use of Rothman's apartment, and the next day we were there.

I had been making one or two trips a year to London, and sometimes on to New York from 1960. If I was going to run a sugar refinery, I needed to know how to manage our raw sugar costs. I was taking things in, and learning how to trade in sugar futures. Nobody spoon-fed me. I went to London and watched how the British firms traded, and asked questions about the mechanics. To test the wind, I might put down five or ten lots (each lot is fifty metric tons). If I lost money it wouldn't hurt me; if I made money it was no big deal. That's how I learned. By experimenting, I began to get a feel for the market.

In 1963, however, I started trading like a house on fire. I made four trips to London that year – spring, summer, autumn and winter – and on each trip I made a fair bit of money simply by trading from my briefcase out of one of the hotels. I made good money in the spring and slightly less in summer. In the autumn, I made a killing, after staring disaster in the face for four weeks. In December, I made almost as much as in the spring, until, at the last minute, a couple of traders sobbed on my shoulders and I forked over part of my profit in sympathy.

Overall, I made a net cash profit for the year equivalent to 14 million Malaysian-Singapore dollars (the equivalent of just under

US$5 million). It was a lot of money: Before that, Kuok Brothers' entire capital was about five million Malaysian-Singapore dollars at the very most.

After years of remaining stagnant, with sugar prices stuck in a range of £22-28 a ton, 1963 brought a rising market. But the market did not only go one way.

In the summer, I had been buying, and the market had gone up in my favour. I found myself sitting on a profit of £50,000; then £100,000. At the end of the summer, I got very bullish. I told my manager in Singapore, "Buy, buy, buy." So we were long in Singapore, with about 20,000 tons of physical sugar. I was also long on futures. My average price was something like £35 a ton. The market was around £40. Suddenly, the price collapsed to £33 and looked like going lower. I could have been wiped out if it had gone down much more. Every trader in London was caught wrong-footed; nobody wore a smile.

I sweated another ten to twelve days. Meanwhile, the market had descended to about £30 before moving sideways, marking time – until, in September, Hurricane Flora started to move across the Caribbean. One of the deadliest storms on record, it hit Cuba (then the world's largest sugar exporter) and severely damaged the sugar crop. The wires were buzzing, the telex machines were going, and sugar took off. For ten or more trading days sugar prices soared, all the way up to over £60 a ton. Of course, when it went up to £48, £49, £50, I was taking my profit. That trip, I ended up making the most money in any short period of my life.

I also made very good money in London during the first two weeks in December. The markets were up because another hurricane was about to hit Cuba. On a Friday, I cleaned up my book and made a reservation to return to Singapore at noon the next day. At 4 pm on Friday, I got a call from one of Woodhouse

Drake's senior traders. "Robert, I'm stuck. I wonder whether you can bail me out."

I said, "What's up?"

He replied, "I fulfilled an order for a client who has now reneged on me. I'm only an employee, so I have to cough up the money from my own pocket. Do you think you could take this position from me?" They make up stories to stoke your sympathy. I agreed to take it off him – big-hearted Kuok.

On Saturday morning, when I was about to leave for the airport, another broker called me for help. It was not my wish to leave London with an open position, but Chinese are sentimental people. I had done well in spring, summer, autumn and December. I did the deal.

I should have liquidated then, taking a chunky loss. Instead, I stubbornly held on and the loss swelled by two to three times. I must have lost about £150,000 in those two deals. So, I forfeited a good portion of my profit from the December trip by helping two friends.

My success in the sugar market in 1963 was due, firstly, to my grasp of the English language and English culture. I adapt like a chameleon to the particular society in which I am at the moment operating. I had grown up in a British colony, with English schoolteachers. When Father received army contracts after the war, I met many army officers – British, Australians and New Zealanders – with whom I became friendly. When in England, I could blend in quite well – except, of course, for the colour of my skin, eyes and hair.

I further won favour through the public-relations skills I inherited from Father. Even as a young immigrant from China, he was extremely popular with the Malays and the ruling circle of Johor. Good social skills are a necessary part of life, but it must emanate from good will in your heart. There I was in England, making friends and, as Dale Carnegie would say, influencing people.

Having made friends with all the major sugar brokers in the City, I was wining, dining and spending money like water on them. It was good public relations as only a Chinese knows how, practicing thrift on yourself, but generosity toward your friends.

To be a successful businessman, you really need to brush all your senses every morning, just as you brush your teeth. I call it "honing your senses" in business: Your vision, hearing, sense of smell, touch and taste. All these senses come in very useful. I would go into a room and spot everything in the twinkling of an eye. If there were more than twenty people, then maybe it took me a few moments to size everyone up. But if there were only six, I would immediately know what was going on. I could sense tension or camaraderie.

Success in futures depends on your feel for the market, your instincts and rhythm. I would talk to different brokers. Each company had bright, young English traders. One or two would be a little cunning, but, by and large, the British are straightforward. I felt every man had his lucky hour or day, and his unlucky hour or day. I would go and chat with all of them.

I would go to Woodhouse Drake for about twenty minutes, then say, "See you," and hop across to Golodetz. Then I'd visit ED&F Man, before calling on one or two more firms. I would think, "Today is Keith Talbot's lucky day or Roy Taylor's lucky day." I would ask a question or two, "How would you trade today?" If Roy Taylor said, "I'd go long," I'd follow him. Three times out of four it worked. I just backed the man I felt had a good hunch – the best judgment – that day.

I never read charts. I don't believe in them. To me, charts are post-mortems, like dissecting a corpse. No chart can tell the future. Charts are another weapon in the brokers' armoury, luring more cannon fodder into the trade.

I kept statistical facts at the back of my head, and constantly updated my knowledge. When Hurricane Flora hit Cuba, I made my own intelligent guesses as to how the market would react. You must not be buying when everybody is buying, and you must not wait to sell until everybody is about to sell. You have to be two or three jumps ahead; one jump may not be enough.

I also benefited from the British class system: they didn't talk to one another. These were full-fledged brokers, full members of the Sugar Terminal Association, while I was just an associate member. Every top trader in these five or six firms was fully abreast of the market – I could be two hours late. If they really communicated well with each other, they would have taken me to the cleaners. Luckily, they didn't talk much. If you came from such-and-such college in Oxford, and the other guy came from an inferior college at Oxford, or Cambridge or Nottingham, they weren't going to talk with you. I could talk with all of them, since I was not part of the system. Once, when visiting Golodetz, I heard them say they couldn't sell a cargo of Polish sugar. I took the lift down, rushed across the street to Woodhouse Drake, and sold the sugar to them for £1 a ton profit. Everybody was happy.

That's why there will always be business on earth. Be humble; be straight; don't be crooked; don't take advantage of people. Even with all the information I had, I never took the market for a ride. I was a principled trader and they all liked me. If our margins went wrong, we coughed up the money straight away. We never argued.

There were other Asian traders in London in 1963, but I don't think anybody worked as hard as I did. The big Japanese *sogo shosha* were all there, but their traders were little cogs in wheels and their overlords in London or in Tokyo treated them as such. Japan is, of course, a large trading nation; but the individuals at the big companies are not skilled commodities traders. They give a deal to a Japanese firm that is related to their company, or to someone who can take them out to a nice dinner that evening. That's how they trade.

In commodity trading, the pain of a loss must hit you straight away. Conversely, the exhilaration from a big, profitable trade must be like champagne to your brain. Therefore, it must be your own capital at risk. The owners of the money in Japan are the banks; it's all a big bureaucracy conducting the trading. Of course, I am making a broad generalization; I am sure that there are brilliant individual Japanese traders. But, in my own experience, I've never met one.

Back in the 1960s and 1970s, the oceans were teeming with fish. In those days, there was only the odd shark or two, and it was fairly easy for me to fish in those waters. While volatility has not changed that much since then, there are many more sharks now. Sometimes, it seems like there are no fish in the sea – only sharks. Honours graduates in science and engineering are being recruited. PhDs are hard at work refining algorithms, and I don't even know what that means. If today's technology and speed of information had existed in the 1960s and 1970s, I would have been like a fish out of water.

I didn't depend on technology for success. People are still making money and people are still losing money, but the floor has gotten much more slippery. You have to be born at the right time.

I went to England four times for sugar trading in 1963, then two or three times in 1964, and in each year after that. Every year from 1958 until 1999, we made good money from sugar due to hard work and a bit of shrewdness. The only time that I stood at the brink of disaster was September 1963, the time that Hurricane Flora saved my hide.

One day – I think it was in December 1964 – one of the London evening papers called me "The Sugar King from the East". The nickname caught on. It came from the fact that I was one of a very few totally integrated sugar-trader industrialists in the world. We are involved in all aspects of sugar operations. But I have always felt that "Sugar King" was a misnomer.

Every time I left London and flew home to Singapore, I realized that I was like a man 8,000 miles away from the fireplace. In London, where they sat in front of the fire with the logs crackling away, they could read how many more logs they needed to add to the fire. From afar, there was no way I could out-trade any of them.

I felt the only way to trade from such a distance was through rhythm trading, a phrase I coined. If you learn to dance the tango or samba, then you know it's all about rhythm. The teacher can tell you it's left leg backwards, backwards, forwards and then sideways. But once you miss your rhythm, you've got to concentrate on the music and regain your poise. Never let anybody – not even your loved ones sitting there – say, "Robert, put your right foot out." The more any bystander interrupts or interferes, the more confused you are likely to become. Even if you make a mistake through poor timing, just by concentrating on the rhythm, you can get back into it. If I felt my rhythm was askew, I would cut back on the volume of trading so that my risk was small. Rhythm became a vital concept for me in my business career.

As a group, the British sugar traders were always the smartest and the shrewdest. The first one I met was Roy Fisher, who came out to Malaysia in 1959. I recall taking Roy, who became a very close personal friend, to a pseudo-French restaurant in Kuala Lumpur called Le Coq d'Or. Roy worked for JV Drake Ltd, which shortly afterwards merged with a coffee and cocoa firm and was renamed Woodhouse Drake and Carey. The chairman of JV Drake was Colonel Tom Drake, a direct descendant of Sir Francis Drake. Roy Fisher was number two in the white sugar department; the director in charge was Allan Arthur, a former senior British colonial civil servant whose wife, Dawn, was a member of the Drake family.

Another excellent trader who became a very close personal friend is Michael Stone of ED&F Man, a venerable broking firm dating from the 18th century. Our first meeting was in 1961, when he popped in out of the blue one day to see me in Singapore. Roy and Michael were two of the outstanding sugar traders of their day.

In around 1958, I recruited Piet Yap who traded sugar in Singapore for Internazio (previously Rotterdam Trading), a Dutch trading house. A Sumatran of Chinese origin, Yap spoke Dutch, Bahasa Indonesia and English. One day, I said to him on the phone, "Yap, why don't you quit this colonial Dutch firm. You know the sun is setting on the Dutch. Sukarno is going to drive them out. Come and join us. We are a young firm, and I could use you."

Yap could secure offers from Indonesia because he was born there. He cultivated the friendship of Sudarso, the aristocratic Javanese director of Gula Negara, the Indonesian National Sugar Board (this was before the Indonesian Bureau of Logistics, Bulog, came into existence). The country was poor and needed foreign exchange, so the government mandated that sugar be made from native plants such as coconut and sago. Gula Negara was then able to export a fair bit of centrifugal sugar from the factories in the early 1960s. Sometimes Sudarso would make offers to us.

We did our first few Indonesian deals jointly with JV Drake. I remember the first one vividly. It was a public holiday in 1962. Yap and I were working in the office when he said, "I have just spoken with Bapak (Father, an Indonesian term of respect) Sudarso of Gula Negara. He has given me a 30,000-ton offer of sugar valid for one week at a fixed price. I am calling up JV Drake on the telex now to make an offer to them. What do you say if we make five shillings a ton?" Yap was already seated in front of the telex machine and had summoned Allan Arthur to the telex in London. He was about to type the offer from Gula Negara when I interrupted, "Yap, Yap; hold on, hold on!"

I started to dictate, "We are holding an offer from the Indonesian Sugar Board of 30,000 tons sugar (we didn't disclose the price). Would you be willing to do this on a joint account with us, sharing it 50:50? If you are willing to consider this, we will disclose the whole deal to you."

Allan Arthur replied, "Delighted."

We did a few joint accounts (deal-by-deal partnerships with unwritten arrangements) with JV Drake. Drake was an established international trader; we were just learning the ropes. By running joint accounts, instead of acting as an agent, we became a principal. We get the offer; we buy, you sell, and we share the profits. Through this strategy, we strengthened the bond between ourselves – an emerging Southeast Asian Chinese firm based in Singapore – and one of the leading sugar brokers in the City of London.

These joint ventures were for export from Indonesia to Europe, the Middle East or Japan. We received the offers; Drake did the marketing. We didn't charge overheads to each other, so we both made tidy profits. If we had served as an agent and merely put across the offer, we could only have added a commission of five shillings a ton. In other words, on a 10,000-ton deal, we would earn £2,500. By operating a joint account, if we bought the sugar for, say, £20 a ton and sold it for £24 a ton, we would equally share a profit of £40,000.

One day in 1963, a request came from Indonesia to amend the terms of a sugar trade. The result would have been to reduce our profit on an offer of 10,000 tons of Java raw sugar from £20,000 to £15,000. Legally, we could have said no, a contract is a contract. But, in Asia, you don't trade only on the basis of legal documents; you trade on give and take and you place great value on friendship.

During the first one or two decades of Indonesian Independence, a lot of the trade between Singapore Chinese merchants and Indonesian Government trading bodies or Indonesian pribumi merchants was conducted on this basis. Most of the Indonesian Government officials who were in charge of their trading organisations in the early years after independence were fairly inexperienced, and they often relied on their Singapore businessmen friends to help them tailor the terms and conditions of their trade. In my chats with Allan, I remembered explaining the whole background to him. Unfortunately, on this particular occasion, he turned stiff and unyielding

When I called Allan Arthur in London, he quickly became very hot under the collar. "We don't trade like this. A deal is a deal. A word is a word."

Gula Negara had trusted us to buy sugar from them, sometimes giving us offers well over and above normal commercial terms, treating us as friends and almost as partners. Now they had got into a jam back home and were asking us for a bit of relief. We could have given way graciously, but Allan was saying, "Hey, this is not done!" In other words, when we make money it's fine; when we're asked to give up a bit, it's not fine.

I tried to make him see sense. "We share the same values as you do. But we are now talking as partners, and Sudarso has given us a helping hand all along with special offers. Can't we just give in to this request? It only involves a tiny bit of money."

Not being born a businessman, Allan went on haranguing me. I lost my temper with him. I told him, "Forget it, Allan! This is my last deal with you!" I felt I could not go on doing joint ventures with him on this basis. Every time something came up, I would feel as if I were a criminal to broach it. So I made a deliberate decision to switch future deals to ED&F Man and Michael Stone, who happily embraced me with both arms. I may have been brutal in my actions, but I have always acted based on fair play.

Allan was a lovely gentleman, a very straight, upright, honourable ex-colonial senior civil servant. Although I chose to no longer use Drake as my London partner for my Indonesian sugar deals, nevertheless, I continued to have a very friendly relationship with Allan and his wife Dawn. Allan was truly a perfect gentleman.

So, 1963 was really the year that I became an international sugar trader, literally trading out of my suitcase from hotel rooms in London. And from 1963, Michael Stone and I became very close friends. A major reason we became close was that most of the other important sugar traders were commuters, meaning that they lived 30-60 miles from the City of London. As soon as trading closed, they very quickly finished off their paper work, shut their desks and headed for the railway station.

Michael was a bachelor. His parents resided in Surrey, but he lived in a flat in Empire House, not far from Harrods. Two or three times a week, he would come to my hotel room after work and we would go out to dine together. We talked endlessly and our friendship quickly flowered. We would talk about everything from sugar, to English politics to Chinese culture.

The only sad part for me was that I could not enjoy his company on weekends, as he would always go back to Surrey. My trips to London averaged about three weeks each, and weekend evenings were particularly hard for me. I'm not one of those lone wolves who enjoy going by myself to nightclubs, and you can do just so much walking in the park, reading in the hotel room or watching TV. It was a great relief for me when, in later years, I often joined Michael in Surrey. I would motor out and he would take me to play golf in St Georges Hill in the beautiful English countryside.

I can honestly say that much of the goodness in Michael, much of his knowledge, his skill in sugar trading and his views on the sugar market – and mine – rubbed off onto each other. There was a tremendous two-way flow, a cross-fertilization, which we both enjoyed immensely. For example, we both did our homework in analysing sugar production and consumption figures. We discussed the different ranges in statistical studies, and analysed the clues as to whether the market would go up or down over, say, a three-month period.

We shared, I think, an amazing ability to spot the important, relevant information. The information is all there; it pours out. The key is your ability to wade through thousands of words very quickly to spot the important points. If he missed something, I would pick it up; what I missed he would pick up. I would give him a call from Singapore or from my hotel room in London and say, "What do you think of this bit of news, Michael?" He'd give his interpretation and ask for mine. Quite often we held the same views.

I realized that in the trading world, if you meet a good sparring partner – and I had met one – the ideas that can flow from the relationship are amazing. It's highly creative. Michael Stone was, more than anyone else in his office, like me. He had the same fast reaction time, impatience and sense of speed and urgency.

Over time, Michael developed in style, forcefulness and temperament. But there was one key difference between us: Michael did not have the authority to trade at the speed and volume that I had. At ED&F Man, he was part of a team; I operated very much as a single trader, taking much bigger risks.

Of course, I didn't know what their book was; neither did they pry into mine. A book means what I call the OP, the Open Position. Are you net short or net long? You may have a long position here and a short position there, but at the end of each day you must know whether you are net long or net short. If you were net long and that day the market rose, you were smiling; the market was running with you. But if you were net long and the market fell, then you were a bit gloomy. If the market went much further down, you would be asked for margin calls. If you had an overweight position and the margin was a big one, you could even be bankrupted.

By the mid-1960s, Michael and I had developed a regular routine. After my plane landed in London in the morning, I headed straight for the public phones in the carousel area to call him while I waited for my check-in luggage to arrive. Once, he said, "There's a lot of activity today, Robert. Can you drop your bag at the hotel and come straight in? We've just sold 66,000 tons to Chile. If you come in fast enough, I may be able to persuade the other partner, Tate & Lyle, to cut you in on the deal."

I put the phone down, grabbed my bag, and hailed a cab, "Dorchester, please." I dumped my bag at the hotel – the concierges all knew me – and continued in the same taxi to the City. The trip from the airport took an hour and a half. I entered Man's office and Mike said, "Come, come, come. We'll go into the conference room now. Alan [Clatworthy], Tim [Dumas], here's Robert. What do you say we cut him in one-third?"

One of them said, "Well, but we ought to get Gordon Shemilt's or Mike Attfield's agreement in Tate & Lyle."

So they called them up and they said, "If it's Robert, okay; one-third each."

I recall that this 66,000-ton trade made about £30 profit a ton, as they had sold it at about £60, while they covered it at about £30. It was for delivery many months forward. When sugar is short in the market, people panic and buy, just like in the stock market. So we made a lot of money. If we earned £30 a ton, then we jointly made nearly £2 million from the deal. My share alone was more than £660,000, in excess of $5 million Singapore dollars, just because I arrived at the right time.

With Michael, I never had to say, "Aren't you taking too much of the cake?" Nor did he have to ask the same of me. We had a common understanding; there was no difference in nuance. Nobody could hide and say, "I thought you meant this or that."

The give-and-take spirit between Kuoks in Southeast Asia and Mans in London was simply amazing. We were people of similar character: Traders who trusted each other and never harboured treachery, selfishness or greed. In fact, it was a virtual partnership. They ran their firm, we ran ours; but in those joint-venture deals we prospered together.

That's the way you keep people happy. If you have a selfish or greedy streak – or a mean streak – and you try to fool your partner, everybody can smell it. A dog that senses hostility in you will go for your heel straight away.

Of course, I was very generous as well. When I had a good deal, I shared it with them. Say somebody gives you a lovely plate of food. Instead of gobbling it all down you say, "Come on, take half of this." Then he, in a similar vein, repays the act of generosity, and that goes on and on. You now have a fusion of real, genuine strength versus the rest of the market. You needn't fear a hidden sword stabbing you in the back. We even got to the stage of forming reversible cable addresses with our three British partners: MANKUOK, GOLOKUOK and KUOKDRAK (Man and Kuok, Golodetz and Kuok, Woodhouse, Drake and Kuok).

The non-British partner we became closest to was Maurice Varsano, by far the ablest of the French sugar traders. I met Maurice – a Bulgarian Jew who ended up in France by way of Morocco – in London or Paris in the mid-Sixties. We hit it off and, from the late 1960s, we entered into joint accounts with his Sucres & Denrées (Sucden), along with Man, Tate & Lyle and others.

Our trading strength in sugar was physical buying and selling in East Asia. Our European partners were stronger in the West. Our greatest strength was the Malaysian market. When I started trading sugar, the Malaysian market was 400,000 tons a year. Malaysian consumption by year 2000 had tripled to 1,200,000 tons.

I travelled alone on most of my sugar trips to London. But, starting in about 1969, I began taking my colleague Richard Liu on virtually every trip. I wanted his company partly to help me, and partly as I felt that it was time to clone someone who could take over from me one day. My brother Philip recruited Richard for MSM in 1964, upon Richard's graduation from the University of Malaya. When I became involved in some of the day-to-day work at MSM, I got to know Richard better. As he was brighter than most of the other young men on the trading side of the refinery, I realized that his talents would be wasted sitting in Prai on the remote northwest corner of the Malay Peninsula. He relocated to Kuok (Singapore) Ltd and soon began covering the London end. Richard was like a mirror image of me, and was fully acceptable to the London brokers.

In the early 1970s, I could have moved to London and become a full-time trader if I had wanted to. I was in Man's office one day with Tim Dumas, the most senior partner, Alan and David Clatworthy and Michael Stone. They said, "Please, can you come into the conference room. We have something serious to discuss with you." Their body language was very warm and open. They made an offer. "Robert, we've had some serious talks here. We have decided that we would very much like you to become a partner. Today, we are offering you one-quarter of ED&F Man." I think the price was £5 million.

I had the feeling that the average English partner only wanted to work until age 55 or 58, so Tim Dumas was getting close to retirement. I figured that when one partner sold shares – and it would always be in a rising market – the others would not always be willing buyers. I might end up being the only one buying, and very soon I would be in control of the firm. That would necessitate my moving to London. My reply to them was, "Let me think it over. It's very kind of you to make me this offer. However, I want to consult my fellow directors back home."

I talked to one or two of the directors, and they responded, "Nien, you do what you think is right." I then communicated with Michael and Alan. I told them, "Thank you all for the offer. You know, businessmen are regarded as rats in a rat race. Therefore, if I am a rat then my sewer is in Singapore." Those were my exact words. For better or for worse, Singapore was still my home.

In the early 1970s, I had a phone call from Hong Kong asking me to go there urgently. The market was abuzz with speculation that the Chinese sugar crop had failed and that China needed to import a large block of sugar. The Cultural Revolution had been raging since 1966. They asked me to go alone, implying that I should not even bring Lim Kai, who had accompanied me on all previous trips to China.

I met two senior officers of Wufenghang: The older man was Pu Jinxin and the younger one, Lin Zhongming, the future Chairman and CEO of COFCO. By then, I had been trading with Wufenghang for about ten years. We chatted on the phone quite a bit. They said they couldn't see me in my Hong Kong office; they wanted to meet in a more discreet place. I suggested we rendezvous at my Hong Kong apartment in Repulse Bay Towers, which I had bought in 1967 when many Chinese had fled Hong Kong following the riots that year.

The three of us sat down together. They first looked at each other. I later realized why: in opening their mouths, they were putting themselves at my mercy. They first spoke a lot of platitudes, "We've worked together for 10 years. We know you; we trust you fully. We don't know who else to trust."

Then they got to the point. "China is desperately short of sugar. In a few months we will run out. You must buy for us. We have cleared it. We have a mandate to request you to be the sole supplier." However, they had a problem. Being in the midst of the Cultural Revolution, China had little foreign exchange to pay for imports.

"We have also learned in our dealings with you that you are very active in the futures market," they continued. "We don't fully understand that market. Can you help us earn foreign exchange for the nation from the futures market?"

I answered, "Everything you have told me and requested of me is logical. But you must know that the minute you told me that China is short of sugar, I could betray you and go out and make a lot of money for myself in the market. However, since you have been honourable and confided in me, I will return the honour by now announcing to you that I will stop trading for three months. I will freeze my positions and devise a scheme to buy the sugar." I added, "The world is heading into a period of shortage. I believe that the only nation that has sufficient surplus to supply you today – and where we can hit the market while it is a bit asleep – is Brazil." We chatted for another hour, had dinner and I flew back to Singapore.

That same night, I started to accumulate futures positions on the London and New York markets on behalf of China, but all in my books. All the trading was conducted at night: London traded with us from about 5 pm to midnight Singapore time, and then New York would trade from 10 pm to about 3 am. I couldn't show my hand too much and place huge orders, so I gradually accumulated positions every day for three weeks. We placed the trades through different brokers whom I knew scarcely compared notes.

Every morning, one of my assistants or I would call up Hong Kong and report to Wufenghang in coded language: say, 20 at what level, meaning we had bought so many lots at what level during the previous night's trading. So they had a record, but we kept nothing in writing. I told them I wanted total secrecy.

Meanwhile, my people flew to London because we didn't want it to look like a Hong Kong/Singapore operation. From London, they contacted the sugar-export monopoly of Brazil, Institute of Sugar and Alcohol, headed by a Señor Watson. We had an agent in Brazil who was of mixed Brazilian and Scottish blood. We told our agent to ask Señor Watson if he was prepared to trade with us directly, not through a London or New York broker. Because of the futures involved, I sensed that there was a risk that London brokers would open up a separate front to trade for themselves. The answer came back positive, so one hurdle was crossed. Piet Yap, James Lim and one other assistant from our firm went to Rio de Janeiro to negotiate.

At this same time, a major international sugar conference was taking place in Geneva. I decided to attend as a decoy. I landed in Geneva and, on my second day, a sugar trader came up to me at the conference. He said, "Oh, Robert, have you heard? There are some mysterious Japanese in Watson's office."

"Oh, that's interesting," I said. "You know, there are lots of Japanese companies and I suppose some of them have made good money and are moving up."

Scarier still, the next day, I was paged through the intercom while I was in the conference hall listening to some discussion: "International call" – luckily they did not say from Brazil – "for Monsieur Robert Kuok."

I went to the phone booth and an operator in Rio de Janeiro connected me. My team wanted guidance on price. I said, "I don't think the secret can be kept very much longer. They're getting very close to the scent here. Close it! Don't bargain for shillings!"

China had given me a mandate up to such-and-such a price. I bettered it for them. I think the tonnage involved was 300,000 tons, which at that time was a large block (today you have to buy a million tons to be a big block). Then, our people gave the Sugar Institute the true picture: the sugar was for China. They were delighted, as they saw the opportunity for large-scale trade between Brazil and China.

We told the Brazilians that we wanted to use Ban Thong, my Hong Kong trading company, rather than Kuok Brothers. They agreed and offered Ban Thong a half-percent commission. Once the deal was signed and announced, the market went through the roof. Over the next three days, I sold all the futures that I had accumulated and kept the profits with the Bank of China (London). I think I handed China about £2,500,000 on a plate, just from the futures. Why? I love China. What do you want money for in life? If you can help a nation, surely it's more satisfying for your heart and soul than just making money for yourself. Our Brazil-China deal was a market coup. The next day, everybody was knocking on China's door.

Not long after this, COFCO gave me a firm bid to buy raw sugar from the Philippines. The bid was valid for three or four days, which was an unusually long period in the trade. China had never before approached anyone and given them a direct bid like this. I felt it was in part a reward for me, demonstrating their gratitude for my role in engineering the Brazilian sugar deal.

But this took place during the reign of Ferdinand Marcos in the Philippines. I detested the Marcos regime. In the early days of his rule, I had met Singapore and Malaysian-Chinese businessmen who kept telling me that Marcos was extremely corrupt. I didn't believe them. I had swallowed some of the stories churned out by gullible foreign journalists who had been wined and dined by Marcos and his cronies.

We tried to do business with the Philippines and soon learned that for every pound of sugar you wanted to sell to or buy from the Philippines, one and a half US cents a pound had to be added on for Marcos and his cronies. One and half cents a pound! To put this in context, an efficient producer such as Brazil or Australia was producing sugar at about seven to eight cents a pound. Prices sometimes went as low as two and a half cents a pound. It stank to high heaven!

When the Chinese extended me their offer, I contacted the Philippine sugar-selling authority. We were told to contact Roberto Benedicto – Marcos' front man on all sugar deals – in Tokyo, where he was serving as Philippine Ambassador to Japan.

Richard Liu contacted Ambassador Benedicto and chatted with him on the phone. Benedicto invited us to visit him in Tokyo. All this was on a very urgent basis, so Richard and I caught the next flight and had a good meeting with him in a hotel on the outskirts of Tokyo. He contacted his boss, Marcos, and we waited a day or two without making any headway. I felt quite deflated and disappointed. We flew back to Hong Kong, and the Ambassador promised to phone or cable us.

Within a day or two his answer came: "Sorry, we have nothing to offer you." A few days after that, we heard that the Philippines had traded sugar with someone else. So it was pretty apparent to me that although they were sellers, the Philippines was picking and choosing whom they wanted to sell to. I felt very badly let down by Marcos and Benedicto.

In the early 1960s, we were also buying sugar from the Soviet Union. Then, from the late 1960s, the Russians turned to become net annual buyers of sugar. They have remained big buyers ever since, and Russian buying is the largest single event in the sugar world every year.

I went to Moscow for the first time in 1972 with Charles Kralj, a senior trader at ED&F Man. Kralj was originally from Yugoslavia. He told me that one day during World War II, the German Gestapo came to his home. He jumped through a window at the back of his house and started running. He walked, hitchhiked and rode on trains and boats until he made his way to England. After the war he joined Man.

I got to know Charles Kralj in 1960 on one of my early trips to London. I was taken ill one night and Charles, who was visiting me in my hotel, cared for me. My friendship with Charles blossomed, and later he arranged to take me to Russia to meet with Prodintorg (the Soviet equivalent of COFCO in China), which held monopolies on imports and exports of commodities like sugar and horsemeat.

The chairman of Prodintorg was a man named Alexeenko; his right-hand assistant was Madame Gaidamoscka. As a very young woman, she had been sent by the Stalin regime as part of the Lend-Lease team of Soviet officers to be stationed in the United States, where she had picked up some English. Alexeenko and Gaidamoscka were both lovely people. They were trustworthy almost to the point of being naïve – not stupid, but just very solid people of high integrity. In none of our trades with them was there ever a whisper of a shady deal.

The Russian trades always involved gigantic quantities that created huge waves, rocking the market. Thus, there was a natural tendency to syndicate the deals, and our joint accounts with ED&F Man, Tate & Lyle and Sucres & Denrées came in useful. We would sell and then buy big blocks of physical sugar or sugar futures to cover our sales to the Soviet Union. We bought futures to cover our risk or ran an open position. Man handled most of the trading, and within Man the chief players were Michael Stone, Alan Clatworthy, David Clatworthy and Charles Kralj.

I remember one funny encounter with the Russians in London in the early 1970s. I had taken an overnight flight from Singapore. After showering, shaving and freshening up, I decided to eat an early lunch. I went to Chuen Cheng Ku, a Chinese restaurant in Chinatown, with two or three of my colleagues. We ordered the food and started to eat.

As I dipped into my meal, I looked up and, at a small table about 15 paces away, I saw Madame Gaidamoscka and her boss, Alexeenko. I thought, "It cannot be them" – even though I had taken Madame Gaidamoscka to this restaurant before.

I would always call ahead and have a chat with my London friends, especially Michael Stone, before getting on the plane to London. There hadn't been a word from Mike about the presence of the Russian buyers. I felt very confused.

Madame Gaidamoscka looked up and our eyes met. She made a sign of recognition. I said, "Madame," got up and quickly strode across the room and shook their hands very warmly. "How are you?" I asked.

The way she behaved gave the show away. She said, "Don't tell anybody I am here. We are just here on a short visit." Everything they volunteered indicated that it was a secret trip. They appeared very embarrassed even to see me.

I finished my meal and went immediately to the City to see Michael Stone at Man. I confronted him. "Mike, why are you keeping all this from me?"

He was genuinely perplexed: "What do you mean, Robert?"

 "Surely you know Madame is in town."

"Madame, which Madame?"

"Madame Gaidamoscka."

"What? Surely you are mistaken, Robert."

"What do you mean by mistaken? I just shook her hand and Aleexenko's."

Then I saw all kinds of question marks on Michael's forehead.

Michael very soon traced them to where they were staying. They were creatures of habit. You knew where they usually stayed and, in those days, hotel staff could be quite unguarded. Alexeenko and Gaidamoscka were both very frank and upright people, and Michael got it all out of them quite easily: Russia was badly in need of sugar so the Russians were in town to buy. They had contacted Czarnikow first on the telephone. Czarnikow enjoined them to secrecy, warning that otherwise they might not be able to get a proper offer out of Australia for them. The Russians were to come straight to the Czarnikow office on arrival in London. Unfortunately, they just liked Chinese food too much.

The Soviets were honourable in their sugar dealings; but not so the North Koreans. We had a very nasty experience with North Korea. They had opened a kind of consular office-cum-residence building in Singapore. Every so often, they would invite us for a simple dinner and then show us North Korean military propaganda films. Once, the day after one of these encounters, they suddenly appeared at our office and said that they had 7,500 tons of sugar to sell us. I think that they had received aid sugar from Poland or somewhere else in the Communist bloc, and they were very short of foreign exchange.

We sold the North Korean sugar to Maurice Varsano of Sucres & Denrées. But when it came time to open our letter of credit, North Korea asked for an extension: "Sorry, our goods have not yet arrived at the port of shipment. Please grant one month's extension." So we negotiated with Maurice. He agreed to a short extension. We went back and extended the letter of credit. Later the Koreans said, "Sorry, we still don't have the sugar; some more extension."

Then Maurice balked. He said, "No, I am not dealing with the North Koreans. I am dealing with you. You are my principal, so you honour." We had to cover the trade. By that time, the sugar price had gone up £15 to £20 a ton higher than what we'd paid the Koreans. We had to buy in the open market and deliver the sugar to Maurice at a large loss – he'd cleverly bought from us at cost and freight. The North Koreans never delivered and they refused to pay demurrage, though theoretically they were required to by contract. We took a great risk hoping to make one or two dollars a ton, and ended up losing quite a large sum of money.

I remember the North Koreans' last cable to us: "We agree that we have been unable to deliver. We will explain our reasons in arbitration court. Please come to Pyongyang to pursue your claims." I kissed everything goodbye and threw that cable into the wastepaper basket.

I made half a dozen trips to Cuba, the first in 1970 with my friend Roy Fisher of Woodhouse, Drake. My experience with Cuba was bittersweet. I met a Cuban named Emiliano Lescano for the first time in London in the late 1960s, and we took an immediate liking to each other. He was then number two man in Cubazucar, the government body in charge of marketing sugar. Cubazucar reported directly to the Minister of Foreign Trade, a Señor Cabrisas, a senior man close to Castro. Soon after I met Lescano, he was appointed President of Cubazucar.

Emiliano Lescano made his mark on every sugar trader from the 1970s to the early 1980s. In Japan he was known as Mr Sugar. He bargained and negotiated with all the figures and statistics of his nation at his fingertips. He never referred to notes. For a young man of about 26, he was a genius of a trader. He never lost his cool.

Lescano was a handsome, graceful, charming man with twinkling eyes. In addition, he was very well built. I remember taking him to the Copacabana Nightclub in Tokyo. At the Copacabana, Lescano was just liquid flowing all over the floor, whether it was a tango or a rumba. The Cubans really have music in their blood.

Then Lescano started to hit the bottle. I could always sense he was under a lot of stress. The American embargo on trade with Cuba made it very difficult for the country to make any sort of progress. Cuba's sugar mills had been established mainly by American interests. When the supply of American machinery and spare parts was cut off, the Cubans went to Eastern Europe and the Soviet Union for equipment, but it was inferior. The Cuban mills were inefficient and often in disrepair, and their sugar industry went into a long, downward spiral. At one time, they produced six million tons of sugar annually, but it later became an almighty struggle for Cuba to make even two million tons. Countries such as Brazil, Thailand and Australia stepped up sugar production while Cuba's production shrank.

Given the circumstances, the man entrusted with marketing the nation's sugar was naturally under a lot of pressure. I think he was expected to do wonders, to create miracles. But he was not a magician. He also had marital problems. Either his wife, a major in the Cuban Army, or the woman he fell in love with, a colonel in Cuban Army Intelligence, fixed him. The Cuban Government lost trust in him.

Lescano hit the bottle harder and harder. My sugar friends who frequented Cuba, including Michael Stone, relayed the news. We heard that he was no longer head of Cubazucar; then we heard that he was jobless; that he was punch drunk, brain sodden; that he had fallen to the level of a beggar. And then he was dead.

When I think back to that lively young Cuban, I am filled with great sadness. This was a tragic story of a man who was just born at the wrong time in the wrong country. He was an upright, honest young man. In his job, he could have made a fortune and run away from the country, claiming political refuge. But there was never a breath of disloyalty to his leader or to his country. He loved his Cuba.

I finally met Fidel Castro in 1990. One evening, I was with a group of sugar traders at a beachside bungalow in Havana. We were casually attired in short-sleeved shirts and slacks. Suddenly, a car drove up and a couple of men jumped out. They shouted, "El Comandante is waiting to see you all. Please get ready." There was no time for us to change our clothes. The eight or nine of us were bundled into two or three cars.

Castro rambled on from about 10.45 pm until 4 am or so. He told us about his cattle-raising and biochemistry and all sorts of things. He had all the air-conditioners going full blast. I think the temperature must have been lowered to 13°C. He wore about three thick cotton tunics while we shivered. It was terrible! At about 3.30 am he sent for brandy. Did I down it in a hurry! It was an awful experience.

Sugar gave me the busiest time in my working life. It started in 1958, and it didn't really ease up for 35 years. From 1963, every year I made at least two or three trips to Europe and America, trips to Japan, the odd trips to Australia, and shorter hops around Southeast Asia. I was seldom home for more than a week, and I hardly saw my five eldest children grow up. I employed trustworthy people who could look after the shop while I was off like a kite, flying here, flying there. I recall that, at one stage, I never slept in the same bed for two straight nights over 20 consecutive nights. I certainly was not doing it for heroics or fun. The business was just such that I had to keep on the move.

When I was young, I used to go to acrobatics shows. It always amused me to see the man juggling balls. From the mid-1960s, I felt as though I was a juggler in the business world. I would look in the mirror and say, "Today you've added another ball and you're now tossing eight balls in the air." By 1964, you might say I was juggling three sugar balls: Refining, imports into Malaysia, and international trading. By the mid-1960s, even before sugar had hardened, I was already juggling new balls in plywood, flour milling, shipping, aviation and steel.

10
ADDING TO LIFE'S ESSENTIALS

ONE THING I LEARNED from the Japanese is that you should focus on products for which there are large, established markets, and for which demand is uniform and sustainable. Your products should not be subject to frequent changes of taste, like, say, plastic pails, where one year the demand is for one colour or shape and the next for another. I realized why the Japanese approached me for sugar and, later, flour milling: the markets for these end products are very simple. Basic processed foods such as sugar and flour have virtually no variation. There is basically only one product, which greatly simplifies factory investment. I eventually added edible oils, to give me rice, sugar, flour and oils – all simple commodities with vast markets.

I learned this lesson the hard way after I entered the plywood business in Malaysia in 1961. Running plywood mills was one of the most excruciating experiences in my life. In basic foodstuff, you deal primarily in single, unchanging products, whereas in the case of plywood, every buyer has his whim and fancy. This furniture maker requests waterproofing; that one wants a walnut veneer; another requires use of urea glue. You're manufacturing to order, and some of the orders were pitifully small. Some logs are diseased, or riddled with pinholes. So, then your plywood gets heavily discounted and you are selling at a loss. If demand shifts, part of your plant is immediately obsolete.

Toiling in the plywood industry was like being born a poor, squint-eyed carpenter who inherits from his father an unbalanced table. The carpenter can't work properly, so he puts the table on its side and saws at one leg. He stands the table up and it still won't balance, so he keeps on sawing the legs. Eventually, all he's left with is the top of the table sitting on the floor.

In other words, there is always unevenness in the plant. You're never able to maximize efficiency in the mill, yet the equipment depreciates every day. Plywood is a terrible, terrible business! You can only succeed if you have the wealth of the Amazon forest behind you, in which case you're really making money from forestry. Humbled, I realized why the Japanese didn't want to enter the plywood industry with me. I exited the business in 1968.

In 1962, Mitsui, one of my two Japanese partners in MSM, and Nippon Flour Mills, approached me about building a flourmill in Malaysia. I went up to Kuala Lumpur to see my old Raffles College friend Raja Mohar, who was then Secretary-General in the Ministry of Commerce and Industry, about the proposal.

Raja Mohar, who was a true Malay gentleman, said, "You know, Hong Kong Flour Mills has already applied for a licence."

So I asked, "But are you going to allow a monopoly?"

Raja Mohar responded, "No, as a top civil servant here, I will not favour any monopoly." He advised me to apply, but said, "Robert, you must not just bring in the Japanese. We don't want our nation to be controlled by Japan or Britain or any single nation. Get another partner, from another nation."

I was already importing flour directly from Australia, thereby bypassing distributors like Sime Darby and Guthrie in Malaysia and Singapore. I always saw the need to cut out layers of middlemen wedged between us and our consumers of flour and sugar. One of the Australian firms that supplied flour to us was William Charlick

Ltd of Adelaide. I asked Charlick if it was interested in partnering in a flourmill in Malaysia. Bang: A man called Jack Dunning, the Managing Director of William Charlick, came up to Malaysia and together we moved very fast.

When it came time to apply for the flour-milling licence, I went to see my old friend Khir Johari (later Tan Sri Khir Johari), who was still Minister of Commerce and Industry at the time. Khir Johari had helped me to break through the obstruction erected by the civil servants when I applied for tariff protection for my sugar refinery. But Khir Johari now remarked, "Aren't you being greedy, Robert? You already have sugar. Why do you want flour milling as well?"

Frankly, I thought this was a rather strange thing for a government minister to say to me, especially since we were already well-established flour traders. Why shouldn't a businessman want to expand? Why must a government decide what's enough for him? But I didn't want to argue with Khir Johari, as he was my friend and had assisted me in the past.

Stung, I went back to see Raja Mohar and told him what Khir Johari had said. Raja Mohar knew the sort of man I was, and he trusted me. He said, "Don't worry, Robert. I'll help you. I don't think he was right to discourage you. Just write in and let the government judge whether you deserve to be a flour miller." In other words, turn the situation from a personal remark by a minister into a government relationship with the business community.

In the end, I was awarded a licence to operate the flourmill. This was the second licence awarded by the Ministry. As Khir Johari had advised, the first went to Hong Kong Flour Mills, which was owned by the Sung family, which founded the first machine-operated flour mill in China in 1890.

Hong Kong Flour Mills was some two years ahead of us, but they moved much more slowly. They started production and selling in Malaysia at the end of 1965. Within about eight months of their flour hitting the market, our mill was up and running. I called our mill Federal Flour Mills (derived from the Federation of Malaya), since Hong Kong Flour Mills had already taken the name Malayan Flour Mills.

As with sugar refining, flour milling was subject to tariffs set by the Tariff Advisory Board (the name had changed from Tariff Advisory Commission). The TAB chairman, who was brought in from New Zealand, had been an ex-Commissioner of Customs there. The Deputy Chairman of TAB was a schoolmate of mine from Johor Bahru, Sujak bin Rahiman. Sujak tipped me off that the chairman might be in favour of granting highly favourable tariff protection to Hong Kong Flour Mills.

I outlined my view of the market to Sujak. An Indonesian Chinese had established Prima Flour Mills in Singapore, and his flour was flooding the Malaysian market. We all bought wheat at similar world prices. Since Prima Flour Mills was based in the large seaport of Singapore, they could, by virtue of cheaper logistics, import wheat slightly more cheaply, although their land transport costs to the Kuala Lumpur market were dearer than ours from Port Klang.

If all three mills – Prima, Malayan and Federal – could produce flour at a cost of say $5.70 per 50-pound calico bag, then we should each make a 30 cent per bag profit if we sold the sack for $6. I wrote in my tariff exercise paper that if we asked for a price above $6.70, it would be tantamount to profiteering. I said the protection should enable us to operate our mill and deliver flour to a shop in Kuala Lumpur at a price between $5.50 and $6.70 per bag. I added that, through competition between the mills – there were more coming on stream – there would be downward pressure on prices.

But, just before the TAB hearing, I received a phone call out of the blue from David Sung Sr, the owner of Hong Kong Flour Mills. He wanted to visit me at my office in Kuala Lumpur.

David Sung Sr grew up in Shanghai. He owned a stable of racehorses and, when he came to Kuala Lumpur, he always lived in grand style, booking the presidential suite on a long-term basis in the then-leading Merlin Hotel. His eldest son was David Sung Jr; he also had a second son, and a nephew called Martin Sung, who eventually ran everything for him.

David Sung Sr climbed the stairs to my office. You would be ashamed to set foot in the place: it was a dingy, narrow room. The bathroom lacked even modern sanitation.

Sung told me that Malayan Flour Mills was already conducting trial runs, and he asked me how I was going to approach the tariff advisory exercise set for the next day. I told him I that would seek a price of between $6.50 and $6.70 per bag. He became very agitated, "No! That's way below my cost of production!" Sung, the experienced miller, was telling me that his cost of production was something like $7.50. Having done my sums, I knew that my production cost was about $5.80, and I estimated that Prima Flour Mills in Singapore was able to produce at about $5.50.

I said, "Mr Sung, I keep telling you what my cost is and you keep trying to convince me that your cost is much higher than mine. It boggles my mind how you can say that! As an experienced flour miller, you should be telling me that you are able to produce more cheaply than I can. You've been in the flour milling business for two generations, so you should be much more skilled than me."

He begged me, "At tomorrow's exercise, please ask for $8.50." He said the TAB Chairman had almost agreed to that price. "If you come in at $6.50," he griped, "the Chairman will be forced to accept your figure because it's more favourable to the local consumer."

I said, "Mr Sung, I'm a Malaysian. I was born and brought up here. It boils down to that. I cannot rape my country or my fellow citizens. At $6.50, I'm still making a very good profit every year. How can I profiteer?"

He could not accept such a blunt statement from me. Sung pleaded, but I said, "I'm sorry, I cannot accede to your request. I don't think there's any point in our continuing this conversation." And that was how the session ended.

After Federal Flour Mills began production on 1 November 1966 – two years after our sugar refinery MSM came on stream – we quickly became Malaysia's dominant miller of wheat flour, a position we have held until today. Our flour market share has typically been more than 40 percent of the market.

One of the first things that I did was to acquire a brand that was already well known to retailers and consumers. I had been buying wheat flour from Sime Darby, which had developed a quality brand called Blue Key. Through this business, I had gotten to know the managers of Sime Darby very well. One day, I told them about my plan to build a flourmill in Malaysia and the looming ban on imports of flour. I asked them to sell me the Blue Key brand. We negotiated, and I think I paid $25,000 to buy over the rights to Blue Key, which is still one of Federal Flour Mills' main brands.

I also managed to scoop up a third flour-milling licence a little later. A Chinese merchant from Kedah had managed to secure a licence for a flourmill in Butterworth, which is on the Malay Peninsula opposite Penang island. He then quietly hawked the licence, but there were no takers because it was very apparent that the first two mills were slugging it out. Then, one of my staff came to me in Kuala Lumpur and reported that the businessman had called to inquire whether we were interested in setting up another mill in Butterworth. At this point he had already held the licence for two or three years.

My staff noted that by buying the licence we would prevent third-party competition. I said, "Yes, that makes sense," but it was apparent to me that Butterworth was the wrong location. I said, "Look here. Get the licence. Then we'll apply for a change of location. We'll take it to Johor Bahru. Let's put the flourmill there and one day we can even sell flour to Singapore."

Sure enough, it became Johor Bahru Flour Mill after we persuaded the government to allow us to change the location of the mill from Butterworth to Johor. Today, Johor Flour is a wholly owned subsidiary of Federal Flour Mills.

Throughout my business career, I have always set a course for deeper and richer seas in which to fish. If we had remained in Johor Bahru, we would have led indolent lives. We would probably have earned MYR$500,000 or so each year, which, split among four or five partners, would have yielded about $100,000 each. I can imagine we would have retired at the age of 55.

By shifting our base of operation to Singapore and looking out onto the international scene, our focus changed completely. We began to import wheat flour, sugar, rice – whatever was in demand. We re-exported some of the foodstuff to Indonesia. If Indonesia wanted glutinous rice (a crucial ingredient in Chinese and Southeast Asian desserts) from Thailand, we supplied it. Relocating to Singapore was really the stepping-stone onto the world stage, and our later move to Hong Kong solidified our position in the first division.

We began trading in Indonesia in the late 1960s in competition with 10-15 very vigorous, shrewd Chinese traders with offices on the five major commodity-trading streets of Singapore: Market Street, Telok Ayer Street, New Bridge Road, Circular Road and Cecil Street. Beside these very active players, there were perhaps another 30-50 commodity traders.

But what is commodity trade? Say somebody comes into a tailor's shop in Singapore. He happens to be a relative of the tailor. He says, "Long-lost cousin, I made it good in Indonesia. I've been given permission by the Indonesian authorities to buy 50,000 tons of sugar. Can you supply it?" If the tailor has any business sense, he will say, "Of course I can." He will then scratch his head and think, "Now, who did I make clothes for who is in the sugar trade?" He has the connection. The tailor will make the sale, but he will draw his supplies from someone else. That, simply, is trade.

After Suharto came to power in 1966, it took him about a year to become firmly entrenched. At the very beginning of Suharto's reign, he ran the country with a management committee comprised of a few generals. The famous ones were Ali Mutopo and Soedjono Humardani, who, between them, ran the army and the security apparatus. General Suryo was put in charge of supplies, and it was he who found able Chinese businessmen to secure supplies for Indonesia.

During the days when Suharto served as a general under President Sukarno, he befriended many Chinese businessmen. They helped to supply the Indonesian military with food and equipment, including military hardware needed for the Irian Jaya campaign against the Dutch. Suharto saw the shrewdness, business cunning, enormous drive and tenacity of the Chinese minority in Indonesia. They were willing to work hard and take chances for greater profit. He saw the Chinese as a people who could deliver and help him to bring up his young nation. In his early years as President, wherever he could he empowered the Chinese to do business as part of his strategy to accelerate economic development.

On the other hand, Suharto was also bound to his own ethnic group. He held the reins, but he constantly came under pressure from other generals, some even senior to him in rank. Many of these harboured anti-Chinese feelings. Suharto had to tread a very fine line to skirt the anti-Chinese elements in his ruling clique. At times, he caved in to the demands of the hotheads to give businesses to the pribumis. But the performance of the pribumis was not half as good as what the Chinese could have done.

Among the Chinese merchants whom Suharto met and befriended in the 1950s was Liem Sioe Liong (Soedono Salim). Sioe Liong was then a shopkeeper selling and repairing bicycles and bicycle tires in a small village in Central Java named Kudus. It was in that village that Suharto cut his teeth as a young army officer.

I met Liem Sioe Liong in the mid-1960s. At this time, my manager in charge of rice in Singapore was Wong Sing Hew, a native of Fuzhou and a bright, young man who joined me in about 1954. Wong spoke hardly any English, but he was very good with Chinese dialects and got along well with the Chinese traders of Indonesia. It was Wong who made the first contact with Liem Sioe Liong.

One day, Wong said, "Oh, would you let me go and call on Liem Sioe Liong to try and offer him some rice?" I said by all means do so. He left our shop on Cecil Street and walked to Telok Ayer Street, where Sioe Liong had opened an office. Wong made them an offer of rice and, as I recall, after a few attempts we closed our first deal. There followed more rice and sugar deals, of 5,000-10,000 tons.

Wong told Piet Yap, the Sumatran Chinese whom I had recruited in 1959, about Liem Sioe Liong. Yap and Sioe Liong, both being Indonesian Chinese, got on like a house on fire. Later, I was introduced to Sioe Liong and had dinner with him and his partner, Liem Oen Kian (Djuhar Sutanto). We communicated in *minnanhua*, the southern Fujian dialect, as well as in Fuzhou dialect and Mandarin. When he turned to Oen Kian, he would speak in Fuqing dialect, which I could scarcely comprehend.

We became quite friendly with Sioe Liong and his company, Waringin, named after an Indonesian wayside tree. (They told me the name was selected by President Suharto himself). Whenever we could, we entertained them to dinner and so on.

In about 1969, I also met General Bustanil Arifin (at that time a Lieutenant-Colonel). General Arifin, who became a very good friend of mine, was number two in Bulog (Bureau Logistics). Under Suharto, Bulog was ostensibly autonomous, but it answered directly to the President. General Arifin later became Director of Bulog. Suharto didn't like criticism. If criticized, he always smiled; but you never knew whether that smile meant your days were beginning or your days were numbered.

One day, Yap gave me a useful tip. He had heard that Indonesia might enter flour milling. Yap was not close to the flour-milling side of our business; he was more involved in sugar. I had my finger on the pulse of everything that I handled; I was as close to shipping as to sugar as to flour as to even plywood adhesives.

Yap brought Sioe Liong to see me in Singapore to discuss flour milling. I told Sioe Liong, "There is a fortune to be made in flour milling in Indonesia." After all, Indonesia had ten times the population of Malaysia.

He responded, "Well, it may be too late. A Chinese businessman from Sulawesi has already convinced the Minister of Industry, General Yusuf, to let him start flourmills there." Sioe Liong continued, "But let me try to get it. I'll rush back to Jakarta and see Suharto." Within 72 hours, Sioe Liong called and said, "I've done it!"

The flourmill project was handed to Liem Sioe Liong. President Suharto named it Bogasari: *boga* is food while *sari* means essence. Sioe Liong, who was new to the flour-milling industry, had a gentleman's understanding with me that we would undertake the project together. He brought Liem Oen Kian to my office for an important meeting to discuss partnership terms in Bogasari. There were actually four partners in his Waringin: Liem Sioe Liong; Liem Oen Kian; Soedwikatmono, who was Suharto's first cousin; and a Sumatran Malay called Ibrahim Rishad. I brought my thirteenth cousin, Hock Toh, a director of Kuok Brothers, to the meeting.

Sioe Liong acted the part of the nice guy and Oen Kian, the toughie. Oen Kian quickly said, "Look here, Brother Robert. I have discussed it with *Oom* (everyone called Sioe Liong '*Oom*,' which is Dutch for uncle). Let's do it this way. Our new company will need US$5 million in paid-up capital. We'll try to raise the rest by loans, since we have got such a tremendous monopoly business. Now, Waringin doesn't have much cash. So, for every dollar of equity in this joint venture, you must put up 75 cents and the Waringin side will put up 25 cents. But since the flourmill is in our country, the shareholding shall be reversed: We will own 75 percent; you will hold 25 percent." Oen Kian also said that Kuok Brothers must provide all of the bank guarantees to import plant and machinery, since their side lacked credit standing with the banks at that point.

On hearing their terms, Hock Toh became irate. I saw from his body language, his expression and particularly his eyes, that he was about to burst out. I signalled him with my eyes to say: "Shut up. Shut up." In other words, it's not your turn to speak. I quickly spoke up before he could start any nonsense, and said, "Sioe Liong, Oen Kian, I understand the situation and I accept. And I will furnish the banker's guarantees for the first flourmills."

Then Liem Oen Kian said, "The President has decided to issue a ruling to restrict the project to Indonesian nationals only. Therefore, you cannot surface. Your 25 percent has to be held by us for you." And so, for 20 or more years from the early 1970s, we owned 25 percent of Bogasari without a scrap of paper to prove it.

Shortly after this encounter, at President Suharto's request,

General Arifin came to see me in Singapore to discuss wheat imports and milling. I remember I did all the sums on the back of an envelope and showed Arifin how profitable the whole venture would be. He asked, "May I keep the envelope?" and took it back to Jakarta.

I moved quickly to order the plant and equipment for the flourmill. We determined that Swiss machinery was too expensive, so we ordered from Miag, a German company in Braunschweig, 20 miles from the East German border (this was 1969). I travelled there with Grant Sansom, an Australian flour miller from Charlick who operated my Malaysian flourmills, to negotiate the details. We received a bank guarantee from Bangkok Bank. About a year later, the machinery arrived in Jakarta. Miag sent installation engineers and we sent our engineering team from Kuala Lumpur to set up the mill.

We had already selected a good-sized site in Tanjung Priok, the port area of Jakarta. The infrastructure was very poor, with old warehouses and huge traffic jams, so I pointed out that the roads had to be widened in order to deliver the flour to the buyers and consumers. We built our own wharves to receive wheat imports. I told them to plan for expansion. Within six months of choosing the Tanjung Priok site, I flew to Surabaya and we picked a plot of land for a second flourmill.

Bogasari began with a tiny plant milling 150 tons of wheat a day in 1971. By the time I left Bogasari in 1992, it was milling over 7,000 tons of wheat a day in Jakarta – making it the world's largest single flourmill at that time – and 5,000 tons per day in Surabaya. Imagine the logistics of that! If you brought in 40,000 tons of wheat (Indonesia had to import its entire wheat requirement), it would last barely five days. The Indonesians developed a ravenous appetite for wheat-flour noodles – fresh and instant – and baked goods like bread, cakes and biscuits.

Kuok Brothers sent over top managers. We seconded Piet Yap to be the General Manager and COO of Bogasari; the Liems served as Chairman and CEO. We also sent the CFO, Chia Pak Chin; the main marketing man; the miller, Grant Sansom, from Federal Flour Mills; and the head of the general affairs department.

We also shipped in nearly all of the wheat to Indonesia. We set up an offshore company called Golden Sari to negotiate the buying and shipping of wheat from Australia, Canada and the US. We held some 43 percent of Golden Sari shares while Liem Sioe Liong owned about 51 percent. We managed this wheat-purchasing and freighting arm out of Hong Kong and Singapore. Pacific Carriers, the Singapore-based shipping company I had established, transported the wheat. Bulog was the offshore buyer of all wheat entering Indonesia. Then Bulog in turn sold the wheat to Bogasari, the sole flour miller, and Bogasari marketed the flour at government-controlled prices.

About six years from that initial meeting with Liem Sioe Liong and Liem Oen Kian – a few years after Bogasari was up and running – they came to me about declaring the first dividend. They were going to declare a dividend of US$5 million. The Liems had a surprise for me. They said, "We must tell you that in our talks with *Bapak* (the President), *Bapak* said the first 20 percent must go to the Armed Forces Fund. The remaining 80 percent shall be prorated according to shareholding." Since our equity stake was 25 percent, we were effectively cut back to 20 percent of that dividend – and to all subsequent dividends.

I often felt short-changed by the Liems. They always offered the Indonesian Government as an excuse, but they didn't even use the word 'government'. They'd just say, Bapak's wish is such. Sioe Liong himself was quite a fair man, especially towards me. Then his third son, Anthoni Salim, grew up and gradually gained management control of the Salim Group.

One day in the early 1990s, Yap called me and said, "At last, we can surface. The Liems want to inject Bogasari into their public company, Indocement."

Two years after Bogasari's establishment, Liem Sioe Liong had invested in a big cement plant. The Liems intended to inject Bogasari into Indocement, converting my flourmill shares to cement shares. It was all cockeyed.

I remonstrated with Yap. I said, "Why should a cement company want to gobble up a wheat-flour factory? One is in building construction; the other is in food." I really had Hobson's choice: I had no proof that I was even a partner! By hinting at morality, I tried to massage them towards my way of thinking and drop the idea of combining Indocement and Bogasari.

The impasse persisted for six or so months. Finally, Yap arranged for a meeting in the Hilton Hotel, Jakarta, for which I flew down. Anthoni Salim brought his young Chinese-Indonesian assistant. We chatted and harangued after dinner from about 10:30 pm until 1 am. Sadly, I realized that there was no way I could dissuade Anthoni from doing it in that way.

That was the end of our involvement in Bogasari, which we had helped to plan, build and operate. We were given overvalued shares in Indocement by Anthoni Salim. We were not compensated for Bogasari's enormous, accumulated undistributed profits: in the latter years, Bogasari was making profits in excess of US$60 million a year after tax, of which they distributed about US$20 million of dividends each year.

Then, a few years later, the Salims took Bogasari out of Indocement and merged it with Indofood, their big instant-noodle manufacturer. We were left holding Indocement shares.

Anthoni Salim approached us in the late 1980s or early 1990s about jointly investing in oil-palm plantations in Indonesia. He sent the message through Piet Yap, who told us, "Anthoni wants us to partner with them in owning and developing oil-palm plantations in Southeast Kalimantan (Borneo)."

If you look at the island of Borneo, Malaysia owns the northern swathe, while the bulk of the island belongs to Indonesia. Anthoni Salim claimed that President Suharto would allow him to gain control of a huge area of land in Borneo. He got me excited about coming in as his 50-50 partner in huge oil-palm plantations. It certainly made geographic and climatic sense, and we had the management expertise.

By this time, the Kuok Group was already enjoying success in palm oil. Originally, we stumbled onto edible oils when we started crushing soybeans in order to obtain the meal to enrich animal feed. We were selling mainly soybean oil until, one day, we woke up and realized that we were living and operating in a region that is a large producer of edible oil in the form of palm oil. I think today the Kuok Group and its sister companies are the world's leading exporters of palm oil, which is principally produced in Malaysia and Indonesia.

I should thank my old Singapore friend Ho Yeow Koon of Keck Seng for steering me into oil-palm plantations. He kept singing the praises of palm oil, which is the lowest-cost agricultural oil on earth. While crops like soybeans must be replanted annually, oil palms are trees that bear oil-rich fruit for about 20 years. The irony was that Yeow Koon miscalculated with his plantations. He went into the southern Philippines, where the soil and climate are suitable, but his operations were disrupted by Maoist guerrillas. He also invested on Hainan Island, which was climatically unsuitable. We invested in oil-palm estates in Sabah, Sarawak and Indonesia.

The largest markets for palm oil are China and India. The fruit of the oil palm has a dark orange colour, which tinges the oil. In India, where they eat a lot of deep-fried foods, the oil imparts a golden hue to the dishes, which is most appealing to the eye. In China, where palm oil is the lowest-priced edible oil, we have been very successful in selling packaged, branded cooking oil like Jinlongyu (Golden Dragon Fish), just as we have marketed the Neptune and Arawana brands in Malaysia.

We almost got to the stage of shaking hands on the deal with Anthoni Salim. I think it was even in writing. By then, Anthoni was seeing President Suharto more often than his father, Sioe Liong, was. Suharto liked Anthoni so much that he even made him a Member of Parliament representing the ruling Golkar Party.

Then Anthoni tried to pull a fast one on me. He attempted to get Yap to persuade me to make the following commitment: in exchange for my being the Salims' equal partner in developing the Kalimantan oil-palm plantations, I would let the Salims come in 50-50 into all the vegetable-oil business and factories that we had established in China over the previous decade. Anthoni had further claimed that he had already made this commitment to Suharto.

Yap said, "I am sure you will agree to this."

I replied, "Nonsense!" I had never asked for a slice of action of the Salims' other successful businesses. What did these established vegetable oil businesses in China have to do with the yet-to-be developed plantations in Indonesia?

Yap said, "Ah, they're part of the marketing."

I responded, "Rubbish! Palm oil is a commodity. China is only one buyer. If Anthoni really wants the China business and factories as a part of the deal, we'll have to sit down and recalculate everything."

The quid pro quo really was our expertise, without which he

couldn't even start. He could attract other partners, but could he find equally honest, capable and efficient plantation partners? In the event, without us, their whole project collapsed.

11

IN INDONESIAN WATERS

THE COLONIAL MALAYA into which I was born in 1923 had a population of about three million. At independence in 1957, when I was busy driving the piles into the ground to establish the Kuok Group of companies, Malaysia's population was ten million. The small population of Malaysia seemed a great blessing for the young nation. But, at the same time, how much of a market can you enjoy in such a small country?

If you are a businessman in the US, you have a giant market, where no man can tap its full extent in his short lifetime. The likes of Wal-Mart, Cargill and Archer Daniels Midland have all feasted on the larger opportunities in the US than any one generation could handle.

In the case of Malaysia, if you start a flourmill, the market is saturated in the twinkling of an eye. Then you must move sideways. So we did feed mills. In another blink you have reached your low ceiling again. Okay, I'll do vegetable oils now; that's a natural extension of animal feed. To produce feed you crush corn or soybeans for the meal, and you can take the oil that flows out and refine it for human consumption. So, we again moved sideways into a new core business because we had reached the limit. I call them shallow ponds.

In Malaysia, I always felt like a little fish swimming in shallow waters. As soon as I tried to dive, I would hit the concrete bottom of this man-made pond. So you need to swim laterally all the time. You couldn't go down deep. In the fishing world, the best fish are those that can dive deep, like the tuna. If I could only dive deep – and that could easily take up 20 years of my life – I might not even have the energy to go sideways. But in Malaysia, the only choice open to me was to expand sideways, so I swam as fast as I could.

If I had been fortunate enough to be born in Indonesia, I would probably have taken a different course. There, the waters are deep; the fish are plentiful. Whatever industry I would enter in Indonesia, which has a huge population and landmass, would last my family three generations. So I envied what the businessmen of populous Indonesia were able to do. I had a seat at the flourmill table in Bogasari; but I was eager for more.

In the early 1970s, I was dining one evening at a Chinese restaurant in Singapore. I had just sat down with my guests when Piet Yap came rushing in and said, "You've got to come with me right away. Jantje Lim, a very influential Chinese businessman in Indonesia, is here in Singapore. He's probably more influential with Suharto than Liem Sioe Liong. He's very hard to meet. He's staying at the Prince's Hotel, across from the Mandarin along Orchard Road. Please come. I know he's got a dinner outside, but he's willing to say hello to you. Hurry, hurry!"

We both rushed off and jumped into a taxi. As we arrived at the hotel, Jantje Lim had just exited the front door to get into his car. We ran up the steps to the entranceway, and then Yap called, "*Pak* Yan, *Pak* Yan. This is Robert, our boss." I shook hands with Jantje Lim and he introduced me to his wife.

When President Suharto was a young commissioned officer in the tiny Central Javanese village of Kudus, he befriended several Chinese businessmen. Two were Liem Sioe Liong and Liem's equal partner, Liem Oen Kian. These two hailed from the same village in

China's Fujian Province, but it was Suharto who put them together in business in Indonesia. Then, in the late 1960s, after Suharto had come to power, the President joined them with a third Chinese businessman, Jantje Lim Poo Hien, who was born in Indonesia. The three formed the company Waringin. But the two Liems soon found they could not work with Jantje Lim, so they parted ways with him. Nevertheless, Jantje remained close to President Suharto.

Jantje Lim had befriended many other Indonesian generals, and one of them one day advised Jantje to take a purely Indonesian name. The general chose a name and thereafter Jantje Lim became known in pribumi circles as Yani Haryanto.

Yani's early business was arms dealing. Through handling weapons he became a big-game hunter in Kenya and a friend of the former President of Kenya, Daniel arap Moi. He had a collection of the most fabulous guns for big-game hunting, rifles capable of bringing down charging elephants and rhinoceroses. Even his pretty little daughter, Susan, was known to have brought down a rhinoceros. Yani employed white hunters. Every time he went hunting, he took along at least one white hunter and one black assistant, crack shots, with loaded rifles. They would provoke the rhinoceros to turn around and charge. There was Susan, standing in the open 200 metres away, firing.

Yani Haryanto came to me unexpectedly in 1974 with a proposal. I was in Hong Kong at the time. He said to me, "*Bapak* has decided to buy all the rice and sugar required for his nation from overseas through me and through nobody else. If the country is short of domestic supplies, I shall be the sole importer." Was I to believe this assertion from a businessman? I decided not to disbelieve it, but to see how things developed.

Yani had a proposition for me: As he was not a commodities trader himself, could he rely on me to provide him with rice and sugar at competitive world prices each time he asked me for an offer? What followed was exactly that. Yani would ask for an offer by phone, cable or telex, and we would make an offer. From Jakarta, he always checked on the world price at any given moment, and then he would come back and either accept our price, counter or bargain with us. If Indonesia needed a million tons of rice, Yani supplied it; if it needed three million tons, he supplied it. Yani contacted General Arifin at Bureau Logistics (Bulog) to suggest the timing of buying rice and sugar to supply the requirements of the country. He himself went to Taiwan to do deals, and when Taiwan sent emissaries to see Suharto, most of them went through Yani. Yani called his company Pipit Indah, named after his youngest son.

The rice volumes – typically 700,000 to one million tons a year – were bigger, but there isn't much margin in rice since the commodity price tends to be non-volatile. Sugar prices, by contrast, can be highly volatile. The sugar volumes were huge, 600,000 tons or more in some years. The average was about 500,000 tons, making Indonesia one of the largest white-sugar importers in the world.

Here's the way a typical sugar deal for Indonesia worked. Yani would require the first sugar delivery to be made three months from the date of signing, followed by additional deliveries at four months, five months and six months. He would study the market and say: "Well, the world futures quotations are this, but I want a $5, $10 discount to that." I had to judge the market and close the contract. I usually covered a portion first and carried the risk for the rest. If the market fell and showed me a better margin of profit because I had already closed my selling price to him, then I would buy in some more futures.

Let's say, theoretically, I made a sale of 100,000 tons. I would quickly cover 20,000-30,000 tons and probably make $3 a ton. Then, say, the market dropped by $8 after 4-6 weeks. I would cover another 25,000-30,000 tons and would probably make about $8-$10 a ton. Since I now had some paper profit under my belt, I could take a bit more risk. Of course, if world sugar prices shot up, we honoured everything and took a hit.

I could see that Yani was adding on huge margins. He was very shrewd. He said, "You and I do a deal first. We sign. But the official contract will be between you and Bulog."

I said, "But how am I to safely operate between doing the deal with you and my contract with Bulog with commodity prices fluctuating so rapidly?"

He answered, "You have my word, because behind me is the President. Arifin will always honour it." And that remained true up to the very end. Whatever I did with Yani was honoured by Arifin.

I would sell to Yani, say, 300,000 tons at US$250 a ton. Then, Yani would ask me to create a fresh contract with Bulog at US$280 a ton. Bulog opened the letter of credit to me, so my contract with Bulog showed me as exploiting Indonesia.

If Kuoks made US$5-6 a ton margin from this Indonesian sugar trade, we were very satisfied. I would say we averaged between US$5-7. Yani began in the mid-1970s with relatively modest margins of US$10-15 a ton. By the end of the early 1980s, he was asking for a US$120 mark-up.

I don't know whether Yani shared his rice and sugar profits with members of the Suharto regime. My guess is that leading Indonesian Chinese businessmen typically coughed up a percentage of their profits. The regime set up units such as armed forces' development or widows' funds.

I met Suharto for the first time in 1974 through Yani's introduction. Liem Sioe Liong never made any attempt to introduce me to the President, but Yani, who lived diagonally opposite Suharto's private residence, made an appointment for me. We walked across the street together – a distance of about 100 metres from Yani's front door – late one evening to meet the President. I remember the young adjutant at the time was a Lieutenant-Colonel called Tri Sutrisno who greeted us and was very polite to Yani. He knew that Yani was one of his boss's favoured friends. After that, I visited with Suharto privately five or six times at his residence.

I also remember meeting President Suharto just a few weeks after he had had gall bladder surgery in December 1975. He was convalescing in his Chiomas home, which was up in the hills near Bogor. I recall driving with Yani up rock-strewn hills to find 100 or more acres of land carved out and owned by Suharto, who reared goldfish and a few cattle there. He invited us for lunch.

In all those early meetings, I grew more and more to like the President. Each time, I came away very impressed and inspired to see that the Indonesian people had found such a dynamic leader. During our conversations, we sometimes had detailed discussions on sugar and rice statistics around the world; which countries had surpluses and which had deficits. Then, if our discussion suddenly veered to shipping, he could talk chapter and verse about shipping. If we moved on to forestry, timber and lumber, he had figures at his fingertips for how many cubic meters his forests in Borneo were producing. The man had stored away a great deal of knowledge; he had a mastery of detail. I found him to be a very fine, warm man who was highly dedicated to serving his country.

The Indonesian sugar business was so enormous that I brought in ED&F Man on joint accounts. Man then called on Woodhouse, Drake because a lot of the trade was white sugar, so then we had Man, Drake and Kuoks.

But our relations frayed when we faced the sordid nature of the business. Man and Drake were sleeping partners when it came to negotiating the sales. From time to time, when I told them of the latest twists and turns of Yani, who was always eroding our positions, my partners in England would show extreme displeasure.

So I decided. I served notice on them: we break. I said, "You know, money-making is one thing, but what I have seen is very distasteful to me. Why are we suddenly sitting in judgment on the morality of the whole thing when we have been a part of these deals? After this, I am on my own."

I had introduced Yani to Man some time before. Yani had said that he'd like to see the sugar markets of London, so I took him to meet Man and Drake. Charles Kralj of Man often went with Yani to the London casinos. Then he taught Yani to play the London sugar-futures market. He made some money for Yani – I wasn't aware of this at the time.

Later, Yani and Charles took the business away from me. But that's business. I knew when I split with Man, that that's how Man would retaliate. It didn't bother me. Everything is fair, I suppose, in business, love and war.

When I sensed that Yani was trying to break away from us to go to Man, I asked Yap to help me do more PR with Yani. Yap was then living in Jakarta, where he worked full-time at Bogasari, the flourmill. He no longer made regular visits to us; he only came calling when it suited him. Yap would say, "Oh, I hate Yani! I don't want to see his face!"

I protested, "Yap, in business we never talk like that. You introduced me to Yani years ago, and now you adopt this attitude. He is around my neck and all you can say is, you don't want to see him." Still, I didn't push Yap, because I knew that I would only be knocking my head against a stone wall.

In about 1980, before Yani broke with me, he came to me and said, "The contract we signed last month: I want you to cut it by $15 a ton."

I said, "Yani, I am making well under $10. How do you expect me to cut by $15?" Yani had already worked on my sugar trader, James Lim, first. James pleaded with me to cut or at least to give in to part of the request. I said no, and James kept warning me there's danger from Yani.

I remember explaining to Arifin, "Yani signed the contract with me, then he wanted a reduction. I have to stand firm. James Lim wants me to give way, but I know that, with Yani, if I give way once I no longer have a real contract with the man, forever. Today, he says cut $15. In future, he'll ask me to cut God knows how much. It's the principle." I could see that the relationship was coming to an end.

When I went to see Yani shortly afterwards, he warned me: "If you don't cut, you won't get the next business." Sure enough, he soon went over to Man.

At Bulog he said, "Arifin, I want this contract to be between you and Man."

Arifin asked, "What about Robert Kuok?"

Yani replied, "No, nothing for him."

Then Arifin called me and said, "I've got *Pak* Yani in front of me, and he is telling me to cancel the contract. What have you to say?"

I replied, "I don't know. It's up to Yani, isn't it?"

Then apparently he turned around to Yani and said, "I can't allow this. The most I can allow is for you to give half to Man. You must give the other half to Kuoks. They have served us well. How can you behave like this to them?"

A few months later, I had another phone call from General Arifin. He said, "Yani is trying to get a huge deal, 1,200,000 tons, and he wants to give it all to Man. I am putting my foot down, because we at Bulog are grateful to you for all the years that you have done business with us. You have honoured every contract. You have even helped us to plan our requirements."

He protested to Yani and told him the business must be shared between Man and Kuoks. Yani said, well, in that case I want to give Man more because I don't want to deal with Kuoks any more.

I think Yani signed a contract with Man for 700,000 tons and with Kuoks for 500,000 tons, delivery commencing about eight months forward. This was 1983, I think. Five or six months later, he still couldn't open the letters of credit. Without comparing notes, Man and we both chased him for the letters of credit, without which you dare not ship the sugar. Then we heard unsettling sounds from Yani's camp, implying that President Suharto had decided not to approve the deal, a ploy that Indonesia had never used before. The sugar market was falling, so it was financially unfavourable for them to honour the contract. Until then, for five or six years, Yani had been giving those same instructions and honouring every contract.

ED&F Man took Yani to arbitration in London, while we stayed our hand. Our finance and trading boys worked out the total amount of our active claim with him. It came to US$105 million, compared to Man's US$160 million claim. Man took Yani to court in England and won; Yani appealed and lost on the appeal.

In this weakened position, Yani came to see me in Singapore. We sat in the lobby lounge of Shangri-La Singapore and came to an agreement. He asked what minimum settlement I would claim from him. I said, "If you pay me US$35 million, I'll forgive the rest. In the past I have made profit from you." I think we settled for about US$33 million and he actually paid us that amount.

After Yani settled with me, he received advice from a lawyer that he could counter-sue ED&F Man in Indonesian courts. So he counter-sued Man, and to make it look real, he counter-sued me.

Round after round, the Indonesian judges decided in favour of Yani against Man. We were summoned, so I went storming down to Yani's house in Jakarta and said, "What's all this about? You asked to settle with me, and we settled in the lobby of the Singapore Shangri-La Hotel. You said that's all you were willing to pay me, and I accepted everything. There are legal papers to prove all this. You may have the judges on your side, but why are you doing this? Ever since you came to Hong Kong to ask me to help you buy sugar and rice on the world markets for you, I have served you properly and correctly. What have I done wrong?"

He muttered, "Never mind, never mind, I'll deal with it," or something like that.

Maybe my haranguing worked, because somehow the matter just died a natural death. But for Man it just went on and on and on. I kept telling Michael Stone: "Settle with Yani, Michael." I think, early on, Yani might have offered Man US$30 million or US$40 million to settle, but Michael refused. Eventually, Man was forced to settle with Yani.

Although I regarded Yani as avaricious, I also saw a different side to the man as Mother showed me. I took Yani to see her a few times. She said, "He is showing typical human frailty. All human beings are afflicted by greed, but our friend Yani seems to have a large dose of it in him." Yet she was always very positive with him.

He told her about his family problems, which were quite terrible. Mother would say, "Well, I think part of your wealth is a case of ill-gotten gains, so you have been punished by the heavens. One way to atone for it is to give part of your wealth to charity. Then God will see it in his heart to forgive you and you will have more peace in your mind."

He always listened to her with great humility and attention, but both Mother and I knew he would not put her words into practice. And so he continued to be afflicted by family problems and mental torment.

With its rich, coffee-coloured volcanic soil, Java has always been the centre of Indonesia's sugarcane industry. In the early 20th century, Java, carpeted with plantations owned by the Dutch and Oei Tiong Ham, was the world's second largest exporter of sugar after Cuba. Java's sugar industry declined during the Pacific War, and declined further during the chaos of Sukarno's rule. But, even in the early 1970s under Suharto, the densely populated island still produced somewhere between 15 million and 20 million tons of sugarcane annually, or some two million tons of sugar per year.

When President Suharto decided that Indonesia should also open up sugarcane plantations in Sumatra, he inquired whether I could start one there. The approach came through Yani – Suharto was aware that Yani was more a dealmaker than an industrialist or businessman. Suharto had shown Yani a map and marked out an isolated area measuring about 25,000 hectares in Lampung Province of southern Sumatra. The closest airport was in Branti, 38 miles away.

Suharto wanted Yani and me to invest and develop the plantations and sugar mills. He indicated that he wanted his eldest daughter Tutu's husband, Indra Rukmana, and his own eldest son, Sigit, to become our partners. Within a few days I was in Jakarta. This was 1974, shortly after Yani and I had started doing business together. We flew across to Branti, and climbed into a helicopter to survey this massive site from the air. I saw one or two herds of elephants and a scraggly jungle with a river or two filled with good freshwater lobsters and fish – so I was told. We landed in a clearing and looked around and soon re-boarded the helicopter. I told Yani, "Good enough," and I dispatched a technical team from Malaysia.

We already ran a much smaller, modestly successful sugarcane plantation and sugar mill in Perlis, Malaysia. The soil in Sumatra is better than in Perlis, though inferior to Java's. But soil is not everything. The more you look at life, the more you see that it is man who makes everything. Java had the superior soil but I knew that Javanese producers would always lobby the government for tariff walls against imported sugar in order to protect their industry. Indonesia is a huge, populous country with a staggering demand for sugar, but it had a shortage of foreign exchange.

Most of the Java plantations were government-owned, so I knew that we would be many lengths ahead of them in efficiency and in plugging leakage. There is always pilferage in a poor country such as Indonesia. When you go to a toilet in an impoverished land there is never any toilet paper. If you put a roll in, the next guy will come and take the whole roll because toilet paper is valuable to him. That is poverty. In the same vein, at a Java mill, the manager may commute in a nice car, but the basic worker pilfers from the mill. A Mitsui corn and rice estate very close to our Sumatran sugar plantation failed for precisely this reason.

I reasoned to myself that the umbrella of tariff protection would always be held high for the Java plantations and mills, and that I would be able to walk right under the umbrella and stay dry and shaded. And that's exactly what happened. We ended up producing about 200,000 tons of refined sugar a year at Gunung Madu (the name was given by Suharto), and earning at least US$10 million profit annually.

However, I faced great scepticism in 1974. I contacted Tate & Lyle and ED&F Man in London about joining in the project. Michael Attfield and Gordon Shemilt of Tate & Lyle and Michael Stone of Man came out to Jakarta in late 1974 or early 1975. Our chief host was General Arifin, who was already head of Bulog. They returned to England and signified agreement to become partners. Thus, the foreign side, holding 45 percent, would consist of Kuoks, Man and Tate & Lyle. The Indonesia side, 55 percent, would be split into half for Yani Haryanto and half for the Suharto clan.

Weeks passed, and we had no confirmation from Tate & Lyle. Man grew embarrassed. Man is a trading house while Tate & Lyle had a sugar-plantation arm, an engineering arm and a technical services unit. As the weeks turned into months, I was getting very hot under the collar. Man was growing more and more agitated at Tate & Lyle's silence, and Man would not come in unless Tate's participated as the technical partner. Meanwhile, Indonesia was chasing me to get on with the project.

After three months, I flew to London. Alan Clatworthy and Michael Stone of Man said, "You know, Robert, we can't get any positive sounds out of Tate's. Why don't you go across and shake them up." So they called over and said to expect Robert in half an hour. I went and had a bit of a row with them.

Gordon Shemilt said, "Robert, you know, but I can't persuade my board. What say you you try and persuade my board?"

I felt that it was an absurd suggestion for me to have to persuade other companies' boards. There was no real guarantee of success – the project itself may encounter many difficulties and problems – and the board of Tate's was evidently unenthusiastic about participating. I therefore decided to do it on my own.

We began work on the plantation. I had a Penang friend, Ong Chin Teik, who ran a transport business ferrying raw sugar from ocean-going vessels to our refinery up the River Prai. He was a capable Chinese entrepreneur. He had no college degree but he was a man of action. I asked him to head my show in Lampung. I also sent Oh Siew Nam, an electrical engineer who today is Chairman of PPB Group, and Ang Keng Lam, who later became Chairman of Kerry Properties Limited. They went down, formed a team and did a lot of backbreaking work.

During this initial period, Tate & Lyle also sent a managing director of technical services, a bespectacled Oxbridge graduate, to advise on the project. I had told ED&F Man and Tate & Lyle that we could buy machinery much more cheaply in Thailand than in Britain. So, on his way to Indonesia, this technical services fellow stopped in Bangkok for three days with his wife, ostensibly to look at Thai sugar machinery. Later, Chanida Asdathorn, a Thai friend (the daughter-in-law of the late Suree Asdathorn) who is a senior executive of one of Thailand's largest sugar exporters, told me that this managing director went sightseeing two out of the three days. Tate & Lyle also sent out a team that included a world-acclaimed agronomist. My people met them at Branti Airport and took them to a little town with an awful little half-star hotel where they had been staying for weeks. The Tate & Lyle people looked around aghast.

The conditions in Lampung were indeed primitive, but why should that scare me? After all, due to poverty my father left China as a boy with a singlet on his back, and probably bare-footed or, at best, wooden clogs on his feet. If he wasn't scared to venture abroad to Southeast Asia in the early 1900s, why should I be scared in modern day 1974? I was born in Malaysia and the language was, and still is, very similar to Indonesia's. The culture in Sumatra was not unlike what we were used to. There's really nothing to be scared of in life.

So the Kuoks took 45 percent of Gunung Madu and the Indonesian side held 55 percent, equally divided by Yani and Suharto's son and son-in-law. The original investment was of the order of US$45 million. We have run the whole plantation operation from day one – the first crop year was 1977 – until today.

Gunung Madu was a major project. We had to build the entire infrastructure for the 25,000-hectare plantation, including more than 5,600 kilometres of plantation roads. Muddy roads are of no use, so we spread chips of granite on the road surface to prevent the equatorial rains from washing the roads away. Trucks are needed to haul out the cane, 15-20 tons per truckload. We feed 14,000 tons of cane a day to the crushing mill.

The cane is harvested from the end of April or early May until about October and November, or about 180 days. There are three principal categories of workers. There are 150-200 resident supervisory managers and workers, from the general manager down to supervisors of trucks and the engineering workshop.

There are infestation and pestilence problems, so scientists, chemists and plant doctors must be present. A few thousand resident full-time workers live on site throughout the year. We also employ about 10,000 seasonal workers who are paid a piece rate to cut cane with machetes for six months of the year. Fortunately, the cane-harvesting season is the off-season for padi, so, after they are done chopping cane, the seasonal workers go back to their villages to grow rice.

How do you get 10,000 people to come onto your land to hack cane every day for 180 days? You must build decent housing for them. We call the long dormitories 'labourers' lines', because they are built in one long line after another. The buildings are raised about 1.5 metres from the ground, so that wild animals such as boars cannot enter. We also put up primary schools and health clinics for the workers' families.

Gunung Madu is probably the only large sugar plantation in the world at about three or four degrees south of the equator. (The ideal climatic range for sugar cane is 14 to 24 degrees north or south of the equator.) With the good soil and lots of rain and sunshine, and very dedicated work by the management and workers, Gunung Madu, after four or five years of teething problems, has been by any measure a great success, making solid profits every year.

It took about 18 months to build the Thai-equipped factory and, as we prepared to harvest our cane crop, we held a grand-opening ceremony. President Suharto agreed to do the honours.

By this time, Yani Haryanto was enjoying life. All the country's sugar and rice businesses passed through his hands, so he was reaping huge profits. His brother-in-law, Tedjo Hartono, did all the work for him. Yani would traipse off to Kenya and go on safari hunts, or holiday in Europe. When he went on vacation, he would disappear from Southeast Asia for about four months.

Yani returned from holiday for the grand opening. Arriving in Jakarta a few days before the ceremony, he then flew to Lampung, where I joined him. On arriving at the plant, he tore into everybody, especially the managing director, my man called Khor Chin Poey. He abused Chin Poey about everything – why this, why that – and cursed everybody. I was furious. Here was this absentee landlord – he was doing nothing – and yet he didn't even have the courtesy and gratitude to thank people for all the hard work they had put in. I let him say his piece and walked away.

Later I said, "Yani, I want to have a private chat with you." The two of us entered a room and then I rounded on him and told him off in no uncertain terms. I scolded him: "It's abominable behaviour. You are behaving like an ungrateful wretch. How can you treat your fellow human beings that way?" The few times I have shown him my temper, he has always been submissive because he knew he was in the wrong.

At the opening, I gave my speech in Bahasa Indonesia, a short one-and-one-half pages that I had rehearsed and rehearsed. When President Suharto got up to make his speech, some careless fellow tripped the wire. Suddenly, nobody could hear Suharto's voice. It was terribly awkward. Since this was a plantation platform, it took a good five minutes for the microphone to be repaired, which was very embarrassing for us. I will never forget that incident.

An event that occurred at Gunung Madu shortly after we began operations sheds light on how we run our organization. We employ ethnic Javanese, Bataks and Sumatrans on the plantation. We had a few crooked Batak workers who falsely clocked in every day for 100-200 absentee seasonal workers who earned a basic daily wage based on clocking in. When the Malaysian Chinese man in charge protested this malfeasance, he was dragged out from behind the counter and beaten up. Before we could report the case to the police, the workers rushed to the local military commander, headquartered in Palembang, 70 miles from Gunung Madu, and alleged that the Gunung Madu workers had been bullied by Chinese from Malaysia.

The military commander climbed in his jeep and brought a truckload of soldiers, fully armed, to confront our Malaysian-Chinese general manager. The commander jumped out of his jeep. He screamed at our people, "You Chinese do this; you Chinese do that."

Our manager kept his cool, and said, "Please come to the operations room. Let me explain the way we run this plantation."

The commander gradually cooled down, listened, and commented, "This is quite an operation. You cannot just wave a wand and produce white sugar." Then, still a bit angry, he said, "Now, what about that incident?"

Our manager replied, "We'll tell you exactly what happened, sir. Let me call my Malay managers to explain."

We have about a dozen top Malay managers, graduates of Bandung Technical College and the like. Addressing the general in the Malay tongue, they explained exactly what had taken place.

The more he heard, the more furious the commander became at the complainant. So he said, "Get me that guy!" He personally boxed the man and said, "Don't you ever dare come and tell funny stories to me again!" That is how we broke that cycle of mischief.

12
REST HOUSES FOR
THE WEARY TRAVELLER

IN 1968, a new ball came into my hands: I was offered a ten percent shareholding in the land where Shangri-La Singapore sits today. This seed eventually sprouted into Shangri-La Hotels & Resorts. As of September 2017, there were 100 Shangri-La hotels in operation, which are widely regarded as one of the finest chains of luxury hotels in the world.

I didn't plan to develop a hotel chain at the outset, but I was eager to diversify from commodity trading. Why? Commodity trading is inherently risky. The only way you can trade commodities and make a fortune is to take substantial risks. You either go long and hope the market will rise, or you go short and hope the market will collapse. There is no joy in getting too big in commodities trading. If you reach too high, you are in danger of going bust. I am reminded of the case of Julio Lobo, a legendary Cuban-born King of Sugar. Once renowned for his judgment, he got it badly wrong in the volatile year of 1963 – and it left him penniless. If I tried to grow bigger and bigger in commodities, I would always run the risk of suddenly losing US$50 or 100 million at a go.

Hotels were one way to diversify, though the seed I planted in Singapore germinated in a fairly convoluted way. It all started when my old friend Ang Toon Chew, the man who had showed me the rice trade in Bangkok in the early 1950s, was approached by a land broker in Singapore in 1967 to purchase the land on which the Shangri-La Singapore sits today. Borneo Company (Inchcape Group) wanted to sell 5.5 hectares on one side of Orange Grove Road, which branches off from Orchard Road, and another 0.8 hectares across the street. Borneo Company bungalows sat on both sites.

Toon Chew very astutely bargained and knocked the price down to S$5 a square foot for the 5.5 hectares and a lower price for what he called the inferior piece across the road. I heard about the land deal through the grapevine.

I eventually built three Shangri-La buildings on the larger site – the original tower block, the Garden Wing and the Valley Wing – and Shangri-La serviced apartments on the smaller lot. But I was not involved in the original acquisition of land.

Toon Chew bought the sites through Petaling Garden, a Malaysian real estate company of which he was founder, chairman and largest shareholder. My old commodity-trading friends Ho Yeow Koon of Singapore and Tan Kim Yeow of Penang were also large partners in Petaling Garden. They planned to build terrace houses on these prime Orange Grove Road sites, until a Cambridge-trained architect named Heah Hock Heng (my second son Ean later married Hock Heng's niece) and my close friend Jacob Ballas both got involved.

Hock Heng had been to see the three Petaling Garden partners and told them, "Don't build terrace houses there. That's a foolish thing to do. It's a waste of prime land. Build a hotel instead." Hock Heng, who was a friend of mine through his older brothers, harnessed Ballas, a leading stockbroker of Singapore. They both urged Toon Chew, Kim Yeow and Yeow Koon to build a hotel, not two-story terrace houses, on such beautiful land virtually in the middle of the city of Singapore.

When the Petaling Garden partners replied, "We don't know

how to build a hotel," Hock Heng and Jacob Ballas suggested that they approach me about joining with them. For one thing, they noted, I got along well with senior Singapore Government officials, so I could help in applying for permission to convert the land from residential to hotel use.

I spurned the idea at first. I showed a bit of temper and said, "I don't want to be mixed up with that crowd in any kind of property development. I have had enough of them."

There was a history to my animosity towards the Petaling Garden partners. I was an original shareholder in Petaling, but had sold my stake in the early 1960s after I had a tiff with Ang Toon Chew. We planned to build a housing development near Kuala Lumpur. I wrote a letter, in English, to a Malay friend who was district officer and could help us to gain government approval for the project. Toon Chew, who didn't know one word of English, wanted to correct my letter. I got very upset with him. "You are picking on nonsense," I said. I went back to my office, called up Kim Yeow and sold all my shares in Petaling Garden to him.

Soon Ballas, who was my stockbroker, started working on me to join in the Orange Grove Road development. "Come on, Robert. Don't always be so quarrelsome and uppity with people. You're just hot-tempered. Cool down. I have talked them around. They are willing to let you come in."

Jacob Ballas was a fantastic friend who taught me a great deal about the Jewish faith and practices. He was born of a poor Sephardic Jewish family in Baghdad, but, through hard work and shrewdness, made money in Singapore and became the leading member of the Jewish community there. He founded the stock-broking firm J Ballas & Co, and was later appointed Chairman of the Singapore Stock Exchange.

Jacob's father, Shua Ballas, emigrated with his family from

Baghdad to Singapore, where he dabbled in various kinds of businesses before going bankrupt during the Great Depression. Jacob's father died when Jacob was quite young, leaving only him and his mother. A very devout Jew, Jacob's life was wound around his mother. I knew I could never call him after 5 pm on Fridays because he rushed home to shave and prepare to observe a proper Jewish Sabbath, which begins at sundown Friday evening. The Ballas family kept a kosher household, and even trained their Cantonese servant to cook kosher meals. So, Jacob grew up with a strong religious discipline.

Jacob only finished O-levels in school, then he started work as a car salesman. His big break in life was with Sun Life Insurance. Jacob had the gift of the gab. He could talk the hind legs off a donkey, and he sold many, many insurance policies. In colonial times, most Chinese tended to be shy and not talk too much in case they fell afoul of the authorities. You were supposed to be obedient, nice and get patted on the head by the colonial governors or the civil servants. It was the same story in Malaysia, Sri Lanka, Hong Kong and the other British colonies. It took a Sephardic Jew, throwing caution to the wind, to talk and talk and talk. He was a roaring success in insurance, and, within two or three years, was the leading agent in terms of sales.

My first encounter with Jacob was an inauspicious one. In his school days, he befriended a bright Eurasian called Hugh Lewis, who went on to Raffles College. After graduating from Raffles post-war, Hugh was appointed a food controller in the Malayan Colonial Government, which was how we became reacquainted. One day in the late 1950s, Hugh called up and said, "I have an old classmate and friend, Jacob Ballas, who is a leading insurance broker in Singapore. He would like to come and see you."

I responded, "Hugh, if it is to sell me an insurance policy, please don't introduce me." Hugh pleaded with me – I think he was under a lot of pressure from Jacob.

Jacob came to my office with Hugh, who left shortly afterwards. Jacob talked a lot and I listened to him, then I counter-argued. I said, "Jacob, you're trying to sell me, what, a £10,000 policy? Now, if you are trying to sell me a £100,000 insurance policy on my life and it's a ten-year policy, I have to contribute around £10,000 every year. It's a big chunk of my income. If I take a policy of £10,000 and I contribute £1,000, which I can easily afford, if I drop dead within the first ten years of my policy, my beneficiaries will receive £10,000. That's not enough to send any one of them to college. In other words, I am chasing my own tail all the time."

Later, we met at the odd party, and, when I began to sniff around the stock market and sometimes trade in shares, Jacob would say, "Oh, do this, do that." He was a shrewd investor and a kind and generous man. We became great friends.

Jacob's favourite hobby was the horse races at the Singapore Turf Club. I wasn't interested in the races, but I saw very early on why Jacob became successful. He was extremely streetwise; not an intellectual.

So how then did Jacob prosper in a Chinese city? It's very simple: Chinese sometimes regard fellow-Chinese as their own worst enemies. When Chinese become super-rich in Singapore, in public they might seem very warm to each other, almost hugging and kissing at the Turf Club or in restaurants. But in their hearts they all had daggers semi-drawn. If Mr ABC had suffered a minor insult at the hands of Mr XYZ, to whom did he go to pour his heart out? On whose shoulder could he cry? Eventually, they all went and cried on Jacob Ballas' shoulder.

That is the human world. It is the world of the butterfly. How do plants pollinate? The butterfly's sticky feet picks up some pollen;

the insect flutters to other plants and the seeds form. Because he was a streetwise man, his pleasure in life was meeting his fellow beings. You never found Jacob spending hours reading, thinking or writing.

So everyone came to him. They talked about virtually everything, from the biggest scandal to the most unimportant little event. And Ballas knew how to coo and to sigh at the right times. He saw cross-sections of strengths and weaknesses in Chinese businessmen and through these insights he even knew how to invest in their companies, when to buy and when to sell.

I have long felt that there are many traits shared by the Jews and the Chinese. For example, when they meet a stranger for the first time, they size him up very fast. How much can they confide in this stranger, where are his sharp edges, should they steer clear of him?

So it was this dear friend, Jacob Ballas, who patched up my relationship with the Petaling Garden crowd.

My indirect talks with the Petaling partners went on for weeks before they officially approached me and asked if I would join them. They needed my help to get the site approved for hotel development. I replied, "Okay, but I am an outsider today. What do you want me to do?"

They said they would cut me in for ten percent, prorated according to their shareholding in Petaling Garden. But, they quickly added, "We've been sitting on the land for a year, so you have to compensate us for it as well as the appreciation in land value."

I thought to myself, "When I invited Ang Toon Chew and Tan Kim Yeow to be my sugar-refinery partners in Prai in 1959, I brought them in on the ground floor. The refinery was already a roaring success by 1966, making them pots of money. I also offered them ground-level entry into my flour-milling business. But now they offer me this piece of land, and it's not at their cost-price. They want paper profits on appreciation of the land. They are bringing me in on the third floor."

The irony was, though I owned only ten percent, it was my personal effort that made the whole project hum. I had stayed in some of the finest hotels in Europe and America in the 1950s and 1960s and made many quiet observations. I take in everything around me deeply. In fact, in my subconscious, I had admired the hotel industry – I don't think I ever voiced my feelings to anyone – and knew that if one day I became a hotel owner or developer I would build some very fine properties.

In the 1960s and the first half of the 1970s, I spent an average of 70-100 days a year in excellent European hotels. I stayed in small hotels in Bury Street, London, such as Quaglino's. Then, Grosvenor House Hotel along Park Lane became my favourite London hotel for many years. I only switched to the Dorchester Hotel down the road because Dorchester installed IDD dialling much earlier. In Grosvenor House, when you picked up the phone, you had to ask the operator to get you an overseas line. For a businessman, that's not only tedious – it was also losing me precious business time. So, I became a frequent guest of the Dorchester and, even during peak season, I could always get a room. I also stayed at Inn on the Park.

Going across to Paris, I stayed at The Crillon and at George V, but my Paris favourite became Le Bristol. In Rome I stayed in Excelsior, and in Munich in two fine hotels. In Geneva my favourite was Hotel D'Angleterre. In 1965, I went on an extensive European trip with Joy, my late first wife. One of our first stops was Vienna, and we stayed in the Imperial Hotel. I was so impressed! From the outside, the building wasn't very much, but as soon as you stepped into the hotel you knew you were in an extremely well run place. The Imperial was a smallish, 200-room property, but each room was beautifully appointed. That hotel grabbed my imagination and made a deep impression on me.

So, I felt that if anyone ever asked me to build a hotel, I would know what I wanted. My mind took mental photographs of everything I saw and experienced – various physical comforts and discomforts and, of course, service qualities.

Probably the best service I ever had was in Grosvenor House and the Dorchester in London. At the Dorchester, it was my good luck to get to know the front-desk reception staff, the butler in my room, the room-service waiters, the Dorchester Grill waiters, and the doormen. I recall that many of the doormen were retired soldiers or policemen, big chaps who stood about 1.9 m tall. The driveway of the Dorchester was very tight. Rolls-Royces drove up, taxis snaked in between limousines, and yet that one doorman could manage everything efficiently. I thought their performance was nothing short of brilliant.

And I could say the same of all the others I met in the Dorchester Hotel. If I must single out two outstanding staff, one would be my butler, Leslie; the other a waiter whose name I have regretfully forgotten. Leslie was a slim, very smart-looking young Englishman. As soon as I arrived, I'd press the button to call for him. Leslie would come in, say, "Good morning, Mr Kuok," open my suitcase and unpack everything for me. Then I'd press a second button for the waiter. When he arrived, I'd say, "The usual," and he'd bring me a pot of hot tea and scrambled eggs on toast.

Meanwhile, Leslie would be collecting my two pairs of shoes for polishing, my shirts and two suits for pressing. I often wondered how he managed all this with just two arms. He opened the door and let himself out. Within 40 minutes, he was back with the two pairs of shoes polished, at least one shirt and both suits pressed. That was real service! I gave him a £1 tip. I am talking about the 1960s, so a pound was fairly large. But I've found that service is not a matter of just tipping. It's a matter of treating the man as a friend: "How are you, Leslie? How have things been in my absence?" And said with true feeling. In other words, I really cared for him, and he felt it, so he responded in like manner. That, I believe, is the way to treat people. It's not just about throwing money around. In none of my travels have I experienced service equivalent to the smartness of the Dorchester in those days.

Nevertheless, learning to become a hotel owner in Singapore was an excruciating experience for me. We groped. Heah Hock Heng, our architect, didn't have real hotel design expertise, but he'd met a Japanese hotel architect named Yozo Shibata, who was involved in the Mandarin Hotel in Singapore. The Mandarin was on Orchard Road about 3 kilometres from our site. By the time we met Shibata, whom we eventually hired as a consultant architect, the Mandarin's foundation and piling were finished and the building was constructed up to level four or so. In other words, George Lien and his team had a head start over us by at least two years.

I remember that at one of our early hotel board meetings, I predicted that we would overtake them, and indicated that that must be our target. I had met Lien and knew he'd be very indecisive and would keep on chopping and changing plans. He didn't like this and he didn't like that; he scrapped this and he scrapped that. We opened the Shangri-La in February/March 1971. George Lien's Mandarin opened a few months later.

Speaking of board meetings, my partners were a joke at the beginning. At the first proper board meeting, I said to them, "We can talk in Chinese, but the records must be kept in English. Don't you agree?" They all said yes. I owned only ten percent, yet I took the chair without formal appointment. Nobody wanted to propose me, but neither did they want to propose anyone else. The meeting had to start, so I called it to order and sat in the chair that became the Chairman's chair. When the minutes came out, I was the

Chairman.

I pointed out that they had not even properly arranged the affairs of the hotel company. I found a shell company and said, "Look here, this company is insolvent, but it's owned by ten firms. So it's insolvent but it's not bankrupt. It's got a tax credit. Let's buy the shell from the other partners." The shell company was called Guan Thong & Company Limited. "Having bought it, we'll inject this Shangri-La land into it. We'll go to the registrar of companies to change the name, and then we'll also recapitalize the company to make it solvent." We did as I proposed.

Now, what's the origin of the wonderful name Shangri-La? The hotel was not named when I joined Ang's group. Credit for the name must go to an old French friend of mine, Georges Toby, a Moroccan-born Jew who worked for many years in Tokyo for Sucre et Denree, the large Paris-based sugar trader. Georges' boss sent him from Tokyo to see me in Singapore sometime in 1968. I didn't have much sugar business with Georges. I took him to the Raffles Hotel grill for lunch; then we ran out of conversation. He was unwilling to leave me, so I said, "Mr Toby, I've got an appointment to go and see a piece of land on which I am building a hotel with my partners."

He said, "Hotel? May I come along?"

We jumped into my car. From Raffles Hotel to the site is about 5.5 kilometers. Georges said, "What are you calling the hotel, by the way?"

"Well, as you can see, this is called Orange Grove Road. I'll call it Orange Grove Hotel," I replied.

Georges shouted in my car, "That's a stupid name!"

I said, "Okay, have you any better ideas?"

Georges hesitated for about two or three seconds and said, "Got it: Le Shangri-La!" I immediately thought: what a wonderful name!

Georges finished his work and left Singapore. I brought the

name "Shangri-La" to my partners. They all shouted me down. Toon Chew cried out, "One of the massage parlours I go to in Bangkok is called Shangri-La." A thought immediately went through my mind: "If my wife's name is Ann and I meet a hooker called Ann, then does that make my wife a hooker?" How irrelevant and illogical! What are these guys talking about? So I said, "Okay, rubbish. No sweat off my brow. If you don't want the name, forget it!" Thank goodness we kept it.

I took to commodities trading like a young duckling takes to water. But hotels – I didn't have a clue! I didn't understand good hotel architecture, interior design, management, or even room size. What I did know from my experience in the business world was that if you meet with the wrong types and you're led up the garden path, you could lose years of time and end up with lawsuits on your hands. Then you would be tied up in knots.

I began to appoint assistants, one of whom was my brother-in-law, Leslie Cheah. I often lost my temper with him. Leslie wasn't streetwise and took wrong turns. I repeatedly had to haul the whole train back to the starting point and turn it left instead of turning right.

The Japanese architect, Shibata, began to play a growing role in designing the hotel. I provided some input, more from the business-economics point of view, leaving the technical design and construction of the hotel to him and an English engineer named Jack Simpson, who had retired from the Malaysian Government and came to work for Kuok (Singapore) Ltd.

In 1968, after Shibata had produced some drawings and plans, he invited a couple of my colleagues and me to meet him in Tokyo. Halfway through the meeting, Shibata could see that we were really greenhorns, totally lost. He asked, "Who is managing the hotel?"

We said, "We're going to try and manage it ourselves."

Shibata said, "That's difficult, Kuok-san. Hilton and Sheraton already have operations in Singapore, but there is a new group called Western International Hotels (later renamed Westin) of Seattle. I recommend you try to get in touch with them."

I had never even heard of the company and asked if I needed to fly to Seattle.

Shibata said, "Wait. According to my information, they will be in Bangkok. They are talking with Dusit Thani Hotel (Shibata was a designer for Dusit Thani, too). I believe the Chairman and Chief Executive, Eddie Carlson, will be there." Carlson would arrive that very evening in Bangkok and stay for two days.

I immediately booked a seat on a flight arriving in Bangkok that evening. I checked into the Erawan Hotel, which was within walking distance of the old Peninsula Hotel (no relation to the Hong Kong firm), where Carlson was staying. The following morning, I waited until 9:15 am to call, in case Carlson was exhausted from the long flight from the US, but not so late that he may already have left for his appointments. An American, Carlson's assistant, answered my call.

"May I speak to Mr Carlson, please."

"Mr Carlson? Yes, this is Mr Carlson's room, but who are you?"

"Robert Kuok from Singapore."

"What business do you have with him?"

"He is not expecting me, but I'd like to have a word with him."

"Oh, you know he is a very busy man and every minute of his time is already arranged. I don't think he can see you."

"Well, could you please ask him for me?"

"All right, hold on."

There was murmuring in the background. The assistant returned to the phone and said, "I am sorry. I have checked with Mr Carlson, and he really is too busy. He won't be able to see you."

I said, "Well, you might let him know that I am going to build what I think will be the best hotel in Singapore. I know that he would like to manage a hotel in Singapore. So if he's not prepared to talk with me, he's going to pass up a very good opportunity."

The man inquired on which road would the hotel be situated. I described it to him. He asked me to hold on for another moment, and went and spoke to Carlson. After a minute another voice came on the line: "Eddie Carlson speaking. Is that you, Mr Kuok?"

I said, "Yes," and we chatted.

He liked what I described and said, "I can spare about fifteen minutes. Where did you say you are staying?"

I had told him that I was in the Erawan, just around the corner. "Okay, I'll come with so-and-so, who's traveling with me, my VP. Expect us in about five minutes' time."

He ended up staying for almost an hour. We chatted and within five minutes hit it off. We were on the same wavelength, talking the same language with the same enthusiasm. We got warmer and warmer. But that was Eddie Carlson, a lovely man with high principles who wanted a good deal. And he was talking to someone who also wanted a good deal. There were no side issues, no lining of pockets; everything was clean and above board. Then we both relaxed. We almost had an agreement; we had only to flesh out certain details. We weren't going to quarrel over terms, because we had discussed and agreed on the broad principles.

Then, somehow, the conversation strayed to politics, culture and the Vietnam conflict. He asked me what I thought about Vietnam. This was, after all, at the height of the Vietnam War and, sitting in Thailand, we were practically next door to the conflict. My Japanese friend at Mitsui & Co, Mizuno Tadao, had fed me information from time to time about the ferocious American bombing of Vietnam. I recall Mizuno saying something like, "According to Mitsui's information, from high up in the Japanese Government, three days of American bombing of Vietnam is the TNT firepower equivalent of the entire 1944 Allied bombing of Japan." I was churned up by all this killing and maiming.

I replied, "Mr Carlson, why are you Americans bullying the Vietnamese? Why go there to bash their heads in, defoliate and contaminate their rivers and their soil – Agent Orange and all that."

His face turned black; he was furious; he grew stiffer and stiffer. In his mind, he must have thought, "I am now talking to a communist." Our relationship soured in that instant; the atmosphere changed and suddenly he was looking for an excuse to end the meeting.

I could see his assistant was as if jumping on hot coals. Now, when I get started, I don't let up. So I rubbed a bit more salt into the wound. I said, "If you have any influence at all back home, you should go back and tell your government to end this monstrous war as soon as possible. You are killing a lot of innocent Vietnamese people, human beings who don't deserve to die. You're pummelling away at these poor people."

Carlson ended the meeting abruptly. We shook hands very coldly. He said, "Goodbye," turned around and left the room.

I was quite taken aback by Carlson's reaction. In my mind, as he was crossing me out of his mind, so was I crossing him out of my mind. I thought, "I am not going to do business with a man who can't even listen to the facts! If he refuses to believe that two plus two makes four, then what sort of management company am I signing up with? Of course I am not going to sign up with him."

The fact is, I very often talk politics in business. That's why I am what I am. I feel that the two are indivisible, and my partner had better know how I feel about life. Otherwise, how can any partnership last?

So I returned to Singapore from Bangkok. Jacob Ballas, who was a director of Shangri-La, had heard of my impending meeting with Eddie Carlson. He asked me, "What happened?" So I told him the whole story. Jacob said with a sigh, "Oh my God, Robert; you and your political views again."

I said, "Ah, never mind, Jacob. You know I am a strong-tempered man. I don't need him either. Forget them."

After that Bangkok encounter, Western went quiet on me for three months. Then, one day, when I planned to leave for London at about nine in the evening, I had a noon-time call from Jacob. "R-o-b-e-r-t," he said. Whenever Jacob's voice started like that, I knew he was onto a thorny subject. "Have you heard that Bob Lindquist and Bill Keithan [both senior vice presidents] of Western Hotels are in town?"

"Yes, I've heard."

He said, "They called me today. They came around to see me, to ask me to please make an appointment with you."

"I don't want to see them," I said. "They were rude to me after a nice meeting. They talked politics. I spoke my mind, and they wanted to play big-power politics. Just because they are American, they are not going to impose their will on me!"

Jacob cajoled me, "Come on, Robert. Cool down. Cool down. Keep your shirt on. Don't fight with everybody. These fellows want to pay a courtesy call on you. Don't be rude."

"I know they've gone around town and discovered there is no better location than ours, no better hotel than what Shibata is designing for us. Forget them!"

Jacob pleaded, "Robert, ten minutes. See them at five o'clock. Your flight is not until nine."

My wife, Joy, was around and, of course, she gave me a glance asking, "Why are you so uppity?" These gestures help in a family. So I relented.

"Okay, I'll see them. What's more, since they've come from

America, I'll put a bottle of champagne on ice. Have them come around four-thirty this afternoon."

They came to my home in Queen Astrid Park. They were very nice, polite and accommodating, almost as if atoning for Eddie Carlson's earlier behaviour towards me. Bill Keithan was in charge of hardware, the look of the hotels; Bob Lindquist, who later rose to become company president, was strong in operations. They said they'd been around Singapore and yes, frankly, they had to admit that we had the best product available. They wanted to recommend to their head office that Western negotiate a management contract with us.

I was accommodating. I said, "Fine. I have not signed up with anyone." I pointed out that my shareholding (at this point) was only ten percent. The conversation ended on a happy note, indicating that we would reopen talks. As they were about to leave, I said, "Bob, I want to ask you a very personal question. The months of silence, was it due to the fact that when the subject came around to Vietnam, Eddie thought I was a communist?" I saw a terrible cloud sweep past his face. They both blushed and gave each other embarrassed looks. So I said, "Well, Bob, if you don't want to answer the question, it doesn't matter. For me, I have my answer." Carlson must have gone back to Seattle, briefed those guys and said, "Kuok is an interesting man, but I think he is a commie." I said to Lindquist and Keithan, "Okay, I am prepared to forget the past, provided Eddie Carlson does the same."

They replied, "Mr Kuok, believe us; that's fine. Otherwise, we wouldn't be here today." Then they returned to Seattle and I flew to England that night for my sugar business.

Within a few weeks, we had an invitation to go across to Seattle. That was in December of 1968. I took Geh Ik Cheong and Tan Chin Nam, Tan Kim Yeow's younger brother. I said to the two of them, "I'll stay in my hotel suite. You two go out as battering rams first." They went off for two and half days of talks. First day, very slow progress. Second day, a bit more progress. I said all along the way, "Don't get bogged down. Wherever you cannot proceed on a point, agree to list it. When you have gone through the whole draft agreement, give me a list of the points where you are bogged down."

Every time Ik Cheong and Chin Nam got stuck on a point, they dealt with Western's executive vice president, Harry Henke III, and narrowed down the list of disagreements. On the third afternoon, Ik Cheong and Chin Nam phoned me. "We are down to about 20 sticking points," they said. "Can you join us now?" I said, "Fine." I put on my shoes, went down, and shook hands with Western's people.

Henke was one of the most marvellous Americans I have met in my life. I said to him, "Harry, now's the time for give-and-take. What do you say someone be the umpire. He'll read out point number one of disagreement and whoever can give way says, 'We concede.' But let's do it as friends." We started and he immediately said: "Concede." Next one, I think I said, "Concede." We breezed through the list in less than half an hour. Once or twice we discussed a point on which either he convinced me and I conceded, or I convinced him and he conceded.

Then Chin Nam, who loved to gamble, said to Ik Cheong and me in Chinese, "Hey, since we have finished, how about the three of us go down to Las Vegas and see a bit of the gambling world?"

I asked Lindquist and the others, "Is it possible to help us hurry up and have this agreement typed so that we can sign it? If it takes two hours, can you get us a flight that leaves between 7 and 8 pm for Las Vegas?" So that was how we left, all in a hurry.

We flew first to Las Vegas, stayed two or three nights, gambled and saw Boulder Dam. Then we flew to Los Angeles – my first trip there – and stayed in a new Western hotel, Century Plaza, and met the general manager, Harry Mullikin, who later rose to Chairman and CEO of the parent company.

Western's terms for managing the Shangri-La Singapore were quite fair: A US$200,000 front-end fee for their expertise during construction, and then five percent of gross operating profit after the hotel opened for business in 1971. But they made a large blunder in the contract. They inserted a clause saying the contract would stretch ten years from the date of signing in Seattle. We didn't open the hotel until two years and four months later, so Western only received seven years and eight months of revenues. They were good hotel operators and a fine bunch of people, but they weren't skilled businessmen.

By the time the contract came up for renewal in 1978, Eddie Carlson was gone, which was a pity since we were close friends whose minds worked virtually on the same wavelength. United Airlines, based in Chicago, had swallowed Western. After United bought Western International Hotels, they took the CEO of Western, Eddie Carlson, and made him Chairman of UAL.

Within the first three or four years of owning a hotel in Singapore, I realized that there was very little magic in running it. So, by 1978, I had already decided to establish my own hotel management company in Hong Kong. However, at that point I was so involved in developing my other businesses that I didn't want to get bogged down with a new venture. So, I offered Western a five-year extension for the Singapore Shangri-La, and they took it.

Around the same time, I built Kowloon Shangri-La Hotel in Hong Kong. Here again, Western blundered by missing an opportunity to invest in a prime piece of Hong Kong real estate before an enormous escalation in property values. I offered them

25 percent ownership of the property, joining me at ground level even after I had already put money in for more than six months. I kept the offer open for two months. They asked for an extension and I said, "Okay, I'll give you one more month." They sent staff over, checked with some locals and kept on looking at this gift horse of mine in the mouth. Maybe all gift horses have bad breath, but they mistook the bad breath for a bad deal. The deadline came and I kept quiet. A few weeks later, they regretted that the deadline had passed and they made many attempts to call me from Seattle.

"Please, we want to come in now," they said.

I told them, "No way. Nowhere on earth can you find a man who will give you an offer for three months, even allowing you to look at the gift horse over and over in the mouth. No way!" I had made up my mind to manage Kowloon Shangri-La, but Western pleaded and I gave in and agreed to a management contract. I bought myself time, really.

Later, Eddie Carlson expressed his deep regret for passing up the offer to invest in the Kowloon Shangri-La. He said to me, "In future, Robert, I want to be in any of your China deals. Please, if you don't mind, be kind enough."

I replied, "You don't want to join me in China, Eddie."

At that time, if China gave you a 20-year cooperation deal they were being generous (Shangri-La Beijing, my first major hotel project in China, was granted only a 13-year cooperation period). "I do it for the love of my motherland, the birthplace of my parents. It's in the marrow of my bones to help the country. Why should you want to help China? Eddie, you must help America." He appreciated my advice. Of course, today China looks good, but imagine what I had to go through in the early days.

In about 1970, I decided that we should try to list Shangri-La Singapore on the local stock exchange, even though we did not have a business record. It was very fashionable then to go public. The Singapore Finance Minister was Hon Sui Sen, who unfortunately died quite young. I went to see him personally for permission to list. We had a quick meeting of minds and he agreed. Then I said, "Can you now wear your hat as Chairman of Development Bank of Singapore?"

He replied, "All right, what do you want me to do?"

I said, "I want to borrow money."

Hon Sui Sen agreed that DBS would lend up to about 20 million Singapore dollars at a favourable interest rate.

We offered shares to the public at $1.20, upon Hon Sui Sen's approval. As the original partners, we had put up front-end money to build the hotel. Since we had incurred costs, we felt that it was only fair to charge a 20 cent per share premium, especially since the value of the land had appreciated.

Shortly after we went public in 1970, the stock exchange collapsed. Stock markets have these bouts of influenza. It was doom and gloom for about three months.

As the market crashed, Shangri-La shares fell to $1.10, to $1.08, to $1.06, and even as low as 92 cents. As the stock dropped, I started to buy. I bought and I bought. In the end, when I looked up, I controlled about 40 percent of Shangri-La shares and had realized my dream of controlling the company. I suppose descendants of those who got watered down by me will say that I contrived the market collapse. I would love to be credited with such supernatural powers, but the truth is that it was pure chance and opportunism on my part.

As I indicated, my entry into hotels wasn't premeditated. But having started one hotel, I realized I couldn't stop there. If you own just one hotel you might as well sell it at the right time – it's more of a burden than anything else. You must expand logically and sensibly.

After Shangri-La Singapore, we moved on to the resort hotels of Rasa Sayang and Golden Sands in Penang, Malaysia, and then on to two resort hotels in Fiji, The Fijian and The Fiji Mocambo. Since these were all resort hotels, I didn't invite Western to participate because I knew they would frown on them; that it was beneath their dignity to get involved.

Then we decided to build big-city hotels, including Shangri-La Kuala Lumpur, Kowloon Shangri-La in Hong Kong, Shangri-La Bangkok, then the Island Shangri-La Hotel in Hong Kong, and many hotels in the major cities of China from the 1980s. All these came along one after the other. As of 2017, we own and/or operate 100 hotels. Of these the Kuoks own 80. We have another 36 projects being planned or under construction.

I never studied hotel management, but whatever I learned at home and in school taught me that everything in life is very simple. So why complicate matters? Weary travellers need to sleep on a comfortable bed; they need to have a good bath; if they're too tired to walk 100 metres to a restaurant, you should provide some good food and beverage outlets for them. Everything else is a gimmick. It's really a hostelry pattern, just as when the tired, dusty horseback rider hitched his horse at the inn, ate and drank and retired to bed to awake fresher and recharged the next morning.

I could make the same statement about the need for simplicity in doing business in general. Mind you, I'm not saying that certain businesses are not more complex in nature, but I am saying that within a complex business you don't have to make it more complex. In each and every business, whether simple or complex, there are simple ways of tackling problems and operating the business. It's those who adopt convoluted ways who never get to the top, because they are tripping themselves up all the time.

I studied the Swiss hotels. But the Swiss run very small hotels ranging from 20 rooms up to about 300 rooms. After all, Switzerland is a very small country. One has to take a blend of the crisp Swiss style of management and the American factory style of management, where they have hotels with 1,000 or even several thousand rooms. To my mind, the optimum scale is somewhere between 800 and 1000 keys (an executive suite with four rooms counts as one key).

As in a factory operation, size gives you economies of scale. You can install bigger, more efficient boilers for hot water and more efficient air coolers; you can hire talented managers, including a top-quality hotel general manager, by spreading the cost over 800 rooms. All business on earth is management. In the hotel world – in any business world – you must look for three ingredients when you hire staff: talent, integrity and the stamina for hard work. If any of these three traits are missing, forget the guy.

When constructing the hotel, you cannot cut the cost to lower than its true value. Everything has a true cost: the cost of good-quality marble, quality timber, quality builders. There's a classic Chinese phrase: *tou gong jian liao* – steal on workmanship, cut back on building materials. If you attempt this, you are really cutting off your own nose. For example, some developing countries have substandard cement, and surely you don't want to be using that. To save money, you need to focus on preventing leakage of expenses that would result in exaggerated costs. If you don't employ good staff, they could steal from you or connive with the various outside contractors to rob you. That happens all the time.

If you build an 800-key hotel sitting on one of the crossroads of the world, you can achieve a high occupancy, which enables you to charge a rate commensurate with the value that you are offering. It's like being a fisherman. Where are the currents flowing that bring schools of fish? You must park your hotel where those schools of fish tend to swim. You shouldn't be fishing in an area of the ocean where there is no current and therefore no fish around.

I don't like hotels that make a practice of overcharging. I think that Shangri-La has got it right: it has a name, a standard, and we are looking to the long term. We, of course, want to make money every year – and we are making money every year – but we are not there to cut the throats of our customers. I want them to go away happy and satisfied.

But I admit to feeling very sorry for hotels – and many of them in my own chain – that are unable to charge decent rates because of over-keen competition. You have nepotism and cronyism in the developing world. When somebody becomes the Prime Minister or President, he may hand out money-making favours.

One of the first things these pretenders think about is building a luxury hotel. They spend money as if it were water and do things such as adorning the bathrooms with gold taps. It's all a lot of nonsense. They spend two to three times what I would spend on the same room. Shangri-La hotels are dressed up smartly to qualify for a five-star hotel appellation, but they are not ornate or fancy. I don't build dream castles.

These favoured businessmen are not interested in hotel management. They want to make money, but they are not managers themselves. They have never managed anything in their lives, so they employ foreign firms to manage the hotels. Most of these companies offer very tough terms. The owners know nothing better, so they accept terms that mean that when the management company makes money every year the owners are in some years still losing. By the time the owners are making some money the management companies are laughing their way to the bank every day. I have seen those contracts.

What distinguishes the Shangri-La is that the owners are very hands-on. We try very hard not to interfere with professional managers, and yet, at the same time, we draw a very fine distinction between the priorities and requirements of an owner versus the priorities of a manager. So, early on, I set up a policy implementation committee mechanism in each hotel. The committee includes the general manager of the hotel and one or two people from the owner's side. If it does its job correctly, management and owner will always work in concert for the betterment of the hotel.

As I stated, we shall never build ornate hotels, or monuments to perpetuate the memory of anyone. I have always felt that business very quickly tends toward the sordid. It may start with noble ideas, but it quickly descends to the sordid. Maybe it's because the extremely competitive nature of business renders it so, and for you to survive you gravitate toward the sordid world. But if you are a member of the sordid world, what noble enterprise or calling are you practicing? There is nothing to create a monument about.

So, I came up with a saying that I constantly repeated at the early board meetings of Shangri-La Singapore. I said, "We must set out to do three things, in this order: To look after our hotel staff; to look after our guests; to look after our shareholders." I quickly explained why I did not put looking after guests first: It was our duty as owners to look after our staff properly; to motivate them; to show them that we are not grasping, selfish owners. By setting good examples – by treating them as kindly and generously as an enterprise is permitted to do, by treating them as fellow human beings (and by not behaving as lords and masters) – we motivate them to provide the best service to the guests, our customers. If we do everything sensibly, we end up rewarding our shareholders with good profits from which we can pay decent dividends.

I would be deceitful if I led you to believe that all Shangri-La projects have gone smoothly. I'll cite four examples, of which only the first, in Bangkok, ended well. The second, in Tokyo, never came off; the third ended maddeningly in Seoul; the fourth was a project in Myanmar which needed time.

I wanted to build a hotel in Bangkok. My old friend Ang Toon Chew recommended a piece of land in the vicinity of the main bus terminus. This was in the late 1970s. Thailand was already a nation of over 45 million people. Bangkok was the hub from which buses departed in all directions. So it's a huge bus terminus, and still is. I went with Toon Chew to see the site, a large piece of land. We were just about to bid at auction to procure the land when I called on another old friend, the late Suree Asdathorn, a leading Thai sugar miller and exporter.

I told Suree, "I am looking at this land. I respect you very much. Will you please join me as a shareholder?"

Suree, who was one of the finest Thai businessmen I have ever met, asked, "What, which piece?" I described it to him again. He said, "I know Bangkok like the palm of my hand." Indeed, he had emigrated there from China at the age of eleven. So he warned, "No, Robert, don't put a hotel there! It's hell! There is noise, smoke and pollution. Why put a nice hotel there? It can't even support a three-star hotel."

"Well, then where?" I asked. Suree introduced me to the present site of the Shangri-La Bangkok on the banks of the Chao Phraya River – and invested in the property.

I sometimes employ this tactic when I'm in doubt about a project: I chat with a man cleverer than myself and offer him a joint-venture deal. If he says, "Oh my God, it's an awful thing," then you know it's poison, and you're able to see the deal clearly through other people's eyes.

The near miss in Tokyo came during Japan's roaring 1980s. Our sugar-refining partner in Malayan Sugar Manufacturing – Nissin Sugar – approached us about building a Shangri-La hotel on reclaimed land in Tokyo Bay. My eldest son, Beau, liked the site. Then I made a trip to Tokyo, and went to have a look at the location, near the Odaiba lighthouse. I thought, "My God, this is way out of the city. It's almost half way to Tokyo Disneyland. What for?"

So, I called up my Japanese architect, Shibata, and he put me right: "Kuok-san, why do you want to build a hotel now? Because of this bubble and inflation in Tokyo, the construction workers have made increasing demands on all the contracting firms. A single Japanese worker is the most costly worker in the world today. None of the big contractors can build cheaply. So you will be building at an astronomical cost. You'll never make money if you build a hotel right now."

After listening to half an hour of Shibata's advice, I made up my mind, then and there, that we must withdraw from the project forthwith. I called up Beau and asked if we were deeply into the deal. He answered, "No." I said, "Cut!"

The epitaph to this story is that on a trip to Tokyo one or two months later, I met young Morinaga Tametaka, the heir to Nissin Sugar. The Morinaga family gave us a dinner at a famous shabu-shabu restaurant near Hotel Okura. After dinner, I rode to a nightclub in young Tametaka's car. He showed great displeasure that I had cancelled the hotel project and made him lose a lot of face. I said, "I am sorry, Tametaka-san. You may have lost face, but if I hadn't saved you and myself from this project, you could have lost your whole company. You could be bankrupted by the failure of such a large project." Reflecting on this episode, it's not hard to understand how so many Japanese firms ran into hot water in the 1990s by "saving face."

The most irritating of these three proposed hotel projects was in South Korea prior to the 1988 Seoul Olympics. Shibata was the intermediary. He was the architect for many of my hotels, including Shangri-La Kuala Lumpur, Shangri-La Bangkok, Shangri-La Kowloon, Shangri-La Singapore and Beijing Shangri-La. He called me one day to say one of his customers in Korea, a Korean Japanese named Kwak Yu Ji, wanted to build a hotel with me in downtown Seoul.

"He's got a beautiful piece of land within 200-300 meters of the mayor's office," Shibata said. "He owns it. He has taken a lot of time and trouble to accumulate this piece of land, buying out small lots and joining them all together. Can we come and see you?"

Kwak, whose Japanese name was Nakayama, had made a fortune in pachinko parlours, a slot-machine game that is a slightly seedy, cheap form of entertainment in Japan. I thought, well, since he comes recommended by this Japanese architect friend, he can't be a bad fellow.

Nakayama came to Hong Kong. He spoke fair Japanese. I don't speak Korean, so Shibata interpreted, translating Nakayama's Japanese into English. We agreed to participate in the project. The reason I accepted the deal was that it allowed me to become a 50-percent partner, meaning he didn't keep majority control. I thought, "Well, that's a nice situation to be in. Of course, I prefer to be 51 percent, but how can you ask a man who is asking you to become his partner to hand over control to you?"

This was late 1985, and I sensed that the Korean won would strengthen very fast, so I told my treasury, "Please remit about US$35 million into Korea straight away." We took advantage of the then-weak won by remitting the money to an American bank in Korea and converting it into won. Then we commissioned Shibata to draw up some hotel schematics.

I went to Korea some ten times for this project. After the fourth or fifth trip, I thought I could safely delegate negotiations to Beau because the trips were coming thick and fast. Beau went up about every three weeks. But our partner, Kwak Yu Ji, gave us a song and dance all the time.

One day I said, "I think this schematic is good."

He replied, "No," and we spent five to six hours trying to redesign the bathroom. He would take out stacks of paper, sketch it himself, then say, "No, no," crumple it up and draw another one. We'd break for lunch, then he would come back and repeat this nonsense. Because of our inability to communicate – Shibata was not at these sessions – he had interpreters, but these aides were terrified of him. I believe he even manhandled some of his assistants; he literally stood them up and slapped them. He was crazy.

At first, I thought I would let him have his way; that the man was just a bit eccentric. But it got to the stage that he never approved plans. Then, one day, I said, "Isn't it your intention to appoint Shibata as architect?"

He said, "No way!"

Everything seemed to fall around me. He had asked Shibata to introduce me to him. He was indebted to Shibata over that, and now he's calmly telling me, "Why do we need to appoint Shibata?"

Shibata was a proven hotel architect. What's this fellow got up his sleeve? It may be that he was trying to drive a hard bargain with Shibata, getting Shibata to work for him for almost nothing. He probably had come up in life the hard way. Probably there were Korean architects available prepared to work for nothing. Our way is, if you want quality service, you pay for it. Shibata had already designed many hotels for me.

Finally, I realized that I couldn't go on like this. More than two years had elapsed. I had wanted to rush the project so that we could build the first 200-300 rooms (the final product was supposed to be 700 rooms) in time for the 1988 Olympics. But the project dragged on and dragged on and dragged on. Every time Beau came back I sensed he was making no headway. So one day I said, "Beau, I am taking it back into my own hands."

I called Shibata and said, "Shibata-*san*, can you meet me in Seoul? This will be a showdown meeting with Nakayama. I don't want anybody else present, just the three of us. You must be the interpreter, because I am going to say some harsh words and I want him to keep his face. The best way of success is if he doesn't lose face."

They came to my hotel suite in Seoul. I said, "Shibata-*san*, please translate what I am going to say. Nakayama, can you give me a deadline by which time you will approve the design? Number two: What influence do you have to get early approval for construction to start? I want to know these two dates." He refused to answer. He said he was still not happy with the design, and sidestepped all my questions. I went on and on and on. I was sidestepped, sidestepped, and red herrings were spread across my trail.

I said to Shibata, "Shibata-*san*, can you hear what's going on? We cannot go on like this. Please tell Mr Nakayama, I have decided as of this moment, after all my attempts to talk with him and getting nowhere, that I want to pull out of this project now. I have made up my mind. I am telling him, serving notice on him, I am pulling out of the project."

When he translated it into Japanese, Nakayama's colour changed. He muttered, "You can't do it."

I said, "Of course I can do it. This has gone on for too long." He kept on protesting that he wouldn't let me out. I said, "Okay. Shibata-*san*, you know the agreement was signed and the land is now all in the company that owns it. He owns 50 percent, I also own 50 percent. In the past, I let him behave as if he owned it all. As from this moment onward, I have as much say as he has. So I am willing to stay in for a few more years, any number of years; but nothing that he wants to build will be approved by me. Let's play the same game together. He's played it against me for two and a half years. I have taken too much nonsense. Now I want to exact my revenge on him. Please translate it."

The man was flustered. Then I said, "You know, I have already confirmed my return flight. I have barely ten minutes to collect my bag and go to the airport. I don't want to say any more. You tell him I am leaving now."

So I got up and said, "Goodbye, Shibata-*san*." I shook hands, went to my room, picked up my bag and left for Seoul airport to catch a flight home.

Within days, Shibata called me from Tokyo. He said Nakayama had called him and said, "I accept your decision to withdraw, but you have made profit on the foreign exchange with your early remittance. I want one-half of that profit."

I responded, "He can have it."

Another businessman's reaction might have been to sue the guy, to litigate. I say: In life, when you can get out, get out. Life is not reasonable. You mustn't face life thinking everybody is going to be reasonable. You must look at life and assume everybody is going to be unreasonable. After all, I was making half of the foreign-exchange profit. I took my money out and quit everything. I didn't even want to talk about the appreciation in real-estate values.

That was the end of my involvement in Seoul. It was a very unfortunate experience. Today, a huge office building sits on that site.

In 1993, my second son Ean and other personnel from Kuok Singapore accompanied a Singapore government delegation on a visit to Myanmar. This was the era of the first opening up of the country. After he returned, we sat down and chatted. He urged our family to invest in Myanmar as a way of helping the country move forward. I knew Myanmar from the rice trade years ago, but my last visit was around 1960. Of course, Myanmar had been under military rule for many decades, and the economy had stagnated for much of that time.

We sent more people to Yangon and, by the following year, we had established good relations with local Burmese businessmen who helped us invest in several pieces of land in downtown Yangon. In 1994, we began building a hotel and apartments, and a Traders Hotel was opened in 1996 at a cost of nearly US$80 million. However, mainly due to the economic sanctions placed on Myanmar by Western nations, the economy went into a long decline. The hotel struggled and did not make a profit. Two apartment blocks built on another site that we acquired were never finished. But I personally sensed that Myanmar would one day change, and we remained committed to the country.

That day came in April 2011, when U Thein Sein took over as President and embarked on a gradual process of opening up Myanmar both politically and economically. Our Traders hotel in Yangon, which was re-branded and re-named Sule Shangri-la in 2014, now sees strong demand for its rooms, as investment and tourism have taken off. In 2013, we completed the two apartment blocks that we had started to build in 1997, and we are operating them as 240 serviced apartments. We have started construction on a 23-storey office tower next to Sule Shangri-la, and within the next three to four years we will open another Shangri-La hotel adjacent to the serviced apartments.

In addition, we are actively exploring investments in the agricultural sector through Wilmar International, as we look beyond Yangon to opportunities throughout the country.

PART IV
–
MALAYSIA

13
AT GOVERNMENT SERVICE

THE 1960S were the busiest years of my life. I seized opportunities as they came along, many of them thrown up by the dismantling of the British Empire. My fertile mind and highly-strung, energetic body pushed me in different directions.

Timing is everything. I figured that if I juggled ten balls and could keep six of them up in the air all the time, I would be way ahead of the fellow who could not even toss two balls in the air. Some people need to concentrate on one task at a time; others have greater flexibility. Fortunately, I was blessed with instinct, rhythm and focus.

Extended as I was in business, I felt that I couldn't turn down requests from the young Malaysian Government to help them to monitor or run new businesses. I was grateful to my country and wanted to lend a helping hand to the leaders. These government appointments provided me with an inside look into the system. What I saw was often not too pretty.

The first of these appointments came in 1965 when the government founded Bank Bumiputra. Tun Razak, the Deputy Prime Minister, asked me to serve as one of two Chinese directors (the other was John Eu) on the first board. As the name denotes, Bank Bumiputra was formed to help the Malay ethnic group (*bumiputra* means indigenous peoples), which, at the time, was significantly under-represented in the economic life of the nation and almost non-existent in banking.

I asked Razak what he expected of me. He noted that the board was mainly comprised of Malays, but that they didn't have a strong background in business. He wanted to ensure that the bank served to foster the economic development of the nation. My role would partly be to ensure sound judgment and prevent any abuse of power. It sounded like a worthy project and a request I couldn't turn down.

I quickly discovered that it was a thankless task. Many of these state projects after Malaysian independence started off as worthy causes, but then got twisted until the result bore no resemblance to the original dream. The promoter of the idea starts it but doesn't align the project properly on the rails. He then bows out and allows others to push it along. If these others are people with clean hearts and minds, then the project may work out. But if they have unclean hearts and twisted minds, the project gets derailed and hijacked. I saw this coming in Bank Bumiputra. It was a very invidious position to be in, so, after serving in Bank Bumiputra for about three years and eight months, I bowed out.

In 1967, some Malaysian cabinet ministers approached me about running Malayawata, a joint-venture integrated steel mill owned by Japanese and Malaysian interests. I had no involvement at the start-up of this company, which, it must be said, was rather half-baked.

In the early 1960s, a few Chinese-Malaysian businessmen went to Tokyo to lobby Mr Inayama, the Chairman and CEO of Nippon Steel. Inayama held talks with Malaysian Prime Minister Tunku Abdul Rahman, and the Japanese agreed to build an integrated steel mill in Malaysia. Coincidentally, the mill was situated in Prai, about 1.6 km from my sugar refinery; when the wind blew in the wrong direction, steel dust would land on our factory.

The project was pushed by the Chinese businessmen, but to

dress it up and make it look very Malaysian, they formed a council of half a dozen Malaysian advisors. One of these advisors was the proprietor-manager of the Railway Station Hotel in Kuala Lumpur. Another advisor was the father-in-law of Tun Razak, the Deputy Prime Minister.

The Japanese sent a middle-senior level manager from Yawata Steel Works called Sakai, a nice enough man. His assistant, Yoshimura, was highly strung. They also sent over an engineer called Kase to head the plant. While I was running my sugar refinery in Prai, I became aware of a growing contingent of Japanese arriving to build the steel mill.

The Malaysian Government grew increasingly uneasy about the direction the company was taking, and finally decided that they wanted me to head the steel factory once it started production. I agreed, but asked first to meet the Japanese with whom I would be working.

When I met them, they spoke in very arrogant language reminiscent of the Japanese occupation period, "Ah, you know, 40 percent of the shares of this company are owned by Japanese. There's Nippon Steel; there's Mitsubishi, Mitsui [I think four or five of the major *sogo shosha* held shares]. The Malaysian Government is the second largest shareholder. Where do you come in?"

I had to remind them that the government had asked me to be Chairman, and I needed to know the company before I said yes or no. "I have asked them for permission to meet you, to seek answers to my questions. So don't talk like that with me." They were very rude.

I went back to the government and relayed my misgivings. "You asked me to go in as Chairman of the Board. Forget it! If you want me to help you, I must be Executive Chairman – Board Chairman and CEO."

About six months went by. They tried unsuccessfully to

negotiate this arrangement with Tokyo. The Japanese had seen my temperament and style and they were worried. I viewed them as arrogant and high-handed, and was prepared to clean them out. But unless I had power there was nothing I could do. Finally, I think the Malaysian Government ordered them to accept me. The Japanese then asked me to share authority with Sakai as co-CEOs. I said, no way. I wanted full authority.

When the grand opening for the mill was about to take place, they finally agreed that I would be Executive Chairman. I remember that my office was inferior in location, layout and decoration to what the Japanese had. It seemed like the Japanese occupation days all over again!

From day one, what I saw at Malayawata was horrendous. I felt as if my role was to clean out the toilets. The plant was initially slated to produce 25,000-30,000 tons of steel per annum, with the iron ore imported and the charcoal made from the mangrove swamps around Prai. The steel mill had about 105 staff members sent from Japan. The average Japanese staff salary was over MYR3,000 per month (there were also about 600 Malaysian workers), so the labour cost of the Japanese alone was more than MYR100 per ton of steel. The finished product should sell for about MYR250 per ton. I warned them that, based on what they were showing me, the steel mill would go bankrupt from day one.

The Japanese said, "Don't worry. Malaysia today is like Japan in 1900. The country has to make sacrifices. We'll ask the government for tariff protection. The price of merchant bars in the country must go up to MYR400." In other words, they would force the whole nation to pay their salaries!

I told the managers, "I want the Japanese staff figure cut down to 80 in three months; and then to 70 till finally 30. I think 30 is more than enough." I had done my homework; I wasn't just pulling figures out of a hat. I also jettisoned the council of advisors and the superfluous members of the board.

Sakai and Yoshimura opposed me every inch of the way. One day, they said, "Kuok-*san*, we must have meeting with you." They repeated the same things I had heard from them before: "Why do you act so rough and tough and talk so big? How many shares do you own in this company? You know, we Japanese have 40 percent. We are the largest single block." I kept my calm and ordered them out of my office.

I realized we couldn't go on like this. I went to see the Minister of Commerce and Industry, Lim Swee Aun, and explained the situation to him. I laid out two scenarios: I could resign, or I could buy shares in Malayawata, turn my back on all my other businesses and devote my life to the steel industry of Malaysia. The Minister said the government was storing 15 percent of the shares with Nippon Steel. He said he'd tell Nippon Steel that the Malaysian Government wanted me to be the buyer, but that Nippon Steel could determine the purchase price.

So I went to Tokyo and met with Inayama, Chairman of Nippon Steel. Sakai and Yoshimura were also present, along with a couple of Inayama's managers. After a few pleasantries, I got down to business. Inayama said, well, the cost in our books today is MYR1.44, so you can buy the block at that price – this at a time when the stock market was depressed.

I replied that, from what I had seen of the company as Chairman and CEO, the shares were barely worth 80 cents. As I was answerable to my own shareholders and board, I could not ask them to pay MYR1.44 for something that was worth only 80 cents. I added that the cost in his books did not concern me. If I continued in the job, I saw a chance for the mill to become successful. If I departed, sooner or later the mill would run into serious financial trouble.

I tried to state the facts. Inayama retorted, "Take it or leave it."

So I quit my government-appointed position after serving for about 20 months. I completely cut my ties with Malayawata, which later lost its leading position among Malaysia's steel mills.

In 1967, word reached my ears that the Blue Funnel Group was coming to set up the national shipping line of Malaysia. Blue Funnel was probably the largest shipping conglomerate in Britain at that time. It owned Blue Funnel, Glen Line, Straits Steamship Co in Singapore, and many other lines. The Executive Chairman, a man whom I recall walked with a bad limp, was making frequent lobbying trips from London to Kuala Lumpur.

I was interested in applying for the licence, so I chatted with a few of my Malay civil-servant friends. They agreed that I should put in a similar application to be considered for the right to establish the national shipping line. My interest was partly patriotism – a desire to help Malaysia to launch its own independent shipping line and not be tied to the apron strings of the ex-colonial government of Britain through Blue Funnel.

I had become interested in shipping from about 1964, due to our large-scale buying of sugar for our refinery, wheat for our flourmill and our international commodities-trading activities. For example, we bought free-on-board sugar from India and delivered it to the Government of Indonesia on a cost-and-freight basis (sellers only wanted to sell on the basis of delivery at their own ports; buyers wanted the sugar delivered to their ports. Thus, covering the span of the ocean was my risk). In those days, shipping was quite volatile and freight rates could sometimes shoot up 25-30 percent. Since margins on sugar trading were small, you could easily make money on your trade, but lose on the freight.

There was one problem: I knew nothing about shipping. I did know that in any business, unless you know the tricks of the trade, you can be badly burnt. I couldn't even submit a decent memo for the application. So I looked for a partner.

On one trip to Hong Kong, I had been introduced by a Malay civil-servant friend to a man called Frank WK Tsao. I remembered that Tsao was a shipping man, Chairman of International Maritime Carriers, so I telephoned him. I said I would like to come and see him to discuss a business proposal. He gave me an appointment and I flew to Hong Kong.

When I went to his office, Tsao was only mildly friendly. I was quite humble in my approach. I told him that we had met. He said, "Oh yes, we have met, we have met." In business life, you learn early on that you must swallow your pride.

I told him that some Malay civil servants, who wanted to stir up competition, were encouraging me to submit an application to set up a national shipping line. I said, "I can't differentiate between the front and rear ends of a ship," which was a bit of an exaggeration, "so why don't you come and help me to set up the Malaysian national shipping line? You're well known in the shipping business. Are you willing to become my partner?"

Without thinking for a second, he retorted, "Do you know, so and so and so and so have also approached me. They are Tan Sris, and I turned them all down." He was virtually saying "And who are you? I've turned down people way ahead of you in the pecking order in Malaysia."

When I heard these remarks and saw his body language, I said, "I'm sorry then. I thought I would give you first crack. I am going to go at it." I didn't tell him what a determined man I am in life. I concluded, "Never mind, nothing has been lost by this little chat we've had. Thank you for receiving me." I got up and was walking out when he shouted, "Oh, no, no. Please, Mr Kuok. Don't go! Don't go! Sit down, sit down." To this day I don't know what made

Frank change his mind.

I had one shipping expert on staff, Tony Goh, a Singaporean-Chinese who was running my plywood factory. Tony had been a manager at Ben Line, a Scottish liner, before he joined me in 1964. So I sent Tony Goh to draft the memo with Frank Tsao. I rewrote certain parts to suit the reading style of the Malaysian civil servants, and we submitted the memo in the joint names of Kuok Brothers and Frank's International Maritime Carriers. A little later, I heard that we were one of the leading contenders.

I asked Frank to meet me in Kuala Lumpur. I had made up my mind that we should pick one day to call on as many important ministers as possible. From eight in the morning we whipped around Kuala Lumpur at a furious pace, such as you can't do today due to the traffic, and saw seven ministers by lunchtime. Some of them gave us good time and good hearings, and we told them the same story. In the afternoon, we visited one or two more. I remember calling on the Prime Minister, the Deputy Prime Minister, Home Minister Tun Dr Ismail, Finance Minister Tan Siew Sin, Minister of Works Sambanthan and Minister of Transport Sardon Jubir. Within two or three weeks, we were picked at a cabinet meeting to start the national shipping line, Malaysian International Shipping Corporation (MISC). We were like a dark horse coming from behind in the last furlong and pipping the favourite at the post!

I was Chairman of the Board and provided business-management guidance. Frank Tsao's side provided the shipping expertise. Just around the time of MISC's formation in 1968, my dear friend Tun Dr Ismail resigned from government when he found that he had cancer. I immediately invited him to be the first Chairman of MISC. Frank Tsao already knew Tun Dr Ismail through a textile-mill investment Frank had made in Johor (Dr Ismail resigned from MISC after the 13 May 1969 riots to return to the Cabinet. I then took over the chairmanship until the 1980s).

Our first two ships came from the Japanese. Simultaneous with our moves to start the shipping line, there was an initiative by the Malayan Chinese Association (MCA) to demand war reparations from Japan. The Chinese community was angry about the Japanese massacre of innocent Chinese and was seeking compensation for this blood debt. Tunku Abdul Rahman, the Malaysian Prime Minister, supported the demand and raised the issue during official trips to Japan. The Japanese finally agreed to give two blood-debt ships to Malaysia, which the Japanese called "goodwill ships."

MISC started with these two cargo ships and paid for them on a monthly bare-boat, hire-charter basis. Frank's ship architects and engineers in Hong Kong supervised the design and construction in Japan. Tunku Abdul Rahman made some very cogent suggestions about the design of the flag for this new national flag carrier.

MISC had an initial paid-up capital of MYR10 million. Since Kuok Brothers led the show, we took 20 percent; Frank Tsao took 15 percent. As the ships were reparation from the Japanese to the Malayan Chinese Association, not to the Malaysian nation, the vessels were assessed a reasonable value and the MCA was given MISC shares in lieu of payment. MCA and other Chinese associations, combined, took 20-30 percent, so in the beginning the holding of Kuok Brothers, Frank and the MCA group together was easily over 50 percent. We had a fairly united board in the beginning.

MISC started business in the second half of 1969 and quickly flourished. Much of the credit must go to Frank, the Deputy Chairman, who recommended capable managers such as Eddie Shih. Shih, another Shanghainese who had settled in Hong Kong, ran the show with Tony Goh. Very early on, Tony recommended his one-time colleague in Ben Line, Leslie Eu, who at the time was manager of Ben Line Bangkok. Leslie, the son of Burmese Chinese who had settled in Malaysia, quit Ben Line and came in as Managing Director of MISC.

Within a year of our launching MISC, Tun Razak, who by then was Prime Minister, sent for me. Razak said, "I want you to make a fresh issue of 20 percent of new shares. I'm under pressure because there is not a high enough Malay percentage of shareholding."

I said, "Tun, are you quite serious about this request?"

He answered, "Yes, Robert." So I replied that I would do it.

I went back and, with a little bit of arm-twisting, persuaded the board to pass a resolution waiving the rights of existing shareholders to a rights issue (MISC was not yet a public company). Razak allocated all the new shares to government agencies. So, I was diluted to 20 upon 120 – the enlarged base – and Frank became 15 upon 120.

One or two years later, Razak again sent for me. He said, "I'm under a lot of pressure at Cabinet meetings. You know, Robert, it's just the price of your success. MISC is doing well, people are getting envious. But now, instead of giving in to those factions, what I've decided is this: Issue another twenty percent, five percent to each of four port cities in Malaysia." This entailed enlarging the capital base to 140 from the original 100, making the Malaysian Government the largest single shareholder and relegating Kuok Brothers to second position. And he again wanted the shares issued at par – the original issue price.

I said, "Tun, I have always cooperated with you, but it's getting very difficult. Three, four years have elapsed from formation, but I would be loath to ask you for a premium since we are a growing company. So I will go back and ask the board again to issue shares at par to you. But Tun, can you please promise me that this is the last time?" He smiled and very gently signified his agreement, without saying the words.

Then Frank and I decided that we should go public. Before we listed in 1987, I made quite a radical move, adopting a practice that I had used within Kuok Brothers. I explained to my Kuok Brothers senior directors that the MISC shares were now worth a lot of money, but only because of the great effort put in by other members of the board and many of the very deserving staff. I wanted to take about 15 percent of our shareholding and sell the shares at par to deserving directors, staff and ship captains. Quite a number of people benefited from this move.

I have always believed in some degree of socialism when you have made money. You know very well that you alone didn't make it; it was a joint effort. I was inspired by the example of Genghis Khan, who, when he conquered cities, usually turned the spoils over to his generals and soldiers. He was not selfish, and that is why he became the greatest general the world has ever seen.

Meanwhile, the ugly head of racism was rising in Malaysia. Razak died in early 1976 in London and Hussein Onn became Prime Minister. The Malaysian Government requested that a man called Datuk Saffian sit on the MISC board. Saffian was virtually head of the Prime Minister's secretariat, a young man who had both ears of the Prime Minister. He was an ordinary board member, but he was quite aggressive at meetings and became increasingly personal.

I must say that Leslie Eu, the Managing Director, was partly to blame. Leslie was in the habit of making European trips himself for MISC. As I was Chairman of the Board, I advised him, "Les, if you are superman and you can go and attend those European meetings, and at the same time you can guide the production of our board papers properly and talk cogently at the board meetings, I'm not against you making those trips. But otherwise, please listen to my advice and don't go. Send someone instead." Leslie is a lovely human being, someone with whom it is very difficult to get angry. But he did not heed my advice.

At one particular board meeting, Les turned up and the board papers had obviously been hastily put together. I tried to start the meeting by confirming the minutes of the last meeting but Saffian interjected, "Before we start, I want to make some statements about our Managing Director." Then he attacked Les aggressively and became quite personal.

I interjected and said, "Can't we take this up under 'Any other matters,' at the end of the meeting, because we have business today and I'm trying to get through item one on the agenda, confirmation of minutes."

Saffian was adamant and his language became acrimonious. I said, "I must ask you to stop making personal remarks and attacks. You are talking about our Managing Director, the Chief Executive, and you must support your allegations with proof. It is very unfair." Mind you, I was one of Les Eu's strongest critics, but, for the sake of the firm, I felt I had to defend him against this surprise attack at the board meeting.

Saffian continued in the same manner. So I said, "I ask you to stop this nonsense. Alternatively, if you wish to pass a motion later on to sack the Managing Director, you can raise it. I'm not against that. But you are holding up the meeting." Saffian insisted that he wasn't suggesting that we get rid of the Managing Director. I demanded, "Then what are you saying?" He got up and we almost came to blows – tempers were so frayed.

I thought to myself: "My God, what is going to be the future of this company?" From then on, I realized how impossible it would be for me to run such a corporation. I felt that in future it would be very difficult to operate this business properly, as for a business to succeed there must always be unity and harmony.

It was likely that some people in the government thought that it was shameful for Chinese Malaysians to run the national shipping line. When I sensed that this was their attitude, it was time for me to call it a day. Kuok Brothers eventually sold all their MISC shares and pulled out of the national shipping company completely.

In the early 1970s, the Kuok Group started its own shipping company, Pacific Carriers, in Singapore. By then I was a semi-expert on shipping. Any business can be learned through hard work, honesty and adherence to basic principles. There are qualified technical people for hire in the world. You can easily employ captains, ship engineers and architects. But most important are your businessmen.

During Pacific Carriers' infancy, we carried mainly our own cargo. Bogasari was already very big, with a ravenous appetite for imported wheat; MSM, the sugar refinery, melted 1,600 tons of raw sugar a day and was steadily expanding its capacity. Our internal demand alone required the chartering of more than 250 vessels a year, including some time charters. I also saw in shipping the potential for a new line of business, another ball to toss, because shipping is a major world industry.

Shipping, of necessity, becomes global once you buy bigger ships. The minute you go into 20,000-ton vessels and upward, you can sail the Pacific, the Atlantic and around the Cape of Good Hope. In the past 20-odd years, we have carried ore, bulk and oil – whatever freight generates a good profit.

Around the time as we were launching MISC, one more job landed in my lap, this time initiated by the Singapore Government. Dr Goh Keng Swee, Singapore's Deputy Prime Minister, asked if I would serve as Chairman of Malaysia-Singapore Airlines (MSA). The Malaysian Government had proposed Dr Lim Swee Aun, the former Minister of Commerce and Industry, who had failed to get re-elected in the elections of May 1969.

"We do not like him," said Keng Swee.

"But he's not a bad fellow," I replied.

"Oh, never!" thundered Keng Swee.

I said, "No, no. I'm overworked and underpaid by my own company." I was joking, though it was true that I hardly had a moment's rest in those days. I told him I couldn't take the job, because I didn't have the time to do it justice and didn't know the airline business. I don't think anybody had talked to Singapore Government leaders like that. They were already known to be very fierce.

As I walked towards the door, Keng Swee said, "Well, you know there are hardly any links left between Malaysia and Singapore. If you don't want to serve, then this link will also go."

It was just like a scene in a Hollywood film. Two steps from the door, I wheeled around and asked, "Are you telling me that if I take the job, that link will be preserved?"

"Yes."

Again, I felt I had no choice. "If I agree to take the job, what do I need to do?"

"Simple things. First, go to see Tunku Abdul Rahman and Tun Razak and tell them we gave you an indication that you're acceptable to us."

"You mean I have to sell myself to my own leaders?"

When he replied in the affirmative, I said, "Give me time to think about it. This is getting very sticky."

So I went away and called up Mother. I explained the situation to her. She said, "Well, if you can help preserve the link, then do it, but for one term only." We belonged to a generation when Malaya and Singapore was one homogenous territory, and felt very strongly that ties should be preserved. So I called Keng Swee and told him that, subject to securing approval in Malaysia, I was prepared to accept the MSA chairmanship for one three-year term. A day or two later I made appointments in Kuala Lumpur and went up.

Relations between Singapore and Malaysia have always been uneasy. I saw signs even during my Raffles College days. Nine out of every ten students from Singapore could be called city-slickers. They were keen to know who your parents and grandparents were, and whether they were rich. By and large, those students who came from Malaya had rural backgrounds. They were usually very charming and uninterested in your wealth or status in life. They were at college just to study and to make friends. Those of us Chinese from Johor had learned to live much more comfortably with Malays. There was far more give and take.

Now relations between Singapore and Malaysia were strained. Singapore felt that I could play a diplomatic role; they knew that I was well connected with the Malaysian Government. I was in Raffles College when Razak was there. In fact, I think two-thirds or three-quarters of the top civil servants in Malaysia had been at Raffles College when I was there; many of the others were in school with me in Johor Bahru.

I first went to see my very close friend Tun Dr Ismail in Kuala Lumpur. He said, "Robert, if you've decided to take it on, take it on, but I don't know whether you can push it through with Tunku." Then Tun Razak called up the Tunku and made an appointment for me the following morning.

I went to Tunku's house at 9 am and was kept waiting for about half an hour. He was a late starter. Then Tunku emerged – it was a big, rambling house – and entered the living room where I was waiting. "Ah, Kuok, Kuok. I know you. Your brother (Philip) is one of our ambassadors."

I said, "Yes, Sir."

"What's this about?" he asked. "You want to become Chairman of MSA?"

I responded, "It's not that I want to, Tunku…"

He didn't sound too enthusiastic about my taking on this role. He made some remarks about the problems he was having with Singapore. I kept quiet, since it was not for me to say anything. Then I prodded him a bit.

"Sir, do you mind if we come back to the subject?"

In the end, he said, "Okay, Kuok. If you want the job, take it. It doesn't matter to me."

So I accepted the position of Chairman of MSA. The board of 15 directors comprised one Chairman, four directors nominated by the Malaysian Government, another four by the Singapore Government, one director from Straits Steamship (then a British shipping company controlled by Blue Funnel Group), two directors each from British Airways and Qantas Airways and the Managing Director, who was on loan from British Airways. So there were six white men, eight Malaysians and Singaporeans, and myself, a Malaysian.

You couldn't have had worse bickering than between the Singapore and Malaysian Government-nominated directors. If one side raised a point and asked for a resolution to be passed, the other side would object. Each side tried to peel off the skin to see what hidden agenda existed under that resolution. The meetings would start at 9:30 am, and quite often I couldn't wind them up until 7:30 pm, this at a time when I was in the thick of my sugar business. I was fortunate that my health held up.

I was not just Chairman of the Board. I constantly had to make peace between the directors from the two governments. I tried every fair and reasonable device I could think of. The evening before a board meeting, I would host a dinner for just the eight government directors and the company secretary. During dinner I would work on them to make peace. "Tomorrow, these are the thorny items on the agenda," I would explain. "Please try to understand both sides." Sometimes, I would obtain a semblance of agreement, only to have bickering erupt at the board meeting the following day. The articles of incorporation granted each of the eight a veto, so I was running a company with eight vetoes. It was horrendous! But I stuck with it for nearly two years.

I should mention that some of the conflicts I had were with one Western director in particular. When I was Chairman, the Managing Director and CEO was David Craig, who came from British Airways. I had acrimonious exchanges with him. He tried very hard to ingratiate himself into the good books of the Malaysian directors, since the Singapore directors were very rigid and severe managers. Whenever David wasn't performing, they were severe, and so he ran to the Malaysian side for protection. He found the Malaysian directors by and large convenient pillars behind which he could hide. I tried to haul him out from hiding, and our relationship soured.

One day, I was in the MSA office on Robinson Road in Singapore, which was a much grander office space than my own humble sugar-trading cubbyhole. David spoke to me about engaging expensive European expatriates for the airline. I asked what was wrong with engaging pilots from Burma, which at that time, under the military regime of Ne Win, was training pilots and sending some of them to aeronautical schools in England. He retorted, "Oh, no, no. Only British pilots are safe."

I pointed out that some of our commanders here were Chinese from the Malay Peninsula. He responded that there were too few. Then I suggested he try Indonesia, since Garuda was a relatively seasoned airline. He responded, "Ah, these guys land their planes in the ocean and in jungles and kill all their passengers."

I rounded on him: "Aren't you being racist?" I noted that a Qantas or British Airways plane piloted by whites had crashed in Singapore's Kallang Basin Airport. We had a very rough exchange. He had his agenda. When I took the job, I had no agenda whatsoever. I just wanted harmony between Malaysia and Singapore.

Meanwhile, the Singapore Government, which was very good with its abacus, was analysing the economics of the airline industry. They began to realize that the Malaysian domestic routes were profit-making, but looking into the future, they could not see such air travel as big-scale business. The international airport in Singapore, and the international traffic, was really the jewel in the crown of the airline industry in the Malaysia/Singapore region. So the Singapore Government felt it would be useful to break Malaysia-Singapore Airlines into two and let each country go its own way.

The Board meetings grew increasingly acrimonious. I made an appointment to see Goh Keng Swee to appeal to him to hold back his aggressive Singapore directors. I hinted that the game was getting very one-sided. I was acting as referee, but I was seeing the poor Malaysian directors slaughtered at every meeting because the Singapore directors had minds as sharp as razors. In fairness, I must say the contribution to running the airline properly and efficiently came almost entirely from the Singapore side. The Malaysian side was too subjective and often allowed their feelings to influence their comments.

The writing was on the wall: the airline would separate. Now, I'm sort of a bulldog. When I want to do something, I am very tenacious. But serving as Chairman of MSA was a thankless task and I was working like a slave, virtually day and night, in addition to juggling all my other balls. Moreover, I had been under the impression that this link between the two countries would be preserved. Now that the decision to split was imminent, I decided to pen a resignation letter that they could not refuse. But how do you write two lines of English words which say just that and nothing more? It took me two days to come up with those two lines. Then there was silence for three or four months.

The Minister of Finance of Singapore then was Hon Sui Sen, one of the finest men to serve as a cabinet minister from the creation of the island state of Singapore to this day. Born in Penang, he graduated in science from Raffles College about two years before I entered the school.

Then came one of the nicest letters I have received in my life. It was penned by Hon Sui Sen himself, and said words to this effect: "I apologize for taking so long to reply. The reason it took so long was we could not find the right successor. This in itself is a compliment to you and what you have done for all of us. Following considerable discussion between the two governments, we have finally come up with a formula of one Chairman from each side to co-chair the board."

They could not have asked for a more classic mongoose and cobra arrangement. The individuals they picked fought each other tooth and nail. When I stepped off, I stepped off completely. I even shut my mind to the whole matter. The Malaysian Government chose Tun Ismail Ali, then Central Bank Governor. The Singapore side picked Joe Pillay, who had been a Singapore director of MSA from the day that I joined the board.

In one sense, you could say Joe Pillay gave me the most trouble. In another sense, you could say he was the single most efficient director on the board. I admired his tremendous intellect, an intellect that had no superior in the Singapore/Malaysia region. His grasp of economics and cost accounting was fantastic. I learned from him, watching the way he worked at his job.

But he was rather highly strung. Joe is a lovely human being and a gentleman, but when it came to protecting his nation's interest and discharging his job, he could come out unnecessarily aggressive.

I remember one unpleasant exchange between Basil Bampfield, a British Airways-appointed director, and Joe Pillay at a board meeting. Joe told Basil that he should go back to British Airways and Qantas and tell them that some of the existing arrangements were unfair, and that the two airlines should make concessions to MSA.

At the next meeting, Basil reported that, on behalf of British Airways and Qantas, he was authorized to agree to every request made at the preceding meeting. I said, "This is amazingly good news. May I on behalf of all of us make a motion to express our thanks to them?"

Joe Pillay interrupted, "No! It is ours by right and we should have gotten it long ago."

I appealed to Joe. Why cry over the past, I thought. Basil Bampfield was a fine English gentleman in an invidious job. He must have gone back and argued MSA's case forcefully.

What the two co-chairmen presided over was like a funeral. To dismantle and separate the whole company was like performing surgery on Siamese twins. It took them a long time to carry out the operation.

14

MALAYSIAN CROSSROADS

I WAS IN SINGAPORE on the morning of 13 May 1969. Weeks earlier, I had called a meeting of Malayan Sugar Manufacturing Co in Kuala Lumpur for 14 May. Elections had just been held in Malaysia and tension was very high throughout the length and breadth of the country. I had planned to fly to Kuala Lumpur and spend the night there for the meeting the next morning.

On the afternoon of 12 May, I had a phone call from Jacob Ballas. Ballas knew that I was planning to travel to Kuala Lumpur. "Robert," he pleaded, "Cancel your trip! Racial tensions are about to overflow, and rioting is likely. Please cancel. I appeal to you." I cancelled.

I was in my Singapore office on 13 May when I had a late morning call from Ismail Ali, Governor of the Malaysian Central Bank in Kuala Lumpur. Ismail was a dear friend of mine. His voice was agitated. "Robert, do you know what's going on up here?"

"I am not up to date, Ismail."

"Siew Sin is threatening to resign. Robert, if Siew Sin resigns, that means the Malayan Chinese Association (MCA) will be out of the government and there may be bloodshed. We've got to try and prevent it. I think you and I are the only two people who can persuade him to change his mind. Can you get on the first plane and rush up here? I need your support. I think our combined voices might just do the trick."

I said, "Okay Ismail. I'll come up."

I had a house in Kuala Lumpur, so I called my secretary and told her to get me on the next flight. I arrived at about 5 pm and four of my managers met me at the airport, which was unusual. Normally, only the driver met me or sent me off. From my very early days of setting up in business, I had told all my managers, "Don't ever send off anybody or receive anybody. You are hired to work and to make money, not to squander your time seeing off and receiving your boss or colleagues." So I wondered why four managers had appeared. One of them was Malay and three were Chinese. They were carefully surveying the surroundings. "We fear there will be rioting. We felt that it would only be safe for you if we all came out."

We separated into three cars. I rode with my brother-in-law, Leslie Cheah. I told him to drop me at Ismail's house, which was on Jalan Natesa (now Jalan Tunku Putra), up on a hill. The convoy escorted me to the foot of the hill; Leslie jumped out of my car and headed home in one of the two other cars. I drove up to Ismail's house and got out. It was almost 6 pm and beginning to get dark.

Ismail and his wife were waiting at the front door. His face was gloomy. He managed to summon a little smile and say, "Hello, Robert. Glad you came." As soon as we shook hands he said, "But too late, Robert. Siew Sin has already resigned." He beckoned me upstairs to a large family room to watch the news on television.

As we chatted, the phone rang. By then it was about 6:30. Ismail said, "Yes, yes, yes," then put down the receiver. "That was the Inspector-General of Police," he said. "A curfew will begin at 7 pm. Rioting has started along Jalan Ampang and there are already some deaths."

Ismail continued, "Robert, it is unsafe for you to go into town. Please spend the night here."

I answered, "No, Ismail. My driver is Malay; I am Chinese and my servant at home is Chinese. It is better that I go home. If we are met by Chinese rioters, I'll try to protect my Malay driver; if we are met by Malays, hopefully he will protect me." These were words of bravado, because the rioting grew very ugly.

We avoided Jalan Ampang, and turned right onto a smaller road. By then, the curfew had begun. Buildings were shuttered. I arrived home safely and went in to have a quick bath. Then I heard the servant shout, "There are fires everywhere!"

I had a small compound, but I walked out onto a side street. My neighbour was Hew Kiang Ming, an accountant who, by coincidence, had also been my neighbour in Raffles College, where he was a year ahead of me. He said, "Hock Nien, you are not supposed to be out in this curfew."

I said, "Then what are you doing out here?"

We laughed.

About a kilometre away in one direction, you could see flames licking up and palls of black smoke above the buildings. We could see another fire and black smoke about three kilometres away in another direction. Afterwards, the government announced that 800-1000 had died in the riots. The Chinese claimed 2,000-3,000 died, predominantly Chinese, many hacked to death.

Simple, law-abiding Malays in the rural villages were stirred up into a frenzy of animosity and anger. They brought out their parangs – crude machetes used to chop firewood or tree trunks. Groups of men drove into Kuala Lumpur from the kampongs. They descended on any Chinese they saw, and sometimes Indians as well. Law and order broke down completely.

Some of the rising politicians of pre-Independence Malaya were my father's good friends when he was alive. The Malay politicians of the Independence generation – men like Tunku Abdul Rahman,

Tun Razak and Tun Dr Ismail – were fine people. They loved and cared deeply for their country and their people.

My closest friend among them was Tun Dr Ismail, a Melbourne-trained medical doctor who became a leader in the struggle for independence from the British. Ismail was always in the forefront of the political ferment. Of the Malay leaders of the time, he was number three after Tunku and Razak – Minister of the Interior, responsible for the police and intelligence.

I was often asked to give substantial donations to the ruling parties, UMNO and MCA, after independence in 1957. I gave willingly, happily and freely.

Malaysia has had six Prime Ministers since independence. I have known all six. The first, Tunku Abdul Rahman, had tremendous rhythm. He was a well-educated man, having graduated with a law degree from Cambridge. If you talk of brains, Tunku was brilliant, and very shrewd. His mother was Thai, and he had that touch of Thai shrewdness, an ability to smell and spot whether a man was to be trusted or not.

Tunku was less mindful about administrative affairs. But he had a good number two in Tun Razak, who was extremely industrious, and Tunku left most of the paperwork to Razak. Tunku was like a strategist who saw the big picture. He knew where to move his troops, but actually going to battle and plotting the detailed campaign – that was not Tunku. He'd say, "Razak, you take over. You handle it now." In that sense, they worked very well together.

In my meetings with Tunku, he demonstrated some blind spots. He had a bee in his bonnet about communism. One day, when we had become quite close, he said to me, "Communists! In Islam, we regard them as devils! And Communist China, you cannot deal with them, otherwise you are dealing with the devil!" And he went on and on about communists, communism and Communist China.

I responded, "Tunku, China only became communist because of the immense suffering of the people as a result of oppression and invasion. I think it's a passing phase."

He interjected, "Oh, don't you believe it! The Chinese are consorting with the devil. Their people are finished! You don't know how lucky you Chinese are to be in Malaysia."

I replied softly, "Tunku, as Prime Minister of Malaysia, you should make friends with them."

Years later, when Tunku was out of office, he was invited to China. Zhao Ziyang, then Premier, entertained him in the Great Hall of the People in Beijing. Tunku travelled with a delegation of 15 Chinese businessmen who were good friends of his.

On his way to China, Tunku stopped in Hong Kong and I gave them dinner. Then on his way out of China, he stopped in Hong Kong and we dined again. I asked him for his impressions. All of his old prejudices had vanished! He didn't even want to refer to them. He just said the trip had been an eye-opener. "They are decent people, like you and me," he said. "We could talk about anything." From then onward, you never heard Tunku claim that the Chinese Communists were the devils incarnate.

One thing I will say for Tunku: he had friends. His friends sometimes helped him, or they sent him a case of champagne or slabs of specially imported steak. He loved to grill steaks on his lawn and open champagne, wine or spirits. His favourite cognac was Hennessy VSOP.

Tunku would also do favours for his friends, but he never adopted cronies. When Tun Tan Siew Sin was Finance Minister, Tunku sent him a letter about a Penang businessman who was one of Tunku's poker-playing buddies. It seems the man had run into tax trouble and was being investigated by the tax department, and he had turned to Tunku for help.

In his letter, Tunku wrote, "You know so-and-so is my friend. I am not asking any favour of you, Siew Sin, but I am sure you can see your way to forgiving him," or something to that effect. Siew Sin was apoplectic. He stalked into Tun Dr Ismail's office upstairs and threw the letter down. "See what our Prime Minister is doing to me!"

Tun Dr Ismail read the letter and laughed. "Siew Sin," he said, "there is a comic side to life." Ismail took the letter, crumpled it into a ball and threw it into the wastepaper basket. He then said, "Siew Sin, Tunku has done his duty by his friend. Now, by ignoring Tunku, you will continue to do your duty properly." That was as far as Tunku would go to help a friend.

Cronyism is different. Cronies are lapdogs who polish a leader's ego. In return, the leader hands out national favours to them. A nation's assets, projects and businesses should never be for anyone to hand out, neither for a king nor a prime minister. A true leader is the chief trustee of a nation. If there is a lack of an established system to guide him, his fiduciary sense should set him on the proper course.

A leader who practices cronyism justifies his actions by saying he wants to bring up the nation quickly in his lifetime, so the end justifies the means. He abandons all the General Orders – the civil-service work manual that lays down tendering rules for state projects. Instead, he simply hands the projects to a Chinese or to a Malay crony. The arms of government-owned banks are twisted until they lend to the projects. Some of these cronies may even be fronting for crooked officials.

Tunku was unnerved by the riots of 13 May. After the riots he was a different man. Razak managed to convince him and the cabinet to form the National Operations Council, a dictatorial organ of government, and Razak was appointed its Director. Parliament went into deep freeze. By the time the NOC was disbanded, Razak had been installed as Prime Minister.

Tunku felt bewildered. He had helped the country gain independence and had ruled as wisely as he could, yet the Malays turned against him for selling out to the Chinese. In fairness to Tunku, he had done nothing of the sort. He was a very fair man who loved the nation and its people. But he knew that, if you favour one group, you only spoil them.

When the British ruled Malaya, they extended certain advantages to the Malays. When the Malays took power following independence on 31 August 1957, more incentives were given to them. But there was certainly no showering of favours. All of that came later, after 1969.

The riots of 13 May 1969 were a great shock to the system, but not a surprise. Extremist Malays attributed the poverty of many Malays to the plundering Chinese and Indians. Leaders like Tunku Abdul Rahman, who could see both sides, were no longer able to hold back the hotheads. The more thoughtful leaders were shunted aside and the extremists hijacked power. They chanted the same slogans as the hotheads – the Malays are underprivileged; the Malays are bullied – while themselves seeking to become super-rich. When these Malays became rich, not many of them did anything for the poor Malays; the Chinese and Indians who became rich created jobs, many of them filled by Malays.

I vividly recall an incident that occurred within a few months after the May 1969 riots. I was waiting to see Tun Razak when a senior Malay civil servant whom I knew very well came along the corridor of Parliament House and buttonholed me. He asked, "What are you doing here, Robert?"

I replied, "Oh, I'm seeing Tun."

He snarled, "Don't be greedy! Leave something for us poor

Malays! Don't hog it all!"

I could see that, after May 1969, the business playing field was changing. Business was no longer clean and open. Previously, the government announced open tenders to the Malaysian public and to the world. If we qualified, we would submit a tender. If we won the contract, we would work hard at it, and either fail or succeed. I think eight or nine times out of ten we succeeded. But things were changing, veering more and more towards cronyism and favouritism.

Hints of change were there even before the riots. I was hell-bent on helping to develop the nation: that's why I went into shipping, into steel – anything they asked of me. Even amongst the Malays there were those who admitted their weaknesses and argued for harnessing the strength of the Chinese. Mind you, that may have created more problems. If they had harnessed the strength of the Chinese, the Chinese would ultimately have owned 90 or 95 percent of the nation's wealth. This might have been good for the Malaysian economy, but bad for the nation.

Overall, the Malay leaders have behaved reasonably in running the country. At times, they gave the Malays an advantage. Then, when they see that they have overdone it, they try to redress the problem. Their hearts are in the right place, but they just cannot see their way out of their problems.

Since 13 May 1969, the Malay leadership has had one simple philosophy: the Malays need handicapping. Now, what amount of handicapping? The Government laid down a simple structure, but the structure is full of loopholes.

Imagine that a hard-working, non-Malay Malaysian establishes XYZ Corporation. The Ministry of Trade and Industry rules that 30 percent of the company's shares must be offered to Malays. The owner says, "Well, I have been operating for six years. My par value of MYR1 per share is today worth MYR8."

Then the Ministry says, "Can you issue it at MYR2 or MYR2.50 to the Malays?" After a bit of haggling, the non-Malay gives way.

So shares are issued to the Malays, who now own 30 percent. But every day after that, the Malays sell off their shares for profit. A number of years pass and then one day the Malay community holds a Bumiputra Congress. They go and check on all the companies. Oh, this XYZ Corporation, the Malay shareholding ratio is now down to seven percent. That won't do. So the Malays argue that they've got to redo the shareholding again. Fortunately, the Ministry usually acts as a fair umpire and throws out such unscrupulous claims.

It's one thing if you change the rules once to achieve an objective agreed to by all for the sake of peace and order in the nation. But if you do it a second time, it's robbery. Why is it not robbery just because the government commits it? And when people raise objections, it is called fomenting racial strife, punishable by three years in jail.

As a Chinese who was born and grew up in Malaysia and went to school with the Malays, I was saddened to see the Malays being misled in this way. I felt that, in their haste to bridge the economic gap between the Chinese and the Malays, harmful shortcuts were being taken. One of the side effects of their zeal to bridge the economic gap was that racism became increasingly ugly.

I saw very clearly that the path being pursued by the new leaders after 1969 was dangerous. But hardly anyone was willing to listen to me. In most of Asia, where the societies are still quite hierarchical, very few people like to gainsay the man in charge. As in The Emperor's New Clothes, if a ruler says, "Look at my clothes; aren't they beautiful?" when he is in fact naked, everybody will answer, "Yes, yes sir, you are wearing the most beautiful clothes."

I made one – and only one – strong attempt to influence the course of history of Malaysia. This took place in September 1975 during the Muslim fasting month. Tun Razak, the second Prime Minister of Malaysia, was gravely ill with terminal leukaemia, for which he was receiving treatment in a London hospital.

My dear friend Hussein Onn, son of Dato Onn bin Jafar, was Deputy Prime Minister, Minister of Finance and acting Prime Minister in Tun Razak's absence. He was soon to become Malaysia's third Prime Minister. I went to Kuala Lumpur and sent word that I wanted to have a heart-to-heart talk. On the phone Hussein said, "Why don't you come in during lunch time. It is the fasting month. Come to my office at about half past one. There will be no one around and we can chat to our heart's content."

Hussein and I go back to 1932 when we were in the same class in school in Johor Bahru. Shortly afterwards, his father fell out with the then-Sultan of Johor and the family moved to the Siglap area of Singapore. My father would often spend weekends with Dato Onn. Two or three years later, Hussein returned to Johor Bahru and we were classmates again at English College from 1935 to 1939.

Hussein's father, Dato Onn, did not have a tertiary education. But he read widely and was very well informed. He was a natural-born politician, a gifted orator in Malay and in English. He was a very shrewd man with a tremendous air of fine breeding even though he was not from Malaysian royalty. When you were in his presence, you knew you were in the presence of someone great.

Dato Onn would go on to found UMNO, the ruling party of Malaysia, and become one of the founders of the independent nation of Malaysia. He set a tone of racial harmony for the nation – and he practiced it. Our families were close.

So, I went to call on his son, my old friend Hussein Onn in 1975. His office was in a magnificent old colonial building, part of the Selangor Secretariat Building. In front of it was the Kuala Lumpur *padang*, where, in the colonial days, the British used to play the gentlemen's games of cricket and rugby.

I climbed up a winding staircase and his aide showed me straight to his room. There was hardly another soul in that huge office complex. After greeting one another, I warmed up to my subject with Hussein very quickly. I said, "Hussein, I have come to discuss two things with you. One is Tun Razak's health. The other is the future of our nation."

I said, "You know, Razak has been looking very poorly lately. We all know he has gone to London for treatment."

Hussein interrupted: "Tun doesn't like anybody discussing his health. Do you mind if we pass on to the next subject?"

I said, "Of course not." I continued, "I had to raise the first subject because that leads to the next subject. Assuming Razak doesn't have long to live – please don't mind, but I have to say that – you are clearly going to become the new Prime Minister in a matter of months or weeks."

"I'm listening," he said.

"Hussein, we go back a long way. Our fathers were the best of friends; our families have been the best of friends. In our young days, you and I always felt a strong passion for our country, which we both still feel. Whatever has happened these past years, let's not go backwards and ask what has gone wrong and what has not been done right. Let's look at the future. If there was damage done, we can repair it."

Hussein listened patiently.

I pressed on, "First, let me ask you a few questions, Hussein. What, in your mind, is the number of people required to run a society, a community, a nation with the land mass of Malaysia?" This was 1975, when the population was about 12.5 million.

He didn't reply. For the sake of time, I answered my own question. "Hussein, if I say 3,000, if I say 6,000, if I say 10,000, 20,000, whatever the figure, I don't think it really matters. We are not talking in terms of hundreds of thousands or millions. To run a society or a nation requires, relatively speaking, a handful of people. So let us say six or seven or eight thousand, Hussein. And of course this covers two sectors. The public sector: government, civil service, governmental organizations, quasi-governmental bodies, executive arms, police, customs and military. The private sector: the economic engines; the engines of development, plantations, mines, industry.

"The leaders of these two sectors are the people I am referring to, Hussein. If we are talking of a few thousand, does it matter to the masses whether it becomes a case of racially proportionate representation, where we must have for every ten such leaders five or six Malays, three Chinese, and one or two Indians?"

I continued, "Must it be so? My reasoning mind tells me that it is not important. What is important is the objective of building up a very strong, very modern nation. And for that we need talented leaders, great leadership from these thousands of people. If you share my view that racial representation is unimportant and unnecessary to the nation, then let's look at defining the qualifications for those leaders.

"Number one, for every man or woman, the first qualification is integrity. The person must be so clean, upright and honest that there must never be a whiff of corruption or scandal. People do stray, and, when that happens, they must be eliminated, but on the day of selection they must be people of the highest integrity. Second, there must be ability; and with it comes capability. He or she must be a very able and capable person. The third criterion is that they must be hard-working men or women, people who are willing to work long hours every day, week after week, month after month, year after year. That's the only way you can build up a nation."

I went on, "I can't think of any other important qualifications. So your job as Prime Minister, Hussein – I am now assuming you will become the Prime Minister – your job will then be from time to time to remove the square pegs from the round holes, and to look for square holes for square pegs and round holes for round pegs. Even candidates who fulfil those three qualifications can be slotted into the wrong jobs. So you've got to pull them out and re-slot them until the nation is humming beautifully."

"We do not have all the expertise required to build up the nation," I added. "But with hard work and a goal of developing the nation, we can afford to employ the best people in the world. The best brains will come, in all shades and colours, all religions, all faiths. They may be the whitest of the white, the brownest of the brown or the blackest of the black. I am sure it doesn't matter. But Hussein, the foreigners must never settle in the driving seats. The days of colonialism are over. They were in the driving seats and they drove our country helter-skelter. We Malaysians must remain in the driving seats and the foreign experts will sit next to us. If they say, 'Sir, Madame, I think we should turn right at the next turning,' it's up to us to heed their advice, or to do something else. We are running the show, but we need expertise.

"You're going to be the leader of a nation, and you have three sons, Hussein. The first-born is Malay, the second-born is Chinese, the third-born is Indian. What we have been witnessing is that the first-born is more favoured than the second or third. Hussein, if you do that in a family, your eldest son will grow up very spoiled. As soon as he attains manhood, he will be in the nightclubs every night because Papa is doting on him. The second and third sons, feeling the discrimination, will grow up hard as nails. Year by year, they will become harder and harder, like steel, so that in the end they are going to succeed even more and the eldest will fail even more."

I implored him, "Please, Hussein, use the best brains, the people with their hearts in the right place, Malaysians of total integrity and strong ability, hard-working and persevering people. Use them regardless of race, colour or creed. The other way, Hussein, the way your people are going – excessive handicapping of bumiputras, showering love on your first son – your first born is going to grow up with an attitude of entitlement."

I concluded, "That is my simple formula for the future of our country. Hussein, can you please adopt it and try?"

Hussein had listened very intently to me, hardly interrupting. He may have coughed once or twice. I remember we were seated deep in a quiet room, two metres apart, so my voice came across well. He heard every word, sound and nuance. He sat quietly for a few minutes. Then he spoke, "No, Robert. I cannot do it. The Malays are now in a state of mind such that they will not accept it."

He clearly spelled out to me that, even with his very broadminded views, it was going to be Malay rule. He was saying that he could not sell my formula to his people. The meeting ended on a very cordial note and I left him.

I felt disappointed, but there was nothing more that I could do. Hussein was an honest man of very high integrity. Before going to see him, I had weighed his strength of character, his shrewdness and skill. We had been in the same class, sharing the same teachers. I knew Hussein was going to be the Malaysian Prime Minister whom I was closest to in my lifetime.

I think Hussein understood my message, but he knew that the process had gone too far. I had seen a picture developing all along of a train moving in the wrong direction. During Hussein's administration, he was only partially successful in stemming the tide. The train of the nation had been put on the wrong track.

Hussein wasn't strong enough to lift up the train and set it down on the right track.

The capitalist world is a very hostile world. When I was building up the Kuok Group, I felt as if I was almost growing scales, talons and sharp fangs. I felt I was capable of taking on any adversary. Capitalism is a ruthless animal. For every successful businessman, there are at least 10,000 bleached skeletons of those who have failed. It's a very sad commentary on capitalism, but that is capitalism and real capitalism, not crony capitalism.

Yet, I've always believed that the rules of capitalism, if properly observed, are the way forward in life. I know that, having been successful, I will be accused of having an 'alright Jack' mentality. But I am just stating facts: capitalism is a wonderful creature – just don't abuse its principles and unwritten laws.

15

BETWEEN KUALA LUMPUR
AND BEIJING

I THINK IT IS FAIR TO SAY that Malaysia regards me as the Malaysian with the best contacts in China. Because of my connections on both sides, I was called upon several times to act as a conduit between the two governments. This led to the ironic role I played in the virtual demise of the Malayan Communist Party; ironic, given that my late brother William had been a senior figure in the MCP. But before I narrate this cloak-and-dagger experience, let me digress to relate how I kept getting dragged into Malaysian politics, even after I had relocated to Hong Kong.

In 1986, I was approached by the Chinese-Malaysian political leadership to post bail for Tan Koon Swan, Chairman of the Malayan Chinese Association (MCA), Malaysia's second political party after Mahathir's ruling United Malays National Organization (UMNO). Tan had fallen afoul of Singapore laws and had been accused of financial crimes. The Singapore judge set bail at MYR 20 million, which was an unheard-of figure at the time.

I was in Kuala Lumpur. My car phone didn't stop ringing. The MCA leadership pleaded with me, "You are the only man who can save our face. We are not judging Singapore's actions, but we cannot bear to see our President go to remand prison. We just want him out on bail. Please, can you stand bail?"

I was in an invidious position. I am a Malaysian; he was accused in Singapore. I said, "Wait, I'll call you back as soon as I can."

From Kuala Lumpur I immediately called Mother for advice, as I so often did. I explained the situation and asked whether I should come forward and stand bail.

Mother asked, "What is your inclination?"

"I'm inclined to help him." I replied. "It's not a matter of the man, but rather for the sake of the political party." MCA was part of the Alliance government.

Mother said, "I agree with you. For political reasons you should stand bail."

So I went forward. I asked for special treatment from the Singapore Government, allowing me to enter court through a side door because there was a media mob on the front steps. After several months free on bail, Tan Koon Swan was convicted and went to jail. When he was released, his first act was to proceed to Johor Bahru to thank Mother.

I was also called in when the MCA was facing financial collapse several years later. The original leader of the MCA movement during the independence era was Tun Tan Cheng Lock, and later the leadership passed to his son, Tan Siew Sin. I got to know Siew Sin when he was serving in government – he was the Minister who had erected roadblocks when I applied for the license for Malayan Sugar Manufacturing.

Tan Siew Sin used to approach me for political donations. He wore two political caps: President of the Malayan Chinese Association, his political party, and treasurer of the Alliance, which included UMNO, MCA and the Malaysian Indian Congress. I contributed funds to the Alliance as well as to MCA, especially when it came to election time.

In the latter part of the 1980s, the MCA leader, Datuk Sri Ling Liong Sik, who is, like me, of Fuzhou descent, came to see me in Hong Kong. He needed urgent help to rescue Multi-Purpose Bhd, which the MCA had set up many years earlier. Poor management had felled the company, which was publicly traded. One of its main holdings was Magnum Corp, a legal gambling syndicate. Another large subsidiary was Bandar Raya, a large property development company; Dunlop Estates was another. In all, there were about half a dozen companies under Multi-Purpose. I took over the chairmanship and, with the help of my Kuok Group colleagues Oh Bak Kim and Ong Ie Chong, we managed to turn it around. In my lifetime I have been given the job of cleaning up three highly controversial projects: Malayawata, the Japanese-invested integrated steel mill; the short-lived Malaysia-Singapore Airlines, and Multi-Purpose Holdings.

My role as an intermediary between the Malaysian and Chinese governments also played out in the 1980s. Tan Sri Abdul Rahim Noor, then Director of Malaysian Special Branch, contacted me first. My contact on the Chinese side, to whom I passed messages, was Zhong *Pak* – Uncle Zhong – an elderly gentleman. I later learned that he had been a respected member of the National Security Ministry, China's equivalent of the CIA.

The Special Branch of the Malaysian Police contacted me often to say, "Can you pass this message to China?" They asked China to silence the MCP radio, which was making broadcasts hostile to the Malaysian Government. I passed the word and the radio was silenced. The Special Branch sent a message of thanks for my intervention through my man in Kuala Lumpur, Datuk Lim Chee Wah.

After that, I carried a flurry of messages between Malaysian security and Uncle Zhong or his assistants. Malaysia wanted assurances, in writing, that China would stop supporting the MCP and Chin Peng, the Malayan Communist Party leader, who was then still active in the jungle. Rahim Noor one day said to me, "We have sent our emissaries to the jungles to talk with Chin Peng's people.

You have already given us some indication of China's attitude, that they are no longer supporting the MCP. This seems to be the case from what our agents are observing. But can we please get something in writing, stating to what extent China is withdrawing its support?"

I returned to Hong Kong and chatted with Zhong *Pak*. I conveyed Rahim Noor's exact words, nuance and all. One or two months after that, one of Zhong *Pak*'s assistants came to see me and said, "A date has been chosen for you to come to Guangzhou. One of us will accompany you, but we won't sit with you. We want you to come by train. You will be met, and we'll take you to meet our head. It's not convenient for him to come to Hong Kong. There is a draft message from a very senior State Leader. We want to consult with you about the message before we send it to the Malaysian Government."

So, on the appointed day, I left about noon and arrived in Guangzhou two hours later. A car met me, and the drive seemed like a James Bond scene. We drove and drove, turning far more corners than was necessary. They were trying to lose anybody who might be tailing us. We went off the main road onto a side road, and from the side road onto a still smaller road. As we turned, I could almost feel people immediately appearing behind us to place a barrier across the road, preventing any more cars from entering.

My car pulled up at a simple, ordinary house which was dimly lit inside. There was a table with chairs. They said, "Please sit down. We'll send word and our Number One will come to meet you within a few minutes."

I waited barely three or four minutes. One man came in first. He said, "Number One is only a few steps behind me." Within seconds, Number One entered. I had met the man before, but I couldn't place where. He had a nice, smiling face. He said, very warmly, "We don't want to keep you too long. We know you are a busy man."

We sat down. He started, "Following upon your various contacts with our people – and we thank you for having played this role so far – can we trouble you now to do one more thing? Here is a draft message. Please read it and give us your comments."

Luckily, by then, I was reading Chinese fairly well. The text was written over two or three pages. It wasn't addressed to anyone; it was just a position statement.

"It's a very good statement," I said. "It will go down well, with two exceptions."

They asked, "Where are the exceptions?"

I pondered for a moment and responded, "You should have stopped here. First you are talking pluses; then these extra few words are like cold water. These are all minus words."

They looked at one another and said, "Mr Kuok is right. If we are willing to stick our necks out and say those positive words, why are we then virtually nullifying the meaning with these other words? Where is the next one?"

I said, "This one is easier. You just have to delete these two or three words. Put a full stop here." Again they agreed.

"Unfortunately, we now have a problem," they said. "This letter has already been approved by a very senior State Leader. How do we get it changed?"

I asked, "Are you going to make me the agent to deliver it?"

They said yes.

I suggested: "One way, subject to your approval, is I will fax this, but before I do that I will obliterate those few words." If I faxed the document after whiting-out the negative words, it would look like the original. I showed them what I meant and they consented. So that is just what I did. The missive was delivered to Tan Sri Rahim

Noor and seemed to do the trick.

A few months later, the Malaysian Government and Chin Peng signed a truce agreement. His people came out of the jungle, symbolically laid down their arms, pledged allegiance to Malaysia and the Malayan Communist Party was no more.

16
OVERSEAS CHINESE

THE OVERSEAS CHINESE made enormous contributions to Southeast Asia. They are the unsung heroes of the region: the poor men and women who migrated and blazed trails into the jungle, accessing the timber wealth; Chinese workers who planted and tapped rubber, who opened up the tin mines, who ran the small retail shops. It was the Chinese immigrants who tackled these Herculean tasks, and created a new economy around them.

The British were good administrators. Many of them in private enterprise were absentee landlords, sitting in boardrooms or plush offices in London, Singapore or Kuala Lumpur. It was the Chinese who helped build up Southeast Asia. The Indians also played a big role, but the Chinese were the dominant force in helping to build the economy.

The transplanted Chinese were born entrepreneurs. The bulk of the Overseas Chinese in Southeast Asia have their roots in the coastal towns and villages of Fujian and Guangdong provinces – and these they have been blessed with some of the best entrepreneurial genes in the world. They came very hungry and eager as immigrants, often barefooted and wearing only singlets and trousers. They would do any work available, as an honest income meant they could have food and shelter. Chinese entrepreneurs are efficient and cost-conscious. When they search for foreign hardware and expertise, they know how to drive hard bargains. They work harder than anyone else and are willing to "eat bitterness", as the Chinese say. The Chinese are simply the most amazing economic ants on earth.

In the Ming Dynasty, the Chinese traded and explored around the South China Sea and the Indian Ocean. But, until the middle or latter part of the nineteenth century, the movement of people was only a trickle. Colonisation opened up Southeast Asia. The Europeans brought a semblance of law and order to the region and opened up rubber, mining and trading operations. Millions of Chinese, a tsunami of human migration, went south in search of better opportunities.

The majority of Overseas Chinese are moral and ethical people who practice fair play and possess a sense of proportion. I will concede that if they are totally penniless, they will do almost anything to get their first seed capital. But once they have some capital, they try very hard to rise above their past and advance their reputations as totally moral, ethical businessmen.

I have not come across any people as loyal as the Chinese. The Japanese have a kind of loyalty, but it's an uncritical, *bushido* type of loyalty: they are loyal even if the boss is a skunk. Unlike the Japanese, every Chinese is highly judgmental, from the most educated to the uneducated. In every Chinese village and community, moral values are drilled into each child during his or her family upbringing.

They are a very clueful people. They may have lived in a village or small town in China and come to Southeast Asia totally ignorant of the world, but they picked up ideas and strategies very quickly. If there is any business to be done on earth, you can be sure that the Chinese will be there. They will know whom to see, what to order, how best to save, how to make money. They don't need expensive equipment or the trappings of office; they just deliver.

If you look at the present generation of achievers in Hong

Kong – men like Li Ka-shing of Cheung Kong, Cheng Yu-tung of New World, Li Shau-kee of Henderson Land, the late Kwok Tak-seng of Sun Hung Kai Properties – they all came from the school of hard knocks. Not one of them went to college.

Since I was mainly brought up in the English-speaking world, I am almost an outside observer of the ways of China-born Chinese businessmen who are steeped in the Chinese language and culture. I can tell you that Chinese businessmen compare notes every waking moment of their lives. There are no true weekends or holidays for them. That's how they work. Every moment, they are listening, and they have skilfully developed in their own minds – each and every one of them – mental sieves to filter out rubbish and let through valuable information.

Good Chinese business management is second to none; the very best of Chinese management is without compare. I haven't seen others come near to it in my 70-year career. This doesn't mean to say that Chinese firms are the wealthiest or the biggest in the world. If you take companies such as GE, or businessmen like Bill Gates or Warren Buffett, their successes and wealth dwarf that of Chinese businesses. But Americans operate in the largest economy in the world, caressed by political and social stability, a strong legal system and generally sound institutions.

The Overseas Chinese in Southeast Asia operate in a much less benevolent environment. Moreover, they flourish without the national, political and financial sponsorship or backing of their host countries. In Southeast Asia, the Chinese are often maltreated and looked down upon. Whether you go to Malaysia, Sumatra or Java, the locals call you Cina – pronounced Chee-na – in a derogatory way.

Around the world, I have seen benevolent governments sponsor and even financially aid their nations' businessmen so that they can compete overseas. It's true in the US, Britain, France, Germany,

Japan, Korea and Taiwan. National banks come to their citizenry's aid; import-export banks subsidize their exports. In the commodity trade, the French and British governments and banks stand proudly behind their commodity brokers, who have lines of credit that I can only dream of. If the commodity traders' capital is US$20 million, they receive US$200 million of credit; while if we have US$20 million of paid-up capital, we can barely hope for credit of US$20 million. When I invested in Sucre et Denree in Paris, I was astonished at the enormous trade facilities Serge Varsano was receiving from the French banks.

The Chinese have no fairy godmothers (I exclude here the type of Chinese who connive with leaders peddling cronyism, and therefore rise and fall with such leaders.) Yet, despite facing these odds, the Overseas Chinese, through hard work, endeavour and business shrewdness, are able to produce profits of a type that no other ethnic group operating in the same environment could produce.

Why did the Overseas Chinese survive, adapt and flourish in Southeast Asia? I say the answer lies in the great cultural strength of the Chinese. When they left their homeland, the Overseas Chinese retained the culture of China in the marrow of their bones. I remember my father had coolies who, after humping numerous bags of rice, stank of sour sweat; their clothes were not properly laundered and they couldn't afford to bathe with perfumed soap. But they were decent human beings at heart and they knew moral values. As a child of three or four years old, I would sometimes sit on their laps and they would regale me with stories of their days in China. Recollecting those stories, I would say they were very cultured people. They knew what was right and what was wrong. Even the most uneducated Chinese, through family education, upbringing and social environment, understands the ingredients and consequences of behaviour such as refinement, humility, understatement, coarseness, bragging and arrogance.

I remember being invited to a brainstorming seminar in Jakarta sponsored by their Center for Strategic and International Studies, headed by General Ali Murtopo, Suharto's head of intelligence. Jakarta was just beginning to stand on its own feet under Suharto. I was interested in further developing my business in Indonesia, and here was a chance to get to know the leaders and to take the economic and political pulse of Indonesia. So I attended. About thirty of us sat around a big oval table. From Malaysia, there was Ghazali Shafie and myself. From Singapore, there was Devan Nair, who later became President of Singapore.

The topic of one session was economic development. When it came to my turn, I spoke into the microphone in front of me: "Gentlemen, I have heard a lot already today from my peers about how Indonesia should develop. Many of you say that we should bring in the multinationals of the world and draw upon their strength to bring up the nation. I beg to differ. European and American multinationals, with their bulldozer-type attitude and mentality, will succeed. I have no doubt of that. But they will also import high inflation and inflationary practices that will enter your bloodstream, into the very marrow of your bones. You will never shake it off! This nation is very poor and cannot afford that style of management."

I continued, "I want to speak today about the Southeast Asian Chinese. The vast majority of Overseas Chinese are decent Chinese. If you go into the smallest Malay kampongs in my country, Malaysia, you will find that a Chinese shopkeeper has set up a tiny provision store. His whole shop may be only 200-300 square feet, but it will be stocked with all the necessities required by that community. If it's a fishing village, there will be many tins of biscuits and canned foods, flashlights and batteries – the food and essentials to keep a fisherman provisioned out at sea for a few days."

"These men are playing sterling roles everywhere." I stressed. "They are entrepreneurs blessed with business brains, though many of them lack financial backing. The mark-up on the goods they sell is very small; thus, they play a vital role in the chain of distribution."

I returned to the subject of Indonesia: "Should not the leaders of this brand-new Indonesian nation harness more of the Chinese entrepreneurs' energies to develop the country? The Chinese can do it, and they will do it economically, not the bulldozing, multinational way. Use the Overseas Chinese, shoestring-economy style and build up your economy like that. That's my plea."

I concluded with this: "Now, before I finish, I want to state one strong caveat. Some of these Overseas Chinese will become very big crooks, and if you let them run rampant they could ruin your nation. Therefore, it is vital that you also build up an executive monitoring arm, one armed with teeth. What I am saying is that in a laissez-faire economy, you must let business develop freely; but at the same time you must have a very well-trained and highly disciplined monitoring arm. Where there is abuse and crimes being committed, you must come down very fast and very hard and punish the crooks severely. You should make examples of them so that the honest Chinese will help your country and the dishonest ones will be deterred."

Later, when I went out to the washroom, I passed a room adjoining our meeting room in which tape recorders were whirring. So what I said – what everyone said – was recorded.

In the ensuing years, Indonesia (and most other countries in the region) didn't heed my warning about the need for watchdog institutions with bite. The decent Chinese have helped to build up Indonesia, Malaysia, Thailand and the Philippines, and made these countries what they are today. But you also had the rise of the unscrupulous and ruthless Chinese, who in turn have devastated many parts of Southeast Asia. Why were these people allowed to wreak havoc? It is because the leaderships have been weak. If the leaders were strong, all these devils would have disappeared overnight.

Singapore had the same number of Chinese crooks, but you try and find one today. They are all hidden, camouflaged, or dormant. The crooks were held on steel leashes by two hands: Lee Kuan Yew's left hand and Lee Kuan Yew's right hand. With the unsavoury elements under control, look what Singapore has been able to accomplish by harnessing the energies of the Overseas Chinese.

PART V
–
CHINA

17
A NEW BEGINNING

TIM DUMAS, one of the senior partners in ED&F Man, once asked me, "Why do you want to go on battling the odds in the business world, Robert? You've made your pile. Why don't you retire?"

My answer may have sounded strange to him: "Tim, can't you see we come from two different worlds? The British Empire spanned the world; wherever the sun rose, there was a Union flag fluttering in the breeze. You had colonies for over 200 years. Even today, Britain punches above its weight because of that history. I belong to a developing Southeast Asia. And now there is China, the land of my parents and ancestors. As long as I can still contribute, I cannot rest."

My 1958 sugar barter deal with India and Mitsui almost led to disaster after the Chinese entered the market as a seller of sugar at the exact same time. However, in the end, it was a blessing in disguise. Through this deal, I got to know the Chinese trading companies based in Hong Kong. They decided that they would rather work with me than against me, and Kuok Brothers gradually built up a strong trading relationship with Chinese-affiliated trading firms in both Hong Kong and Singapore. Business is about one individual getting to know another individual and then another, and so on. We did sugar, we did rice, and then we went sideways into miscellaneous small things like photographic film and dyestuffs.

From 1965, I began travelling to the mainland itself. My first trip took me to the Canton Trade Fair, with a side trip with several busloads of Overseas Chinese to a commune outside the provincial capital. We had a good lunch of simple village-style food at a village community hall. In my early visits, I sensed that the people in China were highly moral and decent. I never felt like a stranger.

China went into a self-imposed period of isolation during the Cultural Revolution, and the China that I returned to in the mid-1970s was a very different place. There was a lot of red tape laced with a high degree of suspicion. Many cadres did not have experience of business, and they feared that every capitalist was coming to try to rob the nation of its national treasures. The cadres didn't know how to develop a business; but neither were they prepared to let you develop it.

Mother warned me against investing in China: "You are going in too soon, my son, too soon. You will meet brick walls. Why bang your head on a brick wall? Your head will only bleed, and you won't achieve anything. Worse still, if you achieve something, then they will take it away from you and you will be back at zero." Mother knew the Chinese makeup and the mindset of her generation.

However, I saw that China was pitifully backward. I felt that the country must wake up and join the modern world. It was much poorer than the Malaya into which I was born. I felt that I wanted to help China and, if possible, push the country to develop faster. Thank God there were good people, and standing above them all was Deng Xiaoping.

I have Mother to thank for my lifelong interest in the birthplace of my parents. Mother always retained a strong and deep emotional tie to her homeland. Yet, she was very objective and critical of all the Chinese faults, including the foibles of successive governments and leaders.

She was travelling regularly between Malaya and China in

Top President Suharto of Indonesia (*middle*) with Yani Haryanto and myself in the President's country home in Chiomas, outside Jakarta, c 1970.

Left Tun Ismail Ali and I on a trip to Lanzhou, Gansu Province, September 1987.

Left At a meeting in Beijing
in May 1984 with Raja Tun
Mohar, Special Economic
Advisor to the Malaysian
Government, Tun Ismail
Mohd Ali, Governor of
Bank Negara, Malaysia,
and Mdm Chen Muhua,
Minister of Foreign
Trade and Economic
Cooperation, the People's
Republic of China.

Below A very dear friend,
Jacob Ballas. He was
head of J Ballas & Co, a
leading stock brokerage
firm of Singapore, and also
Chairman of Singapore
Stock Exchange.

Left At the Joint Venture Agreement signing ceremony for building the China World Trade Centre in 1984. Lei Renmin, then Deputy Minister of Foreign Economic Relations and Trade, signed for China.

Bottom left Greeting Mr Wan Li, Vice Premier of the People's Republic of China, in Beijing, 1984.

Below Meeting with Mr Zhou Nan, Director of the Xinhua News Agency in Hong Kong, c 1993.

Left With Mr Deng Xiaoping and his daughter Ms Deng Rong in Beijing on 15 September 1990.

Bottom left With Mr Yang Shangkun, President of the People's Republic of China, in Beijing, March 1990.

Below With Premier Li Peng in Beijing, March 1990.

Top With Mr Hu Jintao, President of the People's Republic of China, in Beijing, c 2005.

Top right Poh Lin and I with ex-Premier Zhu Rongji and his wife, Mdm Lao An, in Beijing, June 2009.

Right With Mr Jiang Zemin, President of the People's Republic of China, c 2000.

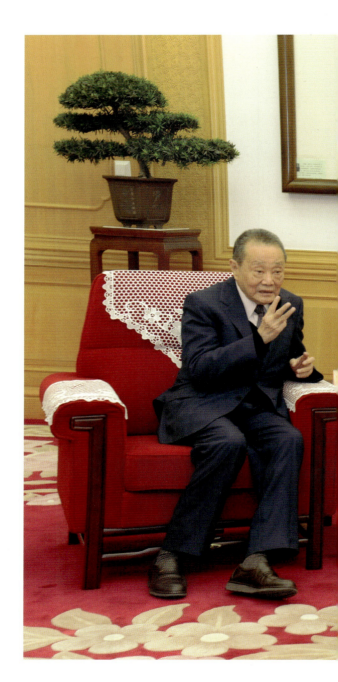

Meeting with Mr Xi Jinping, President of the People's Republic of China, in Beijing, October 2016.

In my office in Hong Kong,
c 2000.

the late 1940s and early 1950s. She welcomed the victory of Mao Zedong and the establishment of the People's Republic of China. Mother always stood up for the poor. In 1951, on one of her trips back to China, she collected all the title deeds for her properties in Shandong province and went north with an assistant. They identified each tenant farmer and made a gift of the land to those who had tilled and maintained it.

Until her death, she said Mao's pluses far outweighed his minuses. But, from early on, she knew that mistakes were being made. She saw the harm that the Great Leap Forward did to the rural areas. I think that, today, we would say Mao didn't really understand how to run an economy. During the war years you needed heroic acts. The tales of daring during the Long March and the call to fight the Japanese resonated with the people. But once all the battles are won, you have to focus on building up the economy and bringing up the standard of living of the people.

Mother was a strong critic of the bad and bullying behaviour of local bureaucrats towards their fellow Chinese. This was particularly so during the Cultural Revolution, which she saw as the dark period in China's history. In the early 1970s, she made a trip to Fuzhou after many years away. She was required to deposit her passport with the Public Security Bureau of Fuzhou. After staying for a few months and feeling unhappy at what she saw around her, she decided it was time to go back to Malaysia. She went many times to retrieve her passport, but the Public Security Bureau always gave her some kind of stupid answer and wouldn't return it to her.

One day, she got really angry. She went to the Bureau, pounded on the desk, and said, "I am an Overseas Chinese citizen of Malaysia. The Chinese Government told us to go overseas and become worthy citizens of the countries of our adoption. Why do you keep my passport? What have I done wrong? Why are you treating me like this? I shall go to Beijing to lodge a strong complaint." Within a few days of that incident, an official brought the passport to her home, and she booked a flight and returned to Malaysia.

Many poor Chinese from Fujian had left to seek a better life abroad, particularly in Southeast Asia, and when they went back to China to visit relatives and asked for assistance, they would often find the bureaucrats at the Overseas Chinese Bureau officious and unsympathetic. On her other trips home to Fuzhou, the Bureau would send someone to greet her who would say, "Madame Kuok, I have come to welcome you. What can we do for you?"

Her response would be: "I have come back to see relatives and to worship at the temples here. I do not need any help from you, but you could offer your help to the many returning Overseas Chinese who are poor and illiterate and who really need your help."

She assessed Deng Xiaoping quite correctly from the beginning. She told me, "Nien, China will go back to capitalism in your lifetime. It's already moving in that direction. I can tell you, son, man can only be driven by the selfishness in his heart and the betterment of himself and his children's well-being. Only that can propel him to achieve more things, to be more creative and productive. China will and must continue to be driven by this."

But in her mind, the ultimate goal of society should be true socialism, where man truly works for all his fellow beings on a totally selfless basis. But that stage is a long way off. Before that, man must complete the long march to becoming truly civilized, and we have only travelled the first few of ten thousand miles.

The principal reason that I elected to move to Hong Kong in the 1970s was taxation. At that time, it almost appeared as though the Singapore and Malaysian governments were competing with each other to see which could levy the highest taxes on those who were generating wealth for the nations. Both were taxing our profits at punitive rates. If you earned a dollar, you barely kept fifty cents.

My main business at the time was in commodities. I was a substantial trader, taking large positions. Three thousand lots is the equivalent of 150,000 tons of sugar. A movement of one US cent a pound would bring huge profits or losses. If I went long and wrong, or short and wrong, margin calls could easily wipe me out. So it was imperative for me to build up my company's cash reserves.

Because of Singapore's steep tax rates, I was handicapped in my effort to build up cash reserves. And without deep reserves, I would be dangerously vulnerable to margin calls if our trading positions went sour. Although Singapore did not tax offshore trading profits, officials imposed extremely onerous conditions on you to prove that your profits were generated offshore. They essentially regarded you as guilty until proven innocent. A tax audit was a bit like the Spanish Inquisition.

By comparison, Hong Kong's tax environment encouraged business. You paid only 17 percent corporate tax, so you were better off by 33 cents on every dollar of profit.

Since I was in the international sugar-trading business, with mobile operations it seemed almost irresponsible not to trade sugar from a low-tax base. Tax policy plays a very important role in encouraging or discouraging business. Hong Kong's policy is very straightforward. Why would I want to hire an army of lawyers and accountants to avoid taxation?

I should stress that I had not – and indeed, have not – lost one iota of my affection for Singapore. It is simply that it made more sense to base my operations in a low-tax jurisdiction like Hong Kong.

In fact, from about the mid-1970s, I often met with Singapore Prime Minister Lee Kuan Yew in a sitting room next to his office. His office would call my office at short notice when he had free time. In an early session, Kuan Yew explained that he wanted to have chats with me because I had a good feel for the scene in Malaysia. He had an embassy in Kuala Lumpur, but he wanted a different perspective. I was always very frank with him. If he asked questions for which I had no answer, I would tell him so. We had many pleasant such sessions, sometimes over lunch. Unfortunately, these informal sessions ended when I moved to Hong Kong, as I could no longer pop around at a moment's notice.

Hong Kong was a much bigger pond than Singapore or Malaysia. I began to see very clearly that the CEOs of the top American, Japanese and European corporations were visiting Hong Kong, if not once a year, then once every two or three years. The senior VPs would go to Singapore and the VPs or departmental managers would visit Kuala Lumpur. That was the pecking order. Today, of course, CEOs are more likely to frequent Beijing and Shanghai.

We had considered relocating part of our operations to Hong Kong from the 1960s. I finally made the plunge in 1974, deciding that I must form a Kuok Brothers Hong Kong.

I summoned several of our executives in Singapore: Richard Liu, Lee Yong Sun, James Lim, Kenny Yeo, and one or two others. I told everyone that we had to act quickly: "I have made up my mind that we will open a branch in Hong Kong. I ask for volunteers. Please give me your answer today. Two weeks from today, I want you to be in Hong Kong, ready to work. On the plus side," I concluded, "anyone who follows me to Hong Kong will be well rewarded."

Lee Yong Sun, Kenny Yeo and James Lim all put up their hands. I asked Richard Liu to commute back and forth, like I was planning to do, to look after both sides of the business for at least a year. I spent about seven to ten days a month in Hong Kong from 1974, and then gradually it became 15 days a month, 21 days, until eventually I moved there in 1979.

We started with about HK$10 million when I formed Kerry Holdings Ltd, the name that we chose for our Hong Kong operation. The executives who relocated to Hong Kong were allowed to apply for the first allotment of shares in the company. Trading, of course, migrated with me; that was unavoidable, as I was the main trader. Within 20 years, Hong Kong has blossomed into by far the largest of our three group companies of Malaysia, Singapore and Hong Kong.

I saw great potential in China, but I can't claim to have had a crystal ball on the momentous changes that would follow the death of Mao Zedong. Luckily or unluckily, I was born Chinese, and I have always remained very proud of being Chinese. The more I heard people call China backward, the more I felt we must show the rest of the world, some day, that China can be advanced. I felt that I had something to offer my fellow Chinese: modern ways of thinking and management, and respect for the value that both sides brought to a business relationship.

However, our focus was most certainly not on China during the first few years after we moved to Hong Kong. Kerry Holdings focused on supplying sugar and rice to Indonesia. That was when Yani Haryanto had his magic arrangement with President Suharto, under which all that vast land's sugar and rice imports passed through Yani's hands.

My first major investment in Hong Kong came in November 1977, when I bought a piece of land in Kowloon at auction and built the Kowloon Shangri-La Hotel. It is still a very important jewel in the Group's hotel crown more than 40 years later.

After that, I plunged into the Hong Kong property market, then into warehousing and local stock-market investing. It is well known that Hong Kong property has created quite a few billionaires. In the hindsight of history, it is not hard to see why.

My first visit to Hong Kong was in 1947, when Joy and I were there on honeymoon. We drove with a friend, Eddie Cheung, past the old Peninsula Hotel in Kowloon. When we were maybe a few hundred metres down Nathan Road from the Peninsula, Eddie said, "Robert, if you have spare money you should buy land here. I think you can buy empty land at about HK$5 a square foot." Well, that is probably the greatest missed opportunity of my life!

Fast forward to the late 1970s, when we had been in Hong Kong for three or four years. We had established a small office, and we rented apartments so that those of us who periodically came over from Singapore would have a place to stay. When a two-year tenancy expired, the rent would always shoot up. The rising rents were creating a strong headwind for our business. So I called several of our executives into my office, and said, "If rents keep going up like this, we will never be able to gain a foothold here. We have to go into property investment."

So, we established Kerry Properties Limited, which is now a public company, and which has been our primary company for investment in Hong Kong and mainland China real estate since 1978.

Even I did not see how important this decision would be. In the 1970s, despite the rising rents, the cost was not that steep. But, as China developed, it became very apparent that rents would continue to soar and soar. We decided not to stop at buying just one or two floors of office space or one or two apartments. We branched into development. We built entire buildings, and then major integrated commercial and residential complexes. We have never looked back.

18
OPPORTUNITIES IN CHINA

OUR BUSINESS IN CHINA really started in earnest around 1982. We started when I was almost 60, when many people are already thinking about retirement, and we have now been going for over 30 years.

I have spent many thousands of hours with many hundreds of people from all over the country, and generally I have found that those who are responsible for commercial matters are very understanding of the needs of business. However, in the initial years, there was a steep learning curve. I had to learn the ropes of how to do things in China, and there were several years of false starts and difficulties. Even as an ethnic Chinese, I found it very complicated to deal with the authorities in China, so I can appreciate how difficult it is for a non-Chinese businessman, even if he knows the language.

The authorities in Beijing knew about my involvement with the Shangri-La Hotel in Singapore. I believe that Lim Kai, my early partner in trading with the mainland and a true friend of China, recommended me to them in strong terms. One day in 1977, Lim Kai passed on the message that China Travel Service was keen to have my help to build hotels in China. I vividly remember flying north on the morning that my daughter Hui was born in Kuala Lumpur.

Most of the existing hotels in China did not qualify for even one star. The bathrooms had filthy toilet bowls and cracked washbasins;

the rooms came with lamps minus lampshades. To a lot of Chinese, working in a hotel was a menial job. Under communism, why should you be a servant to anyone? Why would you demean yourself by serving someone a cup of coffee? As a result, the hotels in China were among the world's worst hostelries.

On 12 November 1977, I flew to Beijing from Guangzhou. Transportation was difficult then; there were few flights between the major cities. Something that would take two days to accomplish in Malaysia might take two weeks or two months in China. You could never line up six or eight meetings in one day. Someone would come and meet you at your hotel, spend an hour or an hour and a half with you, then for two days you met no one.

After Beijing, I went to Shanghai and saw a nice, three-hectare piece of land near where Suzhou Creek flows into the Huangpu River, the site of the former British Consulate General. I also went to Guangzhou and met the authorities there to review possible sites for a hotel.

I soon realized that I was meeting the wrong crowd. Other investors had gone in and met the Beijing City Government or Guangzhou City Government. I had foolishly assumed that under the communist regime there was one employer, one government. I later discovered that in China a single individual's authority can be enormous. China Travel Service may have been responsible for tourism and they may have operated a number of hotels, but they did not have the authority to grant final approval.

I eventually signed a letter of agreement with China Travel Service to build a hotel in Shanghai. I lined up a Hawaii-based firm to design a huge, 1,300-room hotel. We were going to move fast, given the pressing need.

Then the Shanghai City Government came to me and said, "You have to lend us US$50 million because the infrastructure is inadequate. To provide water, waste facilities and electricity, we need to improve the infrastructure, and we are short of funds."

If it were just a closed-ended US$50 million loan, I might have been persuaded. But anybody with common sense knew that Shanghai had been a series of foreign concessions. You had the British settlement, the French settlement and the Japanese area; thus, the infrastructure under the roads was not homogeneous. What if they started tinkering and US$50 million expanded to US$200 million? How did they arrive at that figure of US$50 million in the first place? Where does a pipe or a cable end? I was very worried that I would not see the end of it. But the Shanghai authorities made it clear that unless I was willing to extend the loan, I would not get approval to build the hotel.

So, I told them, "Sorry, I cannot make that commitment." They conceded that they had broken the agreement, but I did not pursue it. It was a valuable learning experience. I had my out-of-pocket expenses and I had to compensate our architect, but it was all manageable.

In about 1982, I took a group of friends to Shanghai. The then-mayor, Wang Daohan, invited me to breakfast at the former French Club. As soon as I sat down to breakfast, Mayor Wang began to apologize for the City's failure to honour the signed hotel agreement. I said, "Mr Mayor, please do not apologize. It is not an important matter to me. The cost was minimal. I feel very embarrassed that a person of your importance should have to say these words to me."

The years 1977 to 1981 were terribly frustrating for me in China. Every time I thought I was near success, I would run into another brick wall. China was crying out for development and in urgent need of foreign investment, yet the people I was dealing with put on all kinds of stupid airs. I met a lot of third-rate officials. But, looking back, I really cannot blame them; it was the early days of reform, and it took a really exceptional individual to break the mould and try something new.

One day, my friend Ho Yeow Koon of Singapore came to me and said, "You know, I think I've got a deal for you. They need someone to renovate and modernize a very elegant but run-down hotel in Hangzhou. Many of the state guests who visit Beijing or Shanghai are put up there for one or two days to enjoy the beautiful environment of West Lake." He was referring to the famous Hangzhou Hotel, which commanded a unique site overlooking West Lake.

I travelled to Hangzhou, one of the most famous resort cities in China, and met the officials in charge. Finally, I succeeded in entering my first hotel venture in China. I signed a contract to renovate the hotel, and we put in US$20 million in cash equity, for which we received a forty-three or forty-four percent stake in the hotel. It was 1982, and I felt I was making quite a sacrifice to commit US$20 million, which I otherwise could have invested in the then-booming Hong Kong real estate market for a quick profit.

We learned some things the hard way in Hangzhou. As elsewhere in China at the time, urban housing was run down; pipes burst and water supply was irregular. Many of the provincial and city cadres and bureaucrats (Hangzhou is the provincial capital) would check into Hangzhou Hotel because it was known to be better maintained. They were used to receiving free rooms and maybe a free meal or two at the hotel restaurant.

Kuok Brothers run hotels as a business. We weren't told anything about these practices and, to preserve face, the local officials were ashamed to inform us. They just expected us to know and to extend the same privileges. We didn't. After all, we had spent US$20 million and were trying very hard to raise room rates, so that we could break even and start to make money. These local practices were draining away resources and interfering with management discipline. We had enough trouble on our hands, what with preventing petty theft inside the hotel and other legacy issues. It took us about 18 months to renovate the hotel, and quite some time after that to root out all the old practices.

Our first hotel in China was Beijing Shangri-La, to which I had committed at the end of 1983. We built the hotel in the educational district of Haidian, in northwest Beijing, where Peking and Tsinghua universities are located. I agreed to invest US$72 million to complete the project on a fully furnished, virtually turnkey basis for the joint venture partners. Our stake in Beijing Shangri-La was about 45 percent.

There was an old hotel next door with about 150 rooms. Our people stayed there and quickly discovered that many of the materials there were highly flammable. If that hotel ever caught fire, everybody inside would be roasted within minutes. We spent over US$3 million to replace all the flammable materials – we couldn't have a disaster on our doorstep!

The China World Trade Center in Beijing was also under negotiation at that time, although we were not part of the talks. The two foreign groups originally competing for the project were led by Chase Manhattan Bank and Industrial Bank of Japan. In 1981 or so, the Ministry of Foreign Economic Relations and Trade (MOFERT) picked Chase as its partner to develop the site, the largest property project in China at the time.

Then, suddenly, everything stopped. Deng Xiaoping was still consolidating power and there was a bit of jockeying for influence within the top leadership. The old guard attempted to block the project, deriding the foreign role and claiming that the project was too grand for a socialist nation.

At least one year passed, and Lim Kai came to me one day

with news that a decision had been made internally to re-start the China World project. But instead of bringing in a foreign bank as a partner, they wanted to see who else may be interested in submitting a bid. Lim Kai's contacts had seen my faith in China when I built the Beijing Shangri-La Hotel. They asked Lim Kai, "Would your partner be interested in taking on this project?" When I expressed an interest, MOFERT assigned Luo Baoyi and Feng Tianshun to talk to me.

I had kept about US$90 million in cash with Bangkok Bank in London and New York, waiting for the day when I could go into China in a big way. With gearing, I calculated that I could probably tackle a US$300 million project. We came in as a dark-horse, submitted a bid, and won the race.

The China World Trade Center negotiations began in the second half of 1983. I rented a two-module suite on an annual basis in the old wing of the Beijing Hotel. Three senior cadres from MOFERT came every day to meet with Lim Kai and me. The five of us talked from nine every morning until seven at night. If I develop lung cancer one day, it will be due to this negotiating experience! The hotel suite was transformed into a smoking room: the cadres and Lim Kai puffed away all day long.

I signed the contract in the Great Hall of the People in 1984. The entire project cost was supposed to be US$300 million — US$200 million of that amount borrowed money. We formed a company with a paid-up capital of US$100 million, of which we put in US$50 million for 50 percent ownership. I recall that Mother didn't agree with my investment in the China World Trade Center. She urged me not to be so hasty. But one good thing about Mother, she knew that I was a strong enough son to disagree with her on occasion.

In China, every contract says the China party is Party A. So we were Party B. But the contract stated that Party B was to take leadership of planning, construction and management, because they accepted the fact that we had the capability. They asked if the Chairman could be Lei Renmin. He was Deputy Minister of MOFERT at the time that I signed the agreement with him. I agreed.

Then, at the first board meeting, Lei asked if the Managing Director could also come from his side. I again gave way. To me the logic was, if they start to ask for it and I say no, it will only lead to tension and stress. They must have talked internally and come to a consensus, like good bureaucrats. If I defy them, what good can come of it? I'm entering their home to do a project – they're not entering my home – so I needed their friendship for smooth cooperation. So I gave way, gave way, and gave way, and all along we worked and worked and made sacrifices. We are very much hands-on managers, not business whiz kids.

I sent in Ang Keng Lam from our side. If we paid him HK$150,000 a month plus bonus, we charged at most HK$50,000 to China World Trade Center, even though he spent 99 percent of his working time on the project. So we subsidized everything, quietly, without asking for credit.

Along the way, the Chinese side brought in a man from Capital Steel Works called Feng Zhicheng, who had gone to some of the best schools in China. He recruited some retiring director-generals from the Ministry, one of whom also always wore a smiling face. Then I began to hear some awful sounds.

The officers from the Chinese side would come to Hong Kong and, as is my style, I gave them a proper lunch or dinner. After that, I left them to look after themselves; not because I didn't want to see them, but because I really was too busy with my own work. I made sure, however, that all their meals were taken care of, and that they were put up in Kowloon Shangri-La. I didn't realize that I had offended some of them; or to put it another way, I had failed to win their hearts and bellies.

Then the rumblings started within the China World Trade Center organization. The divisional and departmental heads would appear to be very cooperative; but these same people would go around backbiting. They'd say, "Oh, such and such a person has been giving away our national treasures to Mr Kuok." In effect, they were accusing me of profiteering at the expense of China.

The first time I heard this story, I told the man who conveyed the rumour to me, "Come on, don't tell tall tales. It's all rubbish. You must have heard wrong. I mean, these guys are smiling in front of me all the time."

Then the murmurings grew so loud and the backbiting so vicious that I realized I could no longer afford to ignore them. At dinners in Beijing, I usually entertained city bureaucrats to make sure that approvals were smooth and that they understood we were forthright, proper businessmen. After dinner one evening, I rushed back to my dingy room in Beijing Hotel and met with Ang Keng Lam. I was seething with anger, and asked for pen and paper. I wrote nonstop for one-and-a-half hours. I wrote a six-page letter in English that began: "Dear Minister Zheng Tuobing." Around midnight, I asked Ang Keng Lam to take the letter down to the photocopying machine, make a copy and keep it.

The next morning, I was playing golf with Minister Zheng at Ming Tombs Golf Course outside Beijing. It was winter, so I wore a coat. I folded the thick letter and put it in the inner pocket. After two holes, I could not contain my anger any longer. I said, "Minister, you are looking at a very unhappy man today."

He responded, "Why are you upset, Mr Kuok?"

I said, "Your old secretary-generals are accusing me of stealing national treasures. They gossip far too much. Mr Minister, I know you understand English. I cannot write a decent Chinese letter. If there is any part you do not understand, please have it translated." I pulled out the letter and gave it to him.

In the letter I said very clearly, "Buy out all my shares at cost plus interest; interest negotiable. I want to pull out of China." I was that upset.

The Minister kept urging me to cool down. I was very rough, even sarcastic. I said, "Minister Zheng, is your country poor or rich?" I didn't say "our country." He was taken aback and didn't answer. I continued, "I'll answer for you. Your country is poor. Therefore, what treasures do you have for me to rob? I came to help, and I have laboured hard. You should not talk behind my back. Please buy me out right away. I want to pull out."

They asked Vice-Premier Gu Mu to see me four months later – this was 1987, at the time of the topping-off ceremony, to plead with me. In that bare-walled, windowless China World building, Gu Mu and I sat two metres from each other across a long table. He said: "Mr Kuok, the attitude and ability of China's bureaucrats is very uneven today. There are still many pockets of ignorance. Please bear with us. We know that you have worked hard and expended your own blood and sweat on this project. All of us in China know it. It would be a great shame if you withdraw now, when you are just about to reap the fruits of your labour. Listen to my urging. Please, Mr Kuok, don't withdraw now."

Fortunately, we remained in the China World Trade Center project, which at today's property prices is worth well in excess of US$1 billion, making the project one of the best investments anybody has made in China. But, at the time, neither party was driven by profit. Of course, as a businessman I would not have allowed the project to operate at a huge loss, but more fundamental was my sense that development in Beijing was about to take off, and this project would help launch that takeoff.

At the time, it was truly a massive undertaking, with more than 400,000 square meters of modern buildings including four levels of underground parking, We built two hotels simultaneously within the complex, China World and Traders Beijing, about 150 metres apart.

Tiananmen Incident in June 1989 delayed construction by about eight months and raised costs by a few tens of millions of US dollars. But we hung on. I was still a raging bull in China after Tiananmen. I remember telling then-Beijing Executive Vice Mayor Zhang Baifa, "You are now going to suffer for about three years. But after three years, you will be forgiven and things will be forgotten."

I believe the success of China World Trade Center, the largest Sino-foreign real estate joint venture up to that date, had a strong demonstration effect on Hong Kong property developers. While a few had invested in China early on, the floodgates opened after the success of the China World Trade Center.

And I also learned from this project. I saw that the good leaders in China far outnumbered the poor ones, especially at the top levels. As long as I see that in a society, then I'm willing to help. When I saw what Deng Xiaoping was doing, I virtually worshipped the man. I have often told overseas friends that, throughout China's 5,000-year history, there has rarely been a period when the leadership has been as committed to providing for the people and nation-building as that since Deng came to power. It has now been more than 35 years since Deng set the country on its current course, and the present leadership continues to put the people first.

We met obstacles and small-minded people in China. Some think you have come to rob them; others just think about themselves, and when you won't line their pockets they turn their backs on you. In some of the provinces, you meet bigoted, narrow-minded officials who are envious before they have given away anything. All you can do is to avoid those places.

Overall, I think my relative success has been due to my willingness to give way. If you were operating in Singapore or Hong Kong, you would not meet with that situation. In China, I was willing to flow with the currents. I was not expecting to make a fortune. I think, in the main, I felt I was there to help the country. But because of all my years of business training and sense of fiduciary values, there were times when I could not compromise. If they were not willing to be reasonable, I could not accept it, and those frustrations sometimes got to me.

Rather than quit the scene, I would just give way. Sometimes, we walked away from projects after expending blood, sweat and money. But more often than not, we tackled the problems and fought our way through. I think I can rightly say we have never compromised with venal officials. You must stand on your principles and be prepared to walk away from a deal if there's a whiff of corruption.

I'll give one example from Beijing. This happened in the early 1990s, not long before the downfall of Party Secretary Chen Xitong. I first met Chen in 1984 when I went to Beijing to undertake the China World Trade Center project. He was then mayor of the city; several years later he was promoted to Party Secretary. Before his downfall, Chen organized a delegation of 399 Beijing bureaucrats to visit Hong Kong. At the last minute he cancelled and let a few vice-mayors lead the group.

One of the vice-mayors, Zhang Baifa, was already a good friend of mine. He was quite determined that my group of companies should try to obtain and develop a huge piece of land right next to Beijing Railway Station. He was grateful that we had come into Beijing when nobody else was willing to do so, and had invested as much as we did in the China World Trade Center.

Ang Keng Lam, who directed our China real-estate projects, ironed out most of the points with the Chinese side for the deal. The Chinese side in the project was a property development company belonging to the Beijing Municipal Government. There was a general manager named Huang or Wang in charge. My limited dealings with the man, and Ang Keng Lam's more frequent contact, told us that he was not a good partner. I thought, "Oh my God, how are we going to live with this man?"

Nevertheless, we signed a basic agreement at the Island Shangri-La Hotel in Hong Kong. Ang Keng Lam and this general manager signed the document. Vice-Mayor Zhang Baifa and I witnessed the signing: that's normal Chinese protocol. So we had an agreement to develop a large piece of land in concert with this Beijing real estate company. Within a few days, Ang Keng Lam went to Beijing to hammer out the last details.

Soon after he arrived in Beijing, I received a frantic phone call. The general manager wanted to make changes to points already agreed. And they were not unimportant changes; they were very major changes.

I asked Keng Lam over the phone: "Can you live with these changes?"

He said, "The truthful answer is no. What is worse, if we give way now, haven't we opened the floodgates?"

So I said, "Keng Lam, if I tell you to go to Vice-Mayor Zhang Baifa, and tell him exactly what has happened and say we feel that the only way out is for us to treat the agreement as null and void and withdraw, would you agree?"

He replied, "I think that is the only way out."

And that is exactly what we did.

I had made many trips to Shanghai on business but, in 1992,

I went on a purely social trip. I brought along two of my closest personal friends so that we could enjoy each other's company, play some golf and dine together. These were the late Ressel Fok and the Shanghai-born CM Woo. After we arrived, I received word that the Party Secretary of Shanghai at the time, Wu Bangguo, wanted to invite me to dinner in one of the city's state guest houses. Wu would be elected Chairman of the Standing Committee of the National People's Congress in 2003, and serve for 10 years before retiring in March 2013.

I accepted, but asked if I could bring my friends along. He graciously consented. I remember sensing on that trip that the ground was starting to move under Shanghai. My instincts told me that we were at the beginning of a new, major wave of development.

As soon as I returned to Hong Kong, I assembled a team led by Wong Siu Kong (Huang Xiaokang) and said, "We must now focus our energies on Shanghai."

During a trip to Shanghai shortly afterwards, Xiaokang said to me, "You know, Charoen Pokphand of Bangkok has established a joint-venture company with the Lujiazui Development Authority in Pudong, under which this joint venture company will decide who is allowed to develop which piece of land in the Lujiazui area. I think one piece is suitable for a hotel. Can we go to see it now?"

Within an hour we were in Pudong. We got out of the car and inspected an old shipyard that was no longer in operation. There were a few shipbuilding cranes, tons of rusting steel and coalyards on the site. Xiaokang said, "If you buy the site, they will close the shipyard and move it within a year or 18 months."

I asked if there would be any further development between the shipyard and the Huangpu River that could block the view. Xiaokang said there would be none. "This will be parkland and pedestrian walkways."

I relied on his judgment and information. Within one and a half days, we signed an agreement to purchase the land, and later built the Pudong Shangri-La Hotel on the riverfront site.

Our first hotel in Shanghai was actually in the Portman Center. Shangri-La was invited to manage the hotel by AIG, which controlled the Portman Center after Hong Kong & Shanghai Hotels dropped out of the project. (We later bought a 30 percent stake in the Center.) I went for the opening ceremony and was given a suite on one of the upper floors of the hotel.

I recall opening my window and looking out on the street, Nanjing Xi Lu. Diagonally across the road, I saw rows and rows of low, old, black-roofed buildings squatting on acres of prime land obviously in need of urban renewal. I immediately sent for Huang Xiaokang, and said, "Xiaokang, look across there. Could we acquire that?"

I must say we approached that land acquisition with gusto. We bought it quite quickly on terms of vacant possession, but paid top prices. Afterwards, we built the Shanghai Kerry Centre on Ci Hou Bei Li (Ci Hou North Lane), which became one of the nicest office blocks in Shanghai. We simultaneously built serviced apartments next door, which were quickly taken up. Thanks to the remarkable growth of Shanghai, it has been a profitable venture, despite the high cost of land. We later bought an adjacent three-hectare lot, where we built Kerry Centre Phase 2, consisting of Puxi Shangri-La, which has become a landmark in Shanghai.

The news of our success in China spread overseas. In late 1992 or early 1993, Coca-Cola contacted us and asked whether we might be interested in acquiring the bottling franchises for certain cities in China. I was very interested. So Coca-Cola sent different groups of officers from their Atlanta headquarters; in between we met the Coca-Cola China Limited people in Hong Kong. After a few months, I was invited to meet with the Asia-Pacific regional chief, an Australian by the name of Douglas Daft, who later became Chairman and CEO of the Coca-Cola Corporation. We met in Singapore in the presidential suite of Shangri-La Hotel. The meeting went well, and we soon drew up a pro-forma agreement.

I was then invited to Atlanta to meet the then-Chairman and CEO, the late Roberto Goizueta, and many of his officers. I flew into Atlanta for a meeting on 30 June 1993. I met with Goizueta in his office. We hit it off virtually at first sight. I was genuinely very fond of the man. He was a straight-talking man; I'm a straight-talking man. We had nothing to hide from each other.

John Hunter, an Executive Vice President of Coca-Cola, hosted me to a meal and asked me a question point-blank: what did I think of being invited to become a member of the Coca-Cola family?

I answered, "To be very candid with you, I think it's the first time in my life that something has fallen into my lap. All my life, I have had to work hard to build up something, but here I am asked to become a bottler of one of the world's leading brands. The business has already been built up. I am just becoming another cog in the wheel of Coca-Cola." I concluded, "It is a godsend opportunity, like a gift from heaven. I hope our relationship flourishes and prospers to mutual advantage." I felt that, in saying those words, I was merely stating a heartfelt truth.

The Coca-Cola people are a fine crowd, but they are very tough businessmen. Their act is, one, to tell their shareholders every year that worldwide total sales have increased so many percent. Two, annual profits from this worldwide increase in sales have risen so many percent. However, no profitable venture on earth can expect annual increases, inexorably. There must be years when there are setbacks. But in order to achieve those flattering results for shareholders, Coca-Cola acts like a bulldozer against the bottler, who has his back to a rock. Soon, we started to feel the pressure. It was up to us to survive and do our best.

The China market is fiercely competitive. There is Pepsi, of course, and many indigenous soft-drink bottlers, with the result that you cannot raise prices. In fact, prices of Coca-Cola products in China are among the cheapest in the world. On top of it, in China, there are multiple Coke bottlers: Coca-Cola first used Swire's and, in addition, invested in some of its own bottling plants in prime locations such as Shanghai. After we came in, China Cereals, Oils and Foodstuffs Corp, a state enterprise, also wanted to get into the act and applied a lot of pressure at the highest levels of government to obtain bottling rights.

For trade purposes, China is one seamless market, like the United States. Bottlers are given rights to cities or provinces, but what's to stop "parallel imports" across provincial borders? If Swire's Coca-Cola attacks Kerry Beverages, should we hit back at them? It was a very tough business.

Despite all this, we made good progress. I signed the initial agreement with Coca-Cola in Atlanta in July 1993. We opened our first plant in China in late 1994, and all 12 plants covered under our agreement by the end of 1998. By then, we had almost caught up with Swire's in total sales, despite their having a head start of a decade or more. Swire's also enjoyed a franchise in the Pearl River Delta, the richest single part of China.

I should mention that apart from the difficulties of doing the business – and every business has its difficulties, otherwise even a fool can be a rich businessman – our business relationship with Roberto Goizueta was one of the best we have had with anyone. His friendship was genuine and warm when I saw him at his once-every-two-or-three years' gatherings of his 30-40 favourite bottlers. He assembled us in Monte Carlo and virtually booked all of the best rooms in Hotel de Paris.

When I saw Roberto at the Monte Carlo get-together in August 1997, I sensed that his health was taking a turn for the worse. I remember telling my wife Pauline that I doubted that Roberto would survive more than six months. Sadly, he didn't.

You are very unlikely to lose your pants in Coke bottling in China, but squeezing out a satisfying profit is backbreaking work. We ultimately decided to leave this business, and sold out around the time of the Beijing Olympics in 2008.

PART VI
–
FAMILY

19
FAMILY MATTERS

THE CHINESE, as a people, are probably the most meticulous group on earth in recording their history. For nearly 5,000 years, national events, community events, and, in many cases, family events have been recorded. I don't know of many other ethnic groups who can trace their roots back for millennia.

Mother believed in karma, and she believed in fortune-telling. After she left Fuzhou for Malaya and gave birth to three sons, someone told her there was a gifted fortune-teller back in Fuzhou. Don't you want your three sons' fates foretold by him? There are different ways of telling fortunes. You can have the lines in your palms or your face read, but the infallible method in Mother's opinion was based on the time when you were born: The day, the hour, and the minute. Thousands of years ago, the wise men of China had already put such matters into diagrams for all time.

She had been careful to record everything about when her sons were born. So, one day, she wrote a letter to a relative in China, asking that these dates and times be taken to the fortune-teller. I was a boy then, and I remember that a long period passed. It was not until many months later that the mail brought our fortunes back, each in a separate envelope for Philip, for William, and for me.

Practice dictates that no one should see our fortunes. Mother locked them up when we went to see her, and she said, "Don't worry, you are still too young." Then the Japanese war came. She took the precious envelopes with her when we moved from place to place. Then William died in the jungle in 1953. She never told me what William's fortune said, and she may have burned the paper it was written on. Nor did she ever tell me what the fortune-teller wrote about Philip, who died in 2003.

When we were together one day in the 1980s, I said, "Mother why is it that I meet near disaster, and suddenly the market turns in my favour and I make money again?"

She said, "Actually, your fortune said you were destined to become wealthy."

"Oh, I see, and what else did it say?"

"You are fairly blessed. Your hard work would be well rewarded by the time you were thirty to forty, and in your fifties you would continue to prosper, and on into your sixties. And this will continue, but at a slower pace, for as long as you live." Those were her words, but she never gave me the writings themselves.

With the inheritance that I received from Father's estate, I bought a house in Johor Bahru and moved there in 1949 with my wife, Joyce, and two baby daughters. There was a gate across a driveway that went down a steep hill from the house to the government road. One day, a young Indian man showed up at the gate at the bottom of the hill. He had a little bundle on a stick over his shoulder, and he shouted up the hill towards the house, "Sir, sir, I come to tell your fortune!"

I shouted back, "No, no need. Please go away!" My daughters were sitting on the doorstep and suddenly became frightened, and started crying. So I yelled, "Please go away. You're frightening my daughters." Well, instead of going away he opened the gate and walked up the driveway. The closer he got, the more the children cried, so I sent them inside the house.

I walked down from the porch and met the man halfway up

the slope. I said, "I told you not to come. I don't want any fortune-telling."

He said, "No sir, never mind, I just tell your fortune. Show me your hand. I will go away after I see." So, to get rid of him, I showed him my hand. He looked at it only for about two or three minutes.

"Ah, sir, you will build many houses," he said, and I laughed.

"What business are you in?" he asked.

"Foodstuffs," I replied.

"No sir, you will build many houses."

So then I said, "Okay, anything else?"

He said, "Oh no sir, you will build many houses, you will not stop building houses, sir." And I thought what a crazy fellow. These are all charlatans. I fished out a dollar from my pocket and gave it to him. He thanked me very graciously, and as he turned he said, "Sir, you will build many, many houses."

At the time, hotels and real estate development were not on my mind at all. I could see myself going into sugar plantations maybe, or flour milling, but building houses was the furthest thing from my mind. Of course, after the decades rolled by, our group of companies became the fastest growing luxury hotel owner-cum-manager in Asia, and one of the leading property developers in China and Hong Kong through Shangri-La Asia Limited, Kerry Properties Limited, and related companies. What did the Indian man see? The Chinese believe in karma. Your fate is already determined.

I hardly saw my five eldest children grow up, the children of my first wife, Joyce Cheah. I was always travelling. I might return to Singapore, only to dash down to Jakarta and spend a night or two there. After 1963, there would be many years when I would run the businesses in Malaysia and Singapore from a hotel room in London for weeks on end. I ran it by telephone and telegram.

I would write lengthy cables late into the night and hand them to the hotel man along with a £5 tip, so he would immediately take them over to the Cable & Wireless office. Then I would have long telephone conversations with Singapore at seven in the morning, while a room service breakfast was getting cold on the table.

I strayed from my marriage with Joy in the early 1970s, around the time of our initial corporate move to Hong Kong as I focussed on building up my business. I had developed a strong feeling of fondness for a young lady named Ho Poh Lin, Pauline, who is now my wife.

Joy helped to shape my life. From the 1940s, she was a wonderful wife and mother to our five children. Like Mother, she was a very virtuous lady. She was also one of the most non-judgmental persons I have ever known.

I find it difficult to talk about this subject without touching on my own attempts over these last 40-odd years to understand why men stray from their marriages. My own father did the same thing. What I am going to say is not meant to whitewash my actions, which brought immense pain and suffering to Joy and others close to me.

Philip was stunned. His wife was Joy's sister, and she would not forgive me. Mother could not understand. I became a pariah, an outcast who had sinned. I felt all of that very deeply. But I weathered my mental storms.

My old schoolmate, Sujak bin Rahiman, who knew Joy and me well, admonished me, "Robert, by falling in love with another woman, you have disappointed your wife. Joy is a highly respectable woman, with noble ideals and values. You must not blame her. She may still love you, but her noble ways will not allow her to live together with you as man and wife."

Several months after Joy discovered that I was in a new relationship, we sat down to talk about it. "Nien, I have been thinking very hard. I have decided you deserve what you find to be pleasurable, and I am prepared to share you with the other woman. And we will continue our lives in that manner."

I was extremely touched. Joy was kind and generous, but also afraid. She said, "I know how hard you have worked all your life. You must have gone through hell in all these years of building up the family company, and I think you deserve this happiness. I mustn't be selfish and stand in your way, so I am prepared to share you."

My instant reaction was: what a fantastic wife I have; what a wonderful human being she is. But something cautioned me, and I said, "Joy, it is a big decision. Why don't you think it over and, if this is well and truly what you want, come and tell me again. Life will change, and we cannot foresee all the twists and turns. For the time being, I am not going to say 'yes' or 'no' to what you have suggested."

The months went by. She never brought the subject up again. She must have sought advice from those closest to her, her siblings. And she was suffering. In her worries and suffering, she suggested that I move out of the house, as she could not take the pressure of my being around. I set up a new home with Pauline, and we moved together to Hong Kong in 1979.

Among Asian societies, there has always been a reluctance to go to the courts for a divorce. In my personal case, when I left the home that I had founded with Joy, she said, "Nien, I will not let you divorce me. I will not divorce you. We will just live separately."

I respected that decision. Joy was a noble person. And that is how it was until the day she died. Tragically, she developed breast cancer and, after a five-year battle, passed away in 1983. I cared for her up to her last breath.

There is probably no joy in life as wonderful as raising young children. I bought a townhouse on Victoria Peak after Pauline and I moved to Hong Kong in 1979, in an area called Strawberry Hill. My children with Pauline, my daughter Hui and son Hua, were infants then, and our daughter Yen, my fifth daughter and eighth child, was born in 1990. All three of them attended Chinese-language and English-language schools in Hong Kong, followed by tertiary education in the US..

We had some lovely times during weekends and holidays on Victoria Peak. We would go for walks early in the morning. The Peak is always cooler and the air fresher than elsewhere on Hong Kong Island. Occasionally, I would take the children along with office colleagues out on a boat that we had moored in Deep Water Bay. We would sail to the middle of the bay, and all go into the sea for a bit of swimming and diving. Alas, those occasions were rare and precious, as I was still chasing my dreams, identifying property development projects in China and expanding the Kuok Group's business.

Pauline is a pillar of support to me. She has given me all her love and cared for me. She won't let me grow lazy and fat. She still walks me up the stairs or outside the house, or takes me out to play golf. I call her my sergeant major. She calls out a marching drill time: "Left… Left… Left, Right, Left." If you add up all the walks in a day, it could be as much as one hour, and this has done me a world of good. And she ensures that my meals are well prepared, and that I get an adequate variety of nourishing foods. She has made sure that our children's lives are filled with love. They have grown up to be wonderful and caring individuals, and I can safely say much is due to their mother's influence on them.

When Pauline and I moved to Hong Kong in 1979, she did not know much Chinese. One day, I said to her, "Pauline, more and more of my business will involve China. I want you to come with me on as many trips as possible, but how are you going to enjoy yourself if you don't know the language?"

Without further ado, she went to the University of Hong Kong and enrolled as a student in a Chinese-language class, with teachers from Beijing. She laboured hard at it. And very soon she was quite good. But as well as she was doing, after a year or two I had to ask her to give up her formal studies. She would sit up at night studying until one or two in the morning. Having my companion's place in bed empty prevented me from sleeping, and I told her that would make it hard for me to find enough energy to run the business. So she stopped. But by then she had acquired a fair knowledge of Chinese, and on all of my subsequent trips to China she has met many officials, both old friends and new acquaintances, and they all took to her.

I am happy to say that, even though Mother was very upset when I left Joy, her relationship with Pauline ended very well. In the end she forgave Pauline, and Pauline developed a deep love for Mother.

20

BREAKING APART
AND COMING TOGETHER

I AM A BELIEVER in karma. One of the most remarkable stories of my life, both as a businessman and as a family man, is how my very able nephew Kuok Khoon Hong in essence repeated what his father had done. His father, my late cousin Hock Swee, had left the Kuok family business in search of greener pastures only to return years later, stronger than ever, and re-entered our lives through a business merger. In Khoon Hong's case, the result is the Kuok Group's interest in Wilmar International Limited, the largest food-related business in Asia. I think this is karma at work.

In my generation – the generation that is comprised of the children of my father and his five older brothers – there were 22 male cousins in all. But, as regards the numbering, we skipped ahead by a few. We ended with 24, because there was a superstition in the Kuok village in Fuzhou about using the numbers seven and nine. Thus, even though I was number 18 by date of birth, I became known as "Cousin Number Twenty."

Kuok Hock Swee (Cousin Number Fourteen) and I are first cousins. In his teens, when he was still in China, Hock Swee was kidnapped by a gang of thieves. They sent ransom notes to his parents, but as there were no means to pay it, he remained a captive for many months. He was kept in intolerable conditions. Fleas and other bugs attacked his body and he was left with ugly scars, but somehow he survived this terrible experience.

Hock Swee was about 20 years old when he came to Johor Bahru. He left China to join my father's firm, like many of my other cousins. But he came much later than the others, I think around 1939 or 1940. As Hock Swee was raised in China, he did not speak any English, but he had very good business genes, was extremely street-wise, and had a fine sense for figures and a strong memory.

Later, he went back to Fuzhou to marry the girl his parents had found for him, and then the couple returned to Johor Bahru. They had a family of two daughters and two sons, the elder son being Khoon Hong. By Chinese custom, I refer to Khoon Hong as "nephew" and he calls me "uncle."

Even though many of the business ventures that my father started up at his Tong Seng & Co. eventually closed, Hock Swee showed that he was the brightest business mind among the many cousins working for Father. I imagine he became exasperated with my father's leadership of his shop – trying to please all his nephews and in the end pleasing no one – so Hock Swee left the family business and struck out for the fishing town of Mersing, 80 miles (130 kilometeres) up the coast from Johor Bahru. He opened his own small shop there with financial help from other cousins.

After Kuok Brothers was established on 1 April 1949, I would sometimes drive up to Mersing with friends to go deep-sea fishing on weekends. The drive would take about two and a half hours. It was a fairly new road, but pretty rough. There were many rivers, and the British armed forces had built Bailey bridges, very simple devices made of steel and wood, across which the cars drove.

I had a very close kinship with Hock Swee. He would greet us at the jetty when we returned from two or three days of fishing with a boatload of Spanish mackerel and jack, and take us out for a fantastic dinner. Business was still thin in those days but, after a few years of effort, Hock Swee had become the largest shopkeeper in

Mersing, and he was a very popular figure there.

On one of my fishing trips to Mersing in about 1951, I took him aside and said, "Hock Swee, I don't see how you can go far in Mersing. You already have the biggest provision store here, and there are no other industries to go into." The main industry was rubber tapping, and the British owned all the big plantations. I said, "Come back to the family company. You are the only one who is outside. I am sure that we can make a good arrangement for you."

At first he was rather shy and noncommittal. I think shyness was a trait in all the Kuok cousins except myself. He must have discussed the idea with his wife. I believe that she had taken the measure of me and decided that I wasn't trying to lure her husband into a bad relationship, and by my third or fourth attempt I saw a light come on in his eyes. So I offered him eight percent of Kuok Brothers at par, and agreed to buy his shop at whatever price Hock Swee thought was fair. We thus merged our two businesses. Hock Swee bought a house in Johor Bahru and brought his family down. While he spent more and more of his time in Johor, he continued to run the shop in Mersing, as he enjoyed the work.

Unfortunately, Hock Swee suffered from high blood pressure and heart problems. Although sturdily built, he passed away in his early seventies in 1990.

Kuok Khoon Hong was born in Mersing in 1949. I barely remember him from those fishing trips, as he and his older sister, Li Lei, would have been in their cribs or upstairs in the shophouse. He graduated from the University of Singapore in the early 1970s, and joined Kuok Singapore immediately after. By that time we were already doing fairly well in both Malaysia and Singapore.

Khoon Hong quickly learned the ropes of the grains commodities business from our managers, buying grains from Canada, Australia, and sometimes the United States, wherever wheat was of good quality and cheapest. Later, he bought other grains too – corn, soybeans, whatever was in demand. Khoon Hong soon began to fill bigger and bigger shoes. Before long, he was literally working on his own without supervision, but coming to see me maybe two or three times a week.

One day, he told me about an enzyme process developed by a Swiss company to extract oil from soybeans. Soybean oil is a very fine quality cooking oil, and the soybean meal residue left over from the crushing process is still rich in oil and protein. In fact, it is probably the most nutritious component of animal feed. Would I give him permission to pursue the idea? That led to ordering and setting up a plant to do soybean crushing, and from that we later became quite big in the feed-milling industry. Around the same time, we also acquired large tracts of land in the East Malaysia states of Sarawak and Sabah, planted oil palms and began producing palm oil.

Khoon Hong became the driving force of these and other ventures, which later came to be known as Kuok Oils & Grains. After building these businesses in Malaysia, he planned and started, in the mid-1980s, the first edible-oil refinery, import base, storage base, and packaging base in Shenzhen, China, next to Hong Kong. He saw that edible oils were an enormous industry, and that China was a yawning market. He went on building up this segment of our businesses into a very major enterprise, developing horizontally, vertically and geographically.

For the first time, I saw in one of my nephews a businessman who was at least as able as myself. It appeared that in Khoon Hong I had the most capable Kuok ever. That is not to take away from the managerial talent and hard work of my own children and other relatives. It is just that Khoon Hong has a special entrepreneurial talent to see an opportunity and turn it into a thriving business.

One day in early 1991, I was in Hong Kong preparing to attend a dinner party at the Kowloon Shangri-La for the first month celebration of my grandson, Meng Xin, Beau's son. Khoon Hong had arrived from Singapore that day, and at about 6 pm he asked if he could pop in to see me. Since I was getting ready to cross the harbour to attend the party, I was pressed for time and already a bit harried. He came in and said, "Uncle, I would like to take up a little bit of your time and discuss the bonus."

I had been following the results of his department for 1990. That year, he wrongly went long or short (I don't recall which) on some of his major futures transactions. I had glanced at his monthly trading statements through the year and knew that he had made mistakes, and hoped quietly that he would change course in midstream. I strongly believe that no outsider should chime in and give an active trader advice, since that would only tend to upset his trading rhythm. Unfortunately, his rhythm was off that year. The results were very thin. There was no profit at the bottom of the barrel.

It was Khoon Hong's practice to come to me once a year to approve his proposals for a bonus. That year, he made no proposal. He just said, "I want your thoughts on it."

I must have been a bit abrupt, although I don't recall being rude. I said, "Khoon Hong, unfortunately along the way during the year, you read the market wrong and you didn't change tack. There is nothing in the barrel. You know that we pay bonus from profits, so I do not know how to advise you. This is a difficult situation."

He suddenly stiffened and said, "Uncle, I have been meaning for some time now to speak to you about striking out on my own. I now wish to tender my resignation."

Well, that took the breath out of my lungs. I remember saying quite quickly, "Khoon Hong, you are free to come, you are free to go, and you go with my blessing. I wish you luck." I asked if he was going to attend my baby grandson's dinner. He said no. He was going to catch the first plane back to Singapore.

Khoon Hong left the company a few weeks later. Not long after that, I was on a visit to Singapore and received a phone call in my hotel room. He said, "Uncle Nien, it's Khoon Hong here. Can I come up and see you?" I agreed to see him.

He came in and after pleasantries came straight to the point. After first telling me he sensed that morale was very low in the department that he had left behind and that a lot of good people may leave, he asked if I would sell the business to him. I was very taken aback and I put him off. After discussing the matter with my senior managers, it was decided that we would not sell such a large part of our business to anyone. So I turned down Khoon Hong, who was already starting his own business. There was no bickering; it was a straightforward attempt at a business deal.

The only acrimony that I recall relating to the breakup was a legal challenge launched by Khoon Hong's new company claiming that a brand that he had developed while working for Kuok Brothers belonged to them. The brand was first registered in Malaysia and Singapore as "Arawana" and in China it was called "Jin Long Yu", or "Golden Dragon Fish." It is the leading brand for edible oils in China. We won the case and kept the brand.

In the following years, I did not follow Khoon Hong's progress closely because my own companies demanded my full attention. Throughout the 1990s and 2000s, I was deeply involved in the development of commercial properties and hotels in China.

Nevertheless, I would hear little snippets of news that indicated that Khoon Hong was doing well. By 2000, his company had established strong footholds in the edible oils and oilseeds businesses throughout Malaysia, Singapore, Indonesia, India, and mainland China. He had help from some former Kuok Brothers managers, including Pu Jinxin (a former COFCO man who was involved in the sugar deal that I did for the Chinese government in the early 1970s), who left us to work for Khoon Hong.

We were competing with them, but then we were also competing with everyone else. I have always felt that competition is a good thing. The market for edible oils was so big that the real overlap and competition was probably minimal, except that Kuok Oils & Grains had the leading brand in China. It was not something that I experienced personally, as I was busy on other matters and did not actually run Kuok Oils & Grains.

Sometime in 2006, I was in my Singapore office chatting with the different heads of Kuok Group businesses in Singapore, as was my habit. I would start off with the Chairman of Kuok (Singapore) Ltd, Teo Joo Kim, whose specialty was the shipping business. I think it was Joo Kim who mentioned that Khoon Hong's company had gone into fertilizers and therefore was competing with our own fertilizer business. He had also gone into shipping, and therefore was competing with us in shipping as well. Joo Kim expressed his great admiration for the successes of Khoon Hong's business. He said, "You know, Khoon Hong is doing very well lately – very well." And that was the first time I heard this stated in such strong terms. Joo Kim also mentioned that Khoon Hong's public company, Wilmar, was looking to place out a block of shares.

Kuok Khoon Kuan, another nephew of mine, is the Managing Director of our Pacific Carriers Ltd shipping line. At that time, I asked Khoon Kuan if he was in touch with Khoon Hong at all. He said he was, but not often.

I said, "Kuan, could you send word to him that I am interested in acquiring some of his Wilmar placement shares and whether he would consider an application for Wilmar shares from me."

A few hours later, Khoon Kuan called up and said, "Khoon Hong is very happy to hear that you are interested, and he asked how much do you want?" I thought about taking the whole block since I had heard such good things about him and I am always a willing backer of a good horse. But not wanting to show myself to be greedy, I said, "Let's say US$15 million worth." Within hours, I got an answer through Kuan that Khoon Hong was very happy that I was backing him, and his answer was "yes" to the whole amount. I was delighted.

Soon after that, I got an email from Khoon Hong. This was after almost 15 years of no direct communications. I had not even seen Khoon Hong at family gatherings. He sent me a brief, lovely message asking whether he could come and see me. Since he had communicated with me directly, I did not go through Khoon Kuan. I emailed back immediately, "Dear Hong, I am more than delighted anytime, now, tomorrow, whenever." So we met, we chatted, and it was like old times again.

Some months later, I managed to get permission from the local government authorities to land a plane on an airstrip near the Wuyi Mountains, one of the most scenic spots in southern China. I asked Khoon Hong and his mother and sisters to join me on the trip, and we had a wonderful time together. On the way back, we stopped in Fuzhou city to see my mother's little temple, which was in the process of being enlarged from a shrine into a full temple.

Then I heard from a friend that Khoon Hong was thinking of expanding further and was approaching investors for a large commitment. I had never suspected that he wanted to grow so fast. I said to myself, Khoon Hong should have come to me. So I called him up and said, "Is it true what I have heard?" Khoon Hong hesitated and seemed a little embarrassed, but admitted that it was true. I said, "Hong, you can go that way or you can talk with me about a possible merger. There is much more synergy in this direction. Such a merger would give enormous strength to your operations."

He said, "I didn't know that you would be willing to talk with me about this." I think he was nervous because of the earlier breakup. He seemed surprised that a merger could be contemplated, and I think he was delighted with my suggestion.

And from then on it was really a matter of mechanics. My team that handled the merger was headed by Chye, my eldest brother's older son who was then Chairman of Kuok Brothers Malaysia, and my son Beau, who by then had officially been appointed as my successor.

I said to both of them, "Get this done with no hiccups and no small-mindedness. If you think he's getting a slightly better part of the deal, give in. We've got to back this horse. Khoon Hong is the most fantastic businessman you can team up with." In any merger there are on-going issues, different warlords fighting to preserve their little bases. That's why I told my side early on, "Give in, give in, give in." I prefer to see life's big picture. If you nitpick you will never get things done.

Khoon Hong asked me what we should name the combined business. "You decide," I said. "If you like the name Wilmar, use it." So the company is called Wilmar International Limited. Today it is one of the largest companies listed on the Singapore Stock Exchange.

The merger and restructuring were completed in June 2007. After the dust settled, our Group owned about one third of Wilmar's shares. Although there is no legal obligation for him to do so, from the day we merged, Khoon Hong talks to me at least briefly before making any major move.

Our shareholding in Wilmar is one of the largest assets of the Kuok Group – an obvious sign of our trust in Khoon Hong's abilities and honesty as a businessman. Khoon Hong, Martua Sitorus, and Archer-Daniels-Midland Company, the large American agribusiness, are also major shareholders. Khoon Hong is Chairman and CEO, while Martua Sitorus served as Executive Director and COO until March 2017 when he became a non-independent Director. My sons Ean and Hua serve on the board of directors.

As part of the merger, Wilmar acquired assets from Kuok Group companies including oil palm plantations and palm oil mills in Malaysia and Indonesia, edible oils refineries and trading operations in Malaysia, and edible oils and grains processing facilities in China, Bangladesh, Indonesia, Vietnam, The Netherlands and Germany. Wilmar had US$41 billion in revenues in 2016, and reported a net profit of US$972 million for that year. The company has continued to grow apace since the merger, and now has over 500 manufacturing plants, an extensive distribution network covering over 50 countries, and owns a fleet of vessels. Wilmar has a multinational workforce of about 90,000 people.

Wilmar is Asia's leading agribusiness group. Its business activities include oil palm cultivation, oilseeds crushing, edible oils refining, specialty fats, oleo chemicals and biodiesel manufacturing, flour and rice milling and sugar milling and refining. It is a globally leading raw sugar producer and refiner, and owns one of the top consumer brands for sugar and sweeteners in Australia. It is also one of the world's largest producers and merchandisers of palm and lauric (coconut) oils. Its edible oils operations stretch from Europe (where it is the largest refiner in Ukraine) to East Africa (where it is the leading supplier) to India to Southeast Asia to China (where it owns the market-leading brand). It is one of the largest oil palm plantation owners in Malaysia and Indonesia; and the world's largest palm biodiesel manufacturer.

Oil palm is the most economical and efficient producer of vegetable oils, especially in terms of land use, and it is important for the industry to conform and work within societies' expectations, the most important aspect being sustainable development.

In December 2013, Wilmar made a commitment to play a significant role towards sustainable practices by announcing its firm policy of no deforestation, no peat and no exploitation.

Wilmar started up with next to nothing in 1991. Its growth prior to the merger, as well as after the merger, saw revenues nearly double from 2007 to 2010. This confirms my belief that Khoon Hong is a master of business. He has mastered strategic and tactical skills and has the ability to translate his vision into action.

Among other things, he has identified certain production practices in China's rural areas that are centuries old but that can be fairly easily updated to modern practices. He notices such things because he is a hands-on manager and has vision – in addition to working 16 or more hours a day, every day of the year. He goes down to the field, goes to his factories and talks to his managers. He sees that the farmers are as hard-working as ever, maybe even more so, but that not enough attention is being given to quality or yield of crops, processing and refining practices, insect resistance and other productivity issues.

He will supply better seeds to rice farmers, and install the best rice-milling machinery. He has corrected the old practice of mixing the best quality rice with the lowest quality rice at time of harvest, and then milling them together without a quality selection process. Rice bran was being fed to livestock, or used for power generation in antiquated boilers. Khoon Hong showed the farmers that by using the best machinery, which he supplied, better quality grains could be produced, and that valuable rice bran oil could be extracted from rice bran.

Wilmar's policy is to improve food production practices and yields, and to share additional profits with the farmers and other processors. That is the reason why Wilmar has been so successful in the places that it does business. That, and taking care of its vendors and customers, the sellers and the buyers. Such things plus vision, hard work and efficiency are what promote a company's growth. You need hands-on, direct management. For a business to be healthy, it needs to keep growing.

Of course too much growth, too quickly, can be unhealthy as well. It can give rise to envy or anger among people who are unable to compete. Wilmar doesn't do anything except be efficient, but resentment can be the price of efficiency. Too much growth can also give rise to environmental issues. It can give rise to questions about "food security," when a government comes to believe that too much of a nation's food is imported or that too much of the food industry is controlled by "foreigners." And in China, the government can decide to try to control inflation by preventing the price of goods like vegetable oils from increasing, notwithstanding increased costs on the part of the producers. From time to time, Wilmar has had to sell at a loss as a result.

But this is part and parcel of the business that Wilmar is in — basic foodstuffs that are vital to the people. China's leaders are not putting money into their own pockets. They do what they do for the good of the country and for the sake of law and order. This is where Chinese morality and philosophy come into play. The majority of Chinese are honest, moral, obedient and law-abiding, and very supportive of fair and reasonable government measures and laws, especially so when the nation's rulers are honest, selfless, patriotic and when they show love and compassion for their countrymen.

On my part, for my entire adult life, I have strived to bring my cousins and their descendants together under one flag, to keep their bellies full and to send their children to the best schools. Unexpectedly, we came together again in Wilmar. We are working as a team and tackling business problems together. That is a source of great satisfaction to me.

I remain confident that the company that was started by five people in 1949, which has expanded into many associated companies controlled by a parent group, can go on for 150 years. There are now three private holding companies: Kuok Brothers Private Limited, founded in Malaysia in 1949; Kuok (Singapore) Limited, founded in Singapore in 1952; and Kerry Holdings Limited, founded in Hong Kong in 1974. These companies in turn own large or controlling interests in a number of substantial public companies and a handful of smaller ones, as well as private interests in shipping, warehouses, fertilizer, sugar, flour, trading, and other businesses.

In 1993, we bought a controlling interest in SCMP Group Limited of Hong Kong, which publishes the leading English language newspaper in Hong Kong, *South China Morning Post*, from Rupert Murdoch. I feel that an independent media is a crucial component of a fair and orderly society. Perhaps I am old-fashioned in believing that print media is important, given all the new media that have emerged. But I believe in the permanence of print, recording events day in and day out. I don't see that books or newspapers will ever become obsolete, although their form may change.

When I read the *Post* in the morning, I wouldn't agree with everything. But that had never prompted me to try and change the contents. However, if the paper ever printed something libellous, I would have come down very fiercely and told them, "If the paper is sued for libel, you have to be responsible and meet the cost, because the owners did not personally print that news." A paper must publish news, not speculation. For every slanted opinion piece, there should be a proponent for the opposite view. Give the reader a choice, and let the reader decide who has the better argument.

In March 2016, a decision was made to sell *South China Morning Post* to Jack Ma of Alibaba. I was pleased for Jack to take over, as the *Post* is a strategically important newspaper and I felt it should be in good hands.

When the sale was completed, friends asked me how I felt after having owned the *Post* for 24 years. I replied by wiping my brow in relief and saying, "pheww!"

21

THE HIDDEN CAPTAIN

WHEN YOU TRAVEL on a ship, you seldom see the captain. You assume he is up on the bridge. When you go to the bridge, you find a simple sailor working the wheel. But the ship has a sense of stability.

Mother was the captain of our ship. She saw and sensed everything, but, being wise, she didn't interfere. She was the background influence, the glue that bound the Group together.

After I co-founded Kuok Brothers in 1949, I must have appeared to my relatives to be a hell of an obnoxious upstart. I was the youngest of all, yet I ordered every one of them around, and in very rough language. I brooked no delay and no interference; nobody could deny me what I wanted done. When they went grumbling to Mother, she was completely impartial. She counselled patience, and explained that I was only intent on developing the business for the common good. I had no personal agenda.

Kuok Brothers was a funny blend of my rough and tough ways and Mother's soft, Buddhist aura. I cannot believe the sort of man I used to be. In the 1960s, when I was trading with London at night, I routinely used to curse and scream at Piet Yap, Richard Liu and my assistant Lean Chye Huat for any perceived mistake. My temper was searing hot every working minute. I had tremendous outbursts of temper, like Mount Vesuvius erupting. I have been so furious that I have literally seen red before my eyes. I was a monster of a man, really.

I scolded them all, and perhaps poor Richard Liu, who became my right-hand man, most of all. On a few occasions I think I pushed Richard to the limit. About to resign from the Group, he went to see Mother. She would somehow talk him out of it, counselling him not to take personally my awful behaviour and temper. She explained that, like a passing storm, my outbursts would end.

Then she would send for me and ask, "Nien, why are you losing your temper again?" Somehow, through her sense of rhythm, she knew that these passing clouds would not fundamentally injure the Group. It was Mother who always kept the peace and unity.

She kept us focused on the big picture. She counselled us to avoid businesses that bring harm, destruction or grief to people. Her principles have steered me away from businesses like hospitals. How can you insist on charging a sick person who needs care but cannot afford it? I have no problem with operating hospitals as charities, but the relationship between a hospital and a patient is not really a normal business relationship: the hospital has the patient's life in its hands.

She taught my brothers and me never to be greedy, and that in making money one could practice high morality. She stressed that whenever the firm does well, it should make donations to local charities.

One day, she brought three metal plaques to me and said, "Nien, you have offices in Kuala Lumpur, Hong Kong and Singapore. You had better put these up to stare you in the face every morning." On the plaques were words enjoining me never to profiteer, never to become greedy, and to think of the requirements of society.

I mentioned that, commencing in 1974, I traded with Yani Haryanto, through whose hands passed all of the sugar and rice import requirements of the Indonesian nation. In those days, I visited Mother at least twice a month in Johor Bahru. I would brief her on the important developments in the Group. She would invariably urge upon me that, as rice and sugar and all such commodities are essential foods, on no account should I engage in profiteering. I knew exactly what she meant by profiteering. In the commodities trade, if you made between one and a half percent and two percent profit, that was considered pretty fair. Once you started to make over two percent you were beginning to stick in your knife, so to speak.

I put her words into practice in Malaysia, which gave me all of my major start-ups in life – my sugar refinery and my flourmill – for which I'm eternally grateful. When the British sterling was devalued in the early 1970s, it coincided with poor harvests that caused great dislocation in commodity prices. Wheat prices doubled. I was fortunate. Before the price jumped, my intuition told me that something dramatic was going to happen. I instructed my wheat buyers to negotiate for a whole year's supply. We secured 12 to 14 months' requirements. Within weeks the world market went shooting up.

When I saw that my instincts had been confirmed to be correct, I very quickly flew to Kuala Lumpur and made an appointment to see Tan Sri Nasruddin bin Mohamud, Secretary-General of the Malaysian Ministry of Trade and Industry. I explained to Nasruddin what had happened in world wheat markets. I suggested that he issue a questionnaire to the flour millers in Malaysia (we occupied nearly 50 percent of the market), asking how much wheat they had bought, at what price, and so forth. I said, "You have to do this, otherwise the price of your bread and other goods will rise immediately."

I brought in wheat at cost price and kept my selling price of milled flour low. In that act, I surrendered MYR30 million or more to the government, which had price controls on essential foods such as flour. It doesn't take a brilliant mind to realize that I could have transferred that contract of purchase to an offshore company in Geneva or Hong Kong, and then my flourmills could be seen to be buying wheat through those offshore entities. In other words, I could have transferred that windfall profit overseas. But instead, I deliberately chose to calm domestic prices, for I was guided by Mother's exhortations. If you have a mother who beats into you: "Never be the cause of high prices of staple foods, because food staples are the food of the poor," then it sticks with you.

Mother had a very good mind – lucid and totally objective. Very widely read, she kept abreast of every development in Malaysia, Singapore, China, and the rest of the world. So, whenever I had a problem, I went to her. Sometimes, I would just chat with her and never even raise the problem directly, just knock on the fence, so to speak. I would hear her comments and receive enough wisdom to know which turning I should take. If I had extreme frustration with colleagues, I might go to see her, since you have to cry on somebody's shoulders. The few words she uttered after hearing me would always cool me down.

Mother was a devout Buddhist and devoted a minimum of two hours a day to deep prayer. She placed one of those musician's stands in front of her, on which she would place the Buddhist sutras, all in Chinese. She kept reciting and chanting to the prayer beat. As I mentioned earlier, subconsciously I always felt that Mother's prayers, her high moral ways and unselfishness, were in some way protecting me from harm or evil in business dealings, which are often fraught with risk.

I'll mention one example which I recall vividly. One day, my dear friend Jacob Ballas introduced me to a Hungarian-Jewish immigrant to Australia, who had started a company called Hartog PLC. This entrepreneur had a bit of a chequered reputation, but

Ballas assured me the man had reformed, had realized his past sins and was now onto a new track.

I was on one of my sugar-business trips to London in the late 1960s or early 1970s when I received a call from this Australian. He was staying at the Hilton Hotel on Park Lane. Invoking Ballas' name, he invited me to meet with him the following day in his suite. I went at about eleven in the morning.

Chatting with this man was the one time in my life that I almost felt as if I'd been hypnotized. He spun yarns and yarns and yarns and mesmerized me. He put a proposition before me that would have cost me US$20-30 million. Three or four times I was on the verge of agreeing and shaking hands with the man. And Chinese businessmen are men of honour: once we give our word, it's tantamount to a written signature. I've always honoured my word.

At the last minute, something held me back from making that verbal commitment. I told him that I needed to consult my other directors in Singapore. He was like a cat already sensing the kill. I could see in his eyes that he was taken aback at my sudden pause; a sort of disappointment crept in, which woke me up from his spell. I said I'd give him a call in the afternoon, as there was still time for me to return to the Dorchester Hotel and call the directors in Singapore.

Noon in London would be eight o'clock in the evening in Singapore. I returned to the hotel and telephoned Mother. I said, "Mother, I need your advice." I explained the situation, telling her of the mysterious Australian with the Ballas connection.

She said, "Give me two or three minutes, but don't hang up."

She went and consulted her book of oracles. The way Mother did it was like this. She would ask me without thinking too hard to come up with a number. Say I'd pick 67. She'd look up page 67. On page 67 there would be many oracles, but where her eyes alighted, she'd pick that sentence and the explanation of that sentence – the oracle.

She came back to the phone and said, "Son, don't touch it! It is bad poison! It is very dangerous! You will lose every cent you invest!" It was as if a bucket of cold water had been poured on me. I called up the man and said, "No thank you." I never saw him again. I believe, a few months later, his business in Australia collapsed.

That is a classic example of the protection Mother offered. Superstition? Yes, but so much of life is superstition. I had nothing else to go by. I didn't know this man from Adam. He had probably hypnotized my friend Jacob Ballas, who was a very fine man. Lucky for me, I loved Mother so much and always believed in her.

In the late 1970s, Mother sent for her four grandsons at the time: Philip's two sons, Chye and Edward, and my sons, Beau and Ean. (Hua was not yet born). Mother said, "I am getting old. I have no need for money. If anything happens to Hock Nien, then this company should be controlled by the unity of you young boys. I am going to give all my shares to the four of you, equally divided." So all her shares in Kuok Brothers Ltd (she held seven percent at that point) were handed over, and she was left with nothing.

After that, from time to time, the boys sent her money. I made an arrangement with my secretary in Singapore, Lim Siew Hong, to send S$5,000 each month to Mother to ensure that she could meet all of her household expenses. I think all she needed was about S$1,500.

Mother's diet consisted of vegetables and soybeans. She prayed four or five times a day and dressed very simply. Her own wants were so limited that most of the money was in turn dispatched by her to local charities and to charities in Fuzhou and other parts of China. She was an avid reader of the local Chinese press, which loved to report on town tragedies. If there was a tragic accident on the road outside Johor Bahru, in which an impoverished taxi driver was killed and left behind a bedridden widow with five young children, Mother would take the newspaper clipping, get into her car and drive into town. She would go to see my secretary and say, "I want you to send these few thousand dollars to this widow. Convert it to a money order and send it to her. No publicity!" And if a widower looking after children became disabled, she would send money to him, always anonymously.

When Mother died in 1995, she left a small trust to support a Buddhist temple that she had single-handedly organized and built in Skudai, a small village ten miles from Johor Bahru.

As for my wealth, Mother left me with this advice: "Don't squander it all on yourself, son. Leave most of it for your descendants and the foundations you have set up." This harkens back to the Chinese phrase *ji-fu*, "accumulate good fortune." This Chinese philosophy teaches that every person in his or her lifetime is given a quota of good and bad, happiness and sorrow. If you don't use up your quota, through your goodness, the God above will help to pass the benefit on to your descendants. I know that I have enjoyed, and continue to enjoy, the goodness of Mother and my ancestors before her.

About eight years after we'd launched Kuok Brothers on 1 April 1949, I went to my relatives who owned Kuok Brothers shares and said, "It's time we brought a bit of socialism into our company." I persuaded all shareholders to give up 30 percent of the stock, which was put into a pool and sold cheaply to our fellow workers. Thus, the Kuoks' holdings dropped to 70 percent. In my case, I was diluted from 25 percent to 17.5 percent; Mother came down to seven percent, and so on.

Similarly, the Singapore holding company, Kuok (Singapore) Ltd, in the beginning was wholly owned by Kuok Brothers. Then we issued new shares in Kuok (Singapore) Ltd to our managers and other staff. We later sold more shares in Kuok (Singapore) Ltd to the recently hired employees. Today, Kuok Brothers as a company owns no shares in Kuok (Singapore); the two are like sisters in the Kuok Group.

When I moved to Hong Kong and set up Kerry Holdings Ltd, those who moved with me, colleagues such as Richard Liu and Lee Yong Sun, each purchased half a percent to three percent of the new holding company's shares. Even though they didn't move to Hong Kong, Singapore managers including Teo Joo Kim and Goh Soo Siah own blocks of Kerry Holdings, because I felt that a bit of the spiritual force from Singapore came to establish the company in Hong Kong. All of the important producers of wealth in Malaysia and Singapore were given a chance to participate in the shareholding of Hong Kong, and I increasingly delegated management of Southeast Asian operations to them.

One technique I employed from an early stage was to maintain reservoirs of shares in each holding company that were not owned by anyone. I had in mind from day one that my co-workers of the 1960s may no longer be the achievers of the 1970s, the achievers of the 1970s may not be the achievers of the 1980s, and so forth. So, we always kept blocks in reserve to reward the new and future achievers. The shares in these reservoirs fill up, too, because many of the old achievers opt for retirement and cash in their chips. These return to the pool and are recycled to the new achievers. Once people turn from an employee to a shareholder, the attitude changes. If we make a foolish investment they feel the pain too. Not only managers are shareholders: clerks and my wonderful secretary in Hong Kong, Miranda Wong – whoever is a performer and achiever – all have shares.

To a Chinese, family ties are paramount. You are expected to show filial piety to your parents and grandparents, as well as to your wife's. You should demonstrate deep love for your brothers and sisters.

Those who work alongside me, for me or under me, mean a lot to me. I call them my working brothers and sisters, for when you start a company you and your colleagues are really like one family. I have worked more than 60 years of my life with these people, sharing tears and laughter. They almost mean more to me than my biological brothers, though this doesn't diminish my fraternal instincts or love for Mother. It's just that I give almost equal importance to my working brothers and sisters.

And yet, once, our Group nearly split apart. My late fifth cousin, Kuok Hock Chin, who had worked with Father at Tong Seng, became a 25 percent shareholder of Kuok Brothers Ltd when we formed the company in 1949. This stake was equal to mine. Hock Chin was the eldest son of my second uncle, who was in many ways the brother most beloved by Father. Hock Chin, who was educated in English, was loyal to Father.

Hock Chin had seven children. The youngest son, David Kuok, studied accountancy in England. We employed his third son, James. James was first assigned to a department headed by my twelfth cousin, who after several months said to me: "Oh, this nephew of ours won't do." James did things in very funny ways. He often disappeared from the office. So, eventually, we had to let him go. He went out and tried various things with other people in town, but nothing worked out.

After a few years, I took pity on James and rehired him. This time I put him directly under me. Then I realized that all the previous complaints about him were quite accurate. He was a very poor worker. After some time, I said, "James, we can't go on like this. I am traveling most of the time and when I come back my colleagues are full of complaints about you." So we had to let him go again.

At an annual shareholder's meeting of Kuok (Singapore) Ltd in the early 1970s, four of Hock Chin's children, including James and David, suddenly showed up. At the time, I was Chairman and I called the meeting to order. When I came to the accounts item, James said, "Chairman, I want to query the accounts. My brothers, sisters and I, who are shareholders, do not trust these accounts. We think they are cooked."

So I said, "James, the accounts have been audited. What do you want to query?"

He responded, "Please, Mr Chairman. I am not your nephew here now. I am a shareholder asking you questions. Let's keep it formal." I looked at Hock Chin who had his head bowed.

Then allegations poured from James' and David's mouths that the accounts had been improperly drawn up and that there was breach of trust. I harangued them a bit and said I couldn't accept these accusations. Two or three times they repeated that they wanted me to act like Chairman: "This is not a family meeting! Why are you talking like that, Mr Chairman?"

After the meeting I sent for Hock Chin. I said, "Hock Chin, what's up?"

He answered, "I don't know. I can't control my children any more." Hock Chin had smoked opium from his twenties, so he was really a victim of drugs. What went through his mind only he and the drugs he took could understand. He could be hallucinating or he could be telling the truth.

I said, "Well, Hock Chin, you know I am working very hard and travelling all the time. I can't go on like this. If you people are trying to mount a palace coup, only two things can happen. Either you promise me today that you can control your sons or you sell and pull out. Otherwise, it is going to lead to total disaster."

This fratricidal struggle continued for two or three years. Hock Chin's children went around town spreading ill rumours about me while I was just looking after the business. I couldn't consult Mother about the problem. I went to see her once, and was about to raise the subject when I saw a shadow of extreme pain cross her face. She said words like, "Nien, they are also my children. You have to resolve it yourself. I cannot take sides in this affair." It pained her enormously to see the rift in the family, yet, she as the elder, felt she had to remain impartial and not pass judgment in any way.

After years of hostile struggle with Hock Chin's children – they repeatedly threatened to take me to court – we finally reached a settlement. They pulled out of the company and were paid S$25 million for all their shares. I remember telling the eldest son, Peter, a trained lawyer: "Peter, if you people can manage this $25 million cash properly you can outstrip this parent company. If you don't manage it well, it will all turn to ashes."

Unfortunately, the latter scenario came true, as I feared. I knew the children. I knew they would quarrel like cats and dogs. Within weeks of the settlement, brothers quarrelled with brothers, brothers quarrelled with sisters, sisters quarrelled with sisters, mother quarrelled with sons. There were lawsuits amongst them.

A year or so after the settlement, Hock Chin made an appointment to see me. I was in Kuala Lumpur at the time in my Malaysian International Shipping Corp Chairman's office. When he emerged from the lift he was panting quite badly. I asked, "Chin, why is your health in such a bad state?" He alluded to extreme stress in his life. He didn't stop panting and gasping for some time.

Hock Chin informed me that his sons were suing him. James, colluding with his other brothers, claimed that the father had withheld dividends rightfully belonging to the children. Hock Chin said that all those years he just thought it was a father and son situation, so he had never given the matter much attention. The children might have the evidence they needed in their hands.

Hock Chin asked for my help. "If the court case takes place," he said, "can you come and, under oath, give evidence in my favour?"

I replied, "Hock Chin, you are asking me to commit perjury. If I were questioned by your sons' lawyers or by the judge, I would have to speak the truth. I am sorry Hock Chin. I advise you to make peace with your sons."

The poor man said, "I understand, I understand. It's too big a request to ask of you. I've got nothing more to say," and he prepared to leave. I told him, "Hock Chin, do take care of yourself." That was the last time I saw him. He died within a few months.

To me, talent and instincts in business are inborn and cannot be learned in the classroom. The best comparison I can give you is the game of soccer. The best soccer players are born with great innate talent. Even if a person is not born with the ability to be a top soccer player, he can learn to be a good soccer player through good coaching. But he will never be one of the great stars of the game, such as a Pele or a Messi, who are gifted people with inborn skills augmented by good coaching.

I don't have any business models or mentors. I don't compare myself with anyone, and perhaps, in this respect, my pride tells me not to compare myself with anyone. I only compare my policies and philosophies with my own conscience, which is often guided by what Mother would have done, or what my late brother William might have done. I don't consider my way particularly outstanding or unusual. I imagine there must be people who are much more generous than I am.

Each successful businessman must develop his own formula. You must have it in you. I don't believe a man can become a successful businessman merely by reading books. I think it's better to observe the falling leaves than to read someone else's advice. I was influenced by what I saw as shrewdness on Father's part and some of the very human qualities in his business relationships. Mother was wise and made a great impression upon me. But, no one else really influenced me. In fact, in everybody else I saw weaknesses first, and I learned through the reverse mirror. If I observed their weaknesses, I made up my mind never to be like that.

When I hire staff, I look for honest, hardworking, intelligent people. When I look candidates in the eye, they must appear very honest to me. I do not look for MBAs or exceptional students. You may hire a brilliant man, summa cum laude, first-class honours, but if his mind is not a fair one or if he has a warped attitude in life, does brilliance really matter? I would rather hire a stodgy, ordinary college graduate, totally trustworthy and clueful, with good street sense. All my life I have abhorred the thought of only engaging elite people to run my company. Something tells me that they would only lead me to an early disaster. The important thing is unity in the Group: Teamwork, hard work and zero treachery. You don't need to employ Einsteins and Nobel Prize winners to build up a solid enterprise.

In my school days, I hardly ever made it into the top five in class. But even then, as a young boy, I knew that none of those top five would make it in life. They were self-opinionated chaps. Most of them had false values and notions. I thought, "Life on earth is not like that." Students who score brilliant results scholastically are the envy of the majority of their peers. Once they have attained success, very often it turns their heads. When you study their progress in life, they often fail in their later years. Conceit crept in too soon, and at a dangerous age.

When I hire or do business with people, I look closely for traits like vanity. I find that, for the majority of men, the hardest thing for them to do is to admit fault. But if you flatter them, their egos go sky high: flattery is the cheapest form of bribery. You'd be surprised that a high percentage of mankind is vain. Indeed, one of the most important ingredients for a man or a woman to become a success in life is humility. Man must always remain humble because no matter how strong you are today, one day there will be someone stronger than you. Even if you have a lot of material wealth, please remember that you cannot live in isolation; you are always just a member of society.

This brings to mind the Chinese saying: failure is the mother of success. It is true that if a person fails but has enough strength of character, he'll bounce back with even greater vigour. But in the last 30 or more years of my business life, I have come to the conclusion that the reverse phrase is even truer of today's world: success often breeds failure, because it makes you arrogant and incautious.

When someone who is close to you and is still able to see the picture clearly says, "Look here, I don't think it's that way," you now brush him aside. Whereas when you were poorer and struggling you'd say, "Now, say it again," and heed the advice more. So always be humble. Humility has only pluses and no minuses – and it costs you nothing.

In the same manner, I believe man should gradually acquire wealth, working hard. By gradually acquiring it, he knows the meaning of thrift and how to conserve wealth. He becomes more aware of the poverty around him in society because he has been working hard all his life, rubbing shoulders with all sections of the community, and has become intimately aware of the needs of the less fortunate.

Mother's plaques still hang in my offices.

PART VII
–
IN CLOSING

22
STRENGTH OF CULTURE

AT A VERY YOUNG AGE, perhaps four or five years old, I was becoming conscious of Mother's stories, and her frequent exhortations to me and my brothers. Father, his associates, and even the Chinese labourers working in the shop also had wisdom. I learned from them and from their behaviour that I belonged to a people with a very rich culture.

As I grew older, through the 1930s and 1940s, I began to realize that what the Chinese lacked most of all was discipline and unity. With our continuous culture going back thousands of years, I think that there are certain good qualities as well as certain defects in the marrow of our bones.

The Chinese are very hard-working. Wherever they go they will try to earn their own living. Some of these migrants started life in their new homes as rickshaw pullers. So the natives of those regions connect the Chinese with the odour of sweat and say they are a miserable lot. I never got taken in by that nonsense. You have to learn to distinguish between form and essence. If your eyes are always glued to form, it is doubtful that you will ever succeed in life.

The Chinese today don't have to learn about Confucius and Mencius from books. The teachings of Confucius and Mencius are part of our culture; these teachings have been with us since birth. Why, then, are so many Chinese running around today in China and all over the world setting bad examples? It is because of greed.

If the journey towards the goal of civilization is ten thousand miles long, I doubt we have gone even one hundred miles. People make a lot of mistakes in their rush. China has been transformed in 30 years. I have seen many mistakes along the way, but I have also seen a serious effort to turn back and correct mistakes when they are made.

Time and again, it has been proven that capitalism is the best system for advancing the economy. Even China has come to realize this. However, it is equally true that if capitalism is allowed to snowball along unchecked, it can be destructive. I have seen so much of what goes on in the capitalist world that I have become a cynic and a sceptic. Capitalism needs to be inspected under a magnifying glass once a day, a microscope once a week, and put through the cleaning machine once a month.

It is good to be ambitious when you are young, but it is not good to be greedy. In capitalism, man needs elements of ambition and greed to drive him. But where does ambition end and greed take over? There are ingredients of greed in every human heart. I think if you take 10,000 businessmen, it would be very, very difficult to find one without greed.

That is why I say that capitalism, if left to its own devices, will snowball along, roll down the hill and cause a lot of damage. A sound capitalist system requires strong, enlightened governments. The leaders must be politician-statesmen willing to put the good of their nations and the people above their individual self-interest. I recoil from politicians who are there for fame and glory, or to line their pockets. True leaders are those who come out of the community and govern to raise the people to greater heights.

I sometimes think that most of the noise made about capitalism and communism is half-truth and half-mirage. There is no absolute thing called capitalism; there is no absolute thing called communism.

The day capitalism becomes oppressive, repressive, selfish and self-centred, it will start to self-destruct. For capitalism to survive, it has to mix its glassful of capitalism from time to time with spoonfuls of communism. By communism, I mean a society must become more compassionate, and must put into practice social institutions that cream the wealth from the rich and spread it on the butter-less bread of the poor.

The American capitalist system is often held up – at least by Americans – as a model for the world. Frankly, I have never had much faith in American capitalism. I have dealt with American businessmen from the mid-1960s. Long before the financial turmoil of the past decade, I recoiled from the capitalism of Wall Street. I think business should be approached with humility, whereas in America I see it being approached with arrogance, roughness and a near total lack of humanity. You almost have to become arrogant, otherwise you won't survive in that hostile world. That kind of environment does not appeal to me.

America's greatest problem is that its culture is based on materialism. The economic tsunami of 2007 and 2008 was fed by no-money-down mortgages and credit card debt, all to support consumption on a crazy scale. The reverberations from that excess are still being felt all over the world.

In its 5,000-year history, I doubt that China has had as enlightened a group of leaders as during the past 30 years. They wanted their country to grow, and their people to prosper. Few leaders today compare with China's in terms of true patriotism, selfless devotion to duty, and complete willingness to dedicate their lives to the causes of nation-building and raising the peoples' standard of living.

There was a period where I think the Chinese leaders misunderstood Confucianism, or they deliberately did not want

Confucian values passed on to young people. They eschewed every religion, and Confucianism was seen as the religion of old China. Mao wanted the people to replace their old thinking with communist idealism. However, in the process, he overlooked the barbarism that still exists in man's hearts and minds. It is easy to talk about all human beings being equal, but all men are not equal, and barbaric instincts still course through our veins.

In my business travels around China, I often came across incompetent or bigoted officials. Nearly every time I had a major tussle with one, or I met a dubious vice governor or mayor, I would come back and, in my judgmental way, tell my colleagues, "How can that man run such-and-such a city?" And sure enough, the next time I visited the place, say a year later, the man had been removed and a better man was in his place. I began to note to myself and to others that in Southeast Asia, a bad egg gets promoted; in China, a bad egg is removed.

Still, I think more can and should be done to root out nonperformers. I have a wonderful colleague named David Pang who helps out with our companies' efforts to lift the poor around China from conditions of extreme poverty. We are trying to open up the sky above their heads and offer them hope. Through this effort, we have come into contact with many local village officials. The quality of these officials varies greatly; the more corrupt ones are all talk and no action.

David Pang told me a sad story about a very bright young man from a small village who made it to the top university in China. After graduating, he went back to his village to share his knowledge. He is a man with a good heart, but after 20 years, he had lost all his vigour and energy and dreams. He became a forgotten soul captured by the bureaucratic web. His superiors think poorly of him because he challenges their intellect. He is bullied and ignored.

There are many individuals like him throughout China, individuals who want to do good things and improve the lives of those around them but who are stymied by vain and arrogant officials.

I was invited to meet Deng Xiaoping in the autumn of 1990. He impressed me as a very fine and humble human being. He was by then an elderly man, but from the moment he saw me his whole behaviour – his smile and his body language – was like that of an eager young man seeking to make a new friend. In none of his actions or words was there a hint of: "I am a great leader of a great nation. Who are you?" You could sense that the man was never thinking of himself. He was all for the people, his people.

When we sat down, his first words were to thank and to praise the Overseas Chinese for their contribution to the birth of the new China, and for the major role they had played and were continuing to play in China's economy. Then he said several things that still stick in my mind. One was: "In 30 years' time, China will be the most important and strongest nation in Asia, which will by then be the strongest continent in the world." There was no hint of arrogance in Deng's voice. It was as if he were a wizened sage looking into his crystal ball and describing what he saw. He stated it very humbly, and then he added words to this effect: "I shall not live to see that day, but I have no doubt that it will become true."

He also said, "Mr Kuok, they all say I am the one that is bringing this huge and rapid development to China. They are wrong. When I opened the door for China, they were all pushing me from behind. They are still pushing me." He wasn't trying to gain more credit by trying to divert the credit. He just said the truth. The people want economic progress.

Then Deng spoke at length on the Taiwan issue. He said, "I have offered them more than I was prepared to give Hong Kong. They will be given everything that I gave Hong Kong, in addition to which they can maintain their armed forces, and renew and update their weaponry. All I ask is that we are one unified nation again; one flag, one foreign ministry, one people. There can be no other way forward for China!"

He smiled throughout the meeting and I thought he was a very kind, friendly man, totally unselfish. But when he spoke on Taiwan, for the first time I saw in the man a sense of extreme frustration.

That was the first and only time I saw Deng. I later heard through Chinese friends in Beijing that mine was the last official meeting granted by the government. After that, a curtain came down and his only visitors were family or close friends.

China is still transforming. When you talk of the transformation of a nation of more than 1.36 billion people, it is too great for one single human mind to follow. Imagine an elephant that is so enormous in girth that if you are standing right in front, you cannot imagine it in its entirety.

The years of experimenting with extreme left-wing communism have had adverse side effects on Chinese society. One effect is that many grew up without a strong moral compass. They acted as though your wealth should be shared with them. While they professed to share their wealth with you – they knew full well that they had nothing. I used to tell Chinese cadres: "That is not communism; it is highway robbery! You people are even indecent in not telling the truth to yourselves."

To my mind, the two greatest challenges facing China are the restoration of education in morals and the establishment of the rule of law.

A moral society cannot be attained through policing. You must begin at the beginning, and infuse the young with a strong sense of morality from a young age, both at home and at school. For centuries, Confucian principles provided China's moral compass;

they can do so again.

The second important point is that China must strive to understand and implement the rule of law. This is more important than implementing democracy. It is a basic principle of the rule of law that everyone is equal before the law. In China today we have rule by man. Under the rule of law, even the General-Secretary of the Communist Party is not above the law.

I know many believe that it is impossible for a communist party to accept the rule of law. But I think that, if the Chinese Communist Party is to survive, the leaders of the Communist Party must adapt. Otherwise, the people of China will reject them and cast them out.

I only hope that the Communist Party will take the lead in implementing the rule of law. It will require a gigantic effort, as the culture must change and the legal infrastructure must be created. You have to train upright judges and lawyers to uphold the legal system. This may take 20-30 years, but it must start today. If the Party succeeds in this monumental task, then the road ahead for China is filled with hope for all mankind.

23
RESILIENCE AND RETIREMENT

I RETIRED, or at least tried to retire, in August 1999. I made up my mind that I would step back from the management of the Kuok Group, although I would still continue my trading activities for the Group, as I had honed my trading skills over the decades. However, it turned out that my retirement was only temporary. For me, work is the permanent state.

What made me think about retirement in 1999 was the knowledge that we are mortal creatures. I have seen friends drop dead at 30 years old, 40 years old, 50 years old; by 1999, I was 76 years. I was suffering from a painful spinal condition, which fortunately was later greatly relieved through surgery. I thought that, for the good of the business, I should distance myself from the company and let others get on with running it.

Thus, I made up my mind to retire, not because I was afraid of work or the challenges I might face, but because I was worried that the grass would not grow where I trod. I wanted to stand aside and see my successors at work. And I had two senior aides who had been with me for decades: my son Beau, whom I put in charge along with several others, and Richard Liu, who had been by my side since 1967.

All of that seemed rational and logical in theory but, in practice, I had always been a strong driver of all things in our businesses – right down to being involved in determining employee bonuses. So, even though I stopped going to the office during those years, I lived just a few kilometres away. There would be many visits to my home, and I was always contactable by phone. I think the people who succeeded me continued to feel my presence. The fact that I was available prevented them from filling the vacuum. Indeed, correctly speaking, there was no vacuum. I was still around. The experiment did not turn out brilliantly.

Two tragic incidents in 2003 were the trigger for my return to the office. I had handed the reins of the Group to my son Beau, and my former chief aide Richard Liu played the same role to Beau as he had to me. Then, in February 2003, without any warning, Richard suffered a fatal heart attack. That same month, the dreadful Severe Acute Respiratory Syndrome (SARS) virus arrived in Hong Kong. The then unknown virus spread rapidly from there. Richard's death and the damage being done by SARS persuaded me to come out of retirement and try to get to grips with the problems facing the Group.

Richard was born in Kuala Lumpur on 6 October 1941. His Chinese name was Liu Tai Fung. He accompanied me on virtually every business trip I took from the late 1960s. He was private secretary, number one aide, and number one pupil. As a consequence, he often bore the brunt of my impatience and temper, and sometimes thought about resigning. On at least two occasions he had gone to Mother to say: "I can't take it anymore, Grandaunt, I can't take it anymore." But he was loyal, honest, and dependable, and he stayed with the Group until the day he died.

My last meeting with Richard was a few weeks before his death. Beau and Richard asked if they could come to see me together. This had never happened before. When they arrived, Beau turned to Richard and asked him to speak first.

Richard was agitated, the most worried I had seen him for a

long time. He said, "Mr Robert (he called me Mr Robert because there were so many Mr Kuoks), things are not going smoothly." Although he was careful not to speak too forcefully in the presence of my son Beau, his current boss, some of his remarks had thorns in them. He concluded by saying, "We can't go on like this."

Now, speaking like that in the presence of Beau was tantamount to disrespect, because Beau was Richard's boss. I thought this was untypical of Richard, very untypical. How could Richard burst out like that? But it was spontaneous, as if a lid on a boiling pot had blown off.

A few weeks after this incident, my wife Pauline and I were in London with our young daughters, Hui and Yen, and were about to take a flight to Geneva for a skiing holiday. It was 1 February 2003, and we had just checked in at Heathrow airport. I went off to buy a magazine and, when I returned, Pauline casually said that Beau had just called, and would call back in five minutes.

Barely three minutes passed and my phone rang. Beau said, "Dad, I have very bad news." My heart fell.

"It's Richard," he said, and my heart fell lower.

"Richard is dead."

Richard had died sitting at the departure gate at Kuala Lumpur airport, about to board his plane.

The scene of Richard's outburst about Beau suddenly flashed through my mind. The Han Chinese have an old saying, a sort of superstition, that goes something like this: "A man who is about to die sometimes displays certain unusual signs." It may have been an omen.

I was completely shattered. We decided that Pauline and I would fly back to Asia, and that the children would continue with their holiday. I am not ashamed to say that I cried for hours on that long journey back to Hong Kong. I was heartbroken that this man who had served me so faithfully for so long, whom I had scolded in my earlier, rough days, had died so young and so suddenly.

As we flew into darkness, I kept my little reading lamp on and handwrote my farewell to Richard in an attempt to rid myself of guilt and doubt and pain. My tears fell on the paper. I hid all that from Pauline. It was as if I were talking to Richard, and Richard alone. I never showed the letter to anyone, but after attending the funeral I gave the letter to his eldest son and told him that I had poured my heart out with grief over his father's death.

I cannot escape the feeling that I might have hastened Richard's death by putting too much pressure on him. At the same time, I wondered how he could allow his health to get into that state without speaking up. I was retired at the time, and I saw no signs – in fact, I rarely saw Richard. I have wondered, if I had not retired, would I have been able to save him? He died at the age of 61.

As the world came to know in 2003, SARS is an acute virus that crossed the species barrier between bats and humans. From the initial detected infection in a doctor from Guangzhou who stayed at the Metropole Hotel in Hong Kong, the disease spread exponentially. At Prince of Wales Hospital, doctors and nurses succumbed. A renal patient who had gone to the hospital for dialysis treatment caught the disease, and infected hundreds at Amoy Gardens, a residential estate in Hong Kong, when he visited his brother there and used the toilet. Sadly, one of those who was infected and died was a project manager in our property development business.

China and Hong Kong were particularly hard hit, and the World Health Organisation issued an advisory against travel to infected areas. Our business suffered greatly. The Island Shangri-La in Hong Kong has 565 keys (rooms and suites), and several restaurants. The place was uncannily silent. I said to the manager, under my breath, "What is the occupancy?"

His reply: "Two percent."

The newspapers were full of stories about companies retrenching. Even then, I refused to think about laying off staff. In the hospitality industry, our employees are the lifeblood of our business. I stood in the shoes of my employees, and thought that I would be casting them out into the desert. How could they go home to face their families, I thought. I urged our managers to show resilience.

So, we waited. And fortunately, about two months later, the dark clouds lifted. International cooperation stemmed the spread of the disease. The amazing researchers in medicine at the University of Hong Kong and the Chinese University of Hong Kong decoded the virus, identified its origins and the path of transmission. Many who were ill were gradually nursed back to health, and with effective isolation of patients the spread of the disease was slowed, and then stopped. SARS had been conquered. The whole world breathed a sigh of relief.

The road to success is paved with challenges, and, with each test or failure, a man must show resilience. If you tread a hard and stony road toward your goal, you develop greater resilience and objectivity as you go along. Worrying never provides the solution to a problem. In fact, worrying exacerbates the problem. It weakens the mind and eventually the physique to the point where people die from frustration, from worrying about their failure.

There must always be a strong degree of resilience in management teams. I think the Kuok Group has displayed this over the years. There is an understanding in the Group that we succeed through knowing our business, through hard work and through a strong adherence to fiduciary values. There is no reason that these same ingredients will not produce new and bigger fortunes down the road, as long as we can bounce back from any setback.

Problems must not be seen as brick walls. You can walk through a problem. Penetrate it and go on to the other side; forget it and start life afresh. Perhaps you have to start from zero again, but you always have a chance in life. You may not make it, but at least you have a chance.

Stay focused, work hard, and work intelligently. Many people think that shyness is a great virtue. Well, if you want to join the business world, leave that outside your door. You have to be thick-skinned, able to take knocks. You will be insulted; you will have people slam doors in your face. But there is always another door, another road, and a way to forge on.

The Kuok Group of companies today is like a banyan tree. It started as a tiny sapling in 1949. Now it has many boughs and branches. Over the course of 60 and some years, I have been responsible for tending those branches, and ensuring they remained healthy. Now, many people are taking care of the branches, including my sons and their senior managers. Still, they turn to me before making major decisions. And because the branches are so numerous, I am kept busy day and night. The conversations end with the ball back in their court. But I suppose I will continue to have such conversations as long as I live. So much for retirement.

24
WHAT IS WEALTH FOR?

THE LAWS OF MORALITY are as sure and powerful as the natural law of gravity. Under this universal law, you reap what you sow. When you violate fairness and true justice, it will come back to haunt you.

When you see a man getting very rich, and you know he's mean, indecent, or even crooked, don't envy him! Businessmen who commit immoral acts will get their comeuppance. Treat people with respect and dignity, and they will do the same to you. If two or three of them are bereft of morality and later turn their backs on you, you still have 97 or 98 who will stand by you. Those without morality will have no one.

Before you enter business, you should vow that in whatever you do, you will be guided by the laws of morality. This will ensure long-term survival. Adopt good, clean and honourable means of doing business; avoid dirty, tricky and unscrupulous methods. Immoral ways will only result in your own character degenerating from good to bad to worse. That is what I have observed in my working life, stretching back over 70 years.

I attribute my attention to principles and morals in conducting business to Mother's influence. She taught me to lead a proper and reasonable life, and not to commit excesses. My upbringing by Mother and her lasting influence have enabled me to stand separate from myself, and study my actions and the actions of other businessmen in an objective way.

Mother was very strict with herself, denying herself pleasure and enjoyment. She told me countless times, "We human beings are born to suffer; we are not born onto this earth to luxuriate or to enjoy life." Leading by example, her message came down loud and clear to all of us. I have, quite frankly, yet to come across anyone who has replicated Mother's strict discipline.

I am made of somewhat different stuff. As a child, I often experienced economic want and hunger. If a servant broke a cup in the kitchen, even Mother would rail at her. I saw misery etched on that servant's face. I was gripped with the question: how do we rise above poverty? Answer: acquire wealth. I am not the arbiter of the good or evil of money, but since wealth is part of our society I felt compelled to step onto the playing field.

But then, having acquired wealth, what do you do with your money? Wealth isn't an end in itself. Wealth helps you to achieve things, but money itself does not make people happy. You soon learn that even the sweetest of material pleasures are at best only a passing cloud. Some of the happiest days of my life were the months that we spent in the pineapple plantation in the Johor jungle from early January 1942 during World War II. We had few material goods, and yet I have fond memories of those days

What makes people unhappy is greed. You have something, but you are still not satisfied. I have seen greed in my lifetime that is beyond human description. Money creates greed, and it can be a horrible thing to witness.

I could leave all of my wealth to my children. I will not. In fact, I am troubled even by the concept of inheritance; it can be corrosive, upsetting their balance and leaving their moral compass askew. Do you really want to harm your children and grandchildren like that? Mother's words make a lot of sense: "If your children are like you, they do not need any inheritance from you. If they are not like you, of what use is your inheritance to them?"

So, then, what is wealth for? Surely, it is to leave the world a better place for your descendants and for all mankind. Wealth should be used for two main purposes. One: to invest and re-invest in creating new and better opportunities. Two: for the betterment of mankind, either by acts of pure philanthropy or by investment in research and development along the frontiers of science, healthcare and so forth.

I derive great satisfaction from creating wealth and jobs through investment. To me that is the positive side of life. The Kuok Group employs tens of thousands of people in Asia, and I believe that we are a decent and caring employer. We also contribute to the daily welfare of society by supplying staple foods in an efficient manner. For example, in Malaysia, we not only grow and refine sugar and mill wheat into flour, but we have also built a very fine distribution chain, so that sugar and flour reach the consumer at very affordable prices. We do the same with vegetable oils.

I have given freely to charities throughout my life. I feel everyone must think of his fellow beings and how you can help those who are less fortunate than yourself. Mother constantly impressed this upon me. If each and every man helped the less privileged, we would all live in a saner world.

My philanthropic views were also very much influenced by some of my dear friends in England. I am by instinct mercenary. Alan Clatworthy, who was a senior partner in ED&F Man, is an especially un-mercenary man. Alan often reminded me: "Robert, you can't take it with you." I have no interest in parading my philanthropy, but the very act of helping my fellow beings gives me a happiness and satisfaction that has no equivalent. And when your mind is happy, then your body is more likely to stay healthy. Hence that wonderful Latin motto: *mens sana in corpore sano*.

The first three charitable foundations I established were the Kuok Foundation in Kuala Lumpur; the Zheng Ge Ru Foundation in Hong Kong, named after Mother; and the Joyce M Kuok Foundation, commemorating my first wife, also in Hong Kong. With the Kuok Foundation, my intention was to have a foundation worth MYR100 million. Through good investments, that foundation is today worth hundreds of millions of dollars, and every year it spends more on charitable activities than the seed money that we put into it.

I thought it was particularly appropriate to name the latter two foundations after the two wonderful women who have had a tremendous influence on me, my children and on my brother Philip's children. Mother and Joy have, in direct and indirect ways, imbued our Group with the values of honesty, integrity and humility, working hard toward our goals of creating more wealth and using that wealth to reinvest in job-creating businesses.

I have established a trust to honour my present wife, Pauline. But as she is in good health, from a sense of karma and to protect her well-being, I added my name to the trust. It is called the He Nian-Po Lin Trust, and one day it will be converted into a full foundation.

The objectives of these foundations are to invest wisely and manage the donated assets, and to dispense the annual proceeds to help the needy and underprivileged. Thus, we keep the golden goose healthy and use its eggs to provide for education and health. These foundations and the private holdings of Kuok family members own a controlling interest in the Kerry Group holding company.

Since charity begins at home, I also established a trust for Kuok Group employees into which fairly significant blocks of shares were transferred. This trust is devoted to paying for the medical and other needs of employees.

I hope and trust that Mother's grandchildren and great grandchildren will carry and pass the baton of unselfishness and generosity towards their fellow beings. Each succeeding generation of Kuok Group leaders should continue to work, not only to feed themselves and their children, but also to try and feed as many of the less-fortunate in society as possible.

Mother instilled this morality and philosophy into me. She taught that a good name and good health are prerequisites for acquiring wealth. If you achieve wealth, but you do not have a good name or good health, then your whole family is travelling on a short, dead-end road. You have no future.

I believe that the ultimate goal in life should be to adopt moral values and to emphasize morality in all actions, so as to achieve a more fair and just world. This is, of course, a lofty ideal that may not be achievable. But so long as you strive toward it, you're contributing to a better world.

What gives me confidence about the next generation of Kuoks is that they each carry with them some of Mother's wisdom. They may not be as steeped in Mother's thinking and philosophy as I am, but they are her disciples. Mother's spirit will live on as the driving force in the Kuok Group of Companies.

How will things turn out? I remember having a visit a few years ago from an American doctor friend. This doctor is a genius of a spinal surgeon in New York, who performed a very complex and successful operation on me in 2000. On the night before he was to return to America, my wife and I gave him and his companion a small dinner at our home in Hong Kong.

Toward the end of dinner, he came up behind my chair, tapped me on the shoulder, and said, "Sometime in the future you'll feel this on your shoulder, and when you turn round it's me."

Now, in the context of our conversation, he meant 50 or 100

years hence. So I said, "Doctor, what do you mean?"

He said, "Because I strongly believe that when we die our souls remain."

And I said, "Doctor, you're a man of science. Do you really believe that our souls remain?"

He was equally amazed, and said, "But don't you believe? Why don't you believe that we have souls?"

I said, "Well, honestly, my most beloved Mother left me 12 or 13 years ago. I have had no feeling, no communication with her whatsoever. How can you expect me to believe there is such a thing as a soul? And my most beloved brother, my second brother who was killed in the jungle tragically in 1953, I have longed somehow to see him, feel him. But there has been nothing."

I am essentially a fatalist. Just as man is mortal, I believe that everything created by man will also perish. The bronze and porcelain objects from China's distant past may be lasting, but most of man's creations have a more limited lifespan. If the Group in something like its present form has a 150-year run, I would be a very happy man indeed.

Over the years, we have established various charitable foundations and trusts that, together with my personal holdings and the shares owned by my children, control the Group. If, after I am gone, my descendants stay united and have a shared purpose in life, and understand that for the Group to survive there must be more to life than the pursuit of wealth, I will be satisfied.

POSTSCRIPT

Years have passed since I wrote most of my memoirs. In this postscript, my aim is to update my thoughts on the rise of modern China and the importance of maintaining personal health and sound values.

XI JINPING'S CHINA

The world is now witnessing a spiritual rejuvenation in China led by Xi Jinping.

In my lifetime, I have followed the astonishing transformation of China. I grew up hearing daily tales of the country being in a horrible state. After many decades of misrule, internal strife and foreign oppression, the country was ripe for a revolution. The People's Republic of China was founded by Mao Zedong and his amazingly able colleagues on 1st October 1949. But Mao was no genius at economics or commerce, and when the economy suffered setbacks, he was criticized by those around him. Mao got mad and thought he would use a fire torch to burn the pestering ants along the edges of the house, not realizing that the house was bone dry, and that it would burst into flames and set off the Cultural Revolution, which eventually left the nation shattered.

After a period wracked by extreme instability and political intrigue, Deng Xiaoping came to power. He saw the right direction for his people and personally led them for about fifteen years. I met him in the Great Hall of the People in Beijing in September 1990 and was struck by his humility. He said that he did not deserve the peoples' acclaim that he was responsible for the country's booming economy and rising prosperity. He said: All I did was to open the door, but it was the people charging up behind and they pushed me through the door. I found Deng to be a wise and compassionate leader: a great man indeed.

After Deng had ushered in a time of increasing prosperity, there developed the disease of greed and decay.

Fortunately for China and its people, Xi Jinping assumed leadership of the country in November 2012. What he has accomplished in just five years is truly amazing. He has greatly reduced corruption in the government bureaucracy, in state-owned enterprises and in the armed forces. The economy had been developing in too uncontrolled a manner (excess capacity in steel, cement, and aluminium, etc.), and some of the agonies due to enforced adjustments are now being felt.

Xi realized it was not just the body but also the mind and spirit where decadence had entered Chinese society and systems. He is fostering mental, physical, moral and spiritual rejuvenation. It is a difficult job because China is relatively affluent now. Leaders have an easier job when the people are poor and have nothing to lose.

Xi is effectively bringing China into the modern age by dismantling, step by step, the feudal attitudes and officious practices which have been deeply ingrained in Chinese society.

From my knowledge of Xi Jinping, he is selfless, compassionate, patriotic, with a profound knowledge of Chinese history and culture. He is putting good practices in place, which will further transform China. He may need several more years to put his imprint on the country, but I firmly believe that history will honour him as one of China's greatest leaders.

A HEALTHY MIND IN A HEALTHY BODY

I am now in my tenth decade. Reflecting back on 75 years in business, I realize that strong physical and mental health are vital for a long and successful business career and critical for the ability to bounce back from the inevitable adversities along the way. I have always liked the Latin phrase *mens sana in corpore sano*, "a healthy mind in a healthy body," which was my early school's motto. Nearly everyone I meet now asks how I keep so healthy at the age of 94.

The golden rule for good health is to lead a simple life, physically and mentally.

From my teens until the age of 90, I was, fortunately, able to turn adverse situations into a positive shaping of my life. After the Japanese Fascist regime invaded and conquered Malaya, they forced us to advance our clocks 1½ hours to Tokyo time.

I would sleep at Tokyo time 9 pm (7.30 pm Malayan time). Early every weekday morning I would ride my bicycle through darkened streets to a small Indian vegetarian restaurant four doors away from the Mitsubishi office where I worked. There I would sit among Indian workers and enjoy a simple vegetarian pancake dipped in curry sauces, followed by a cup of very hot coffee with fresh milk.

This simple living turned out to be the strong foundation for my health.

From 1942 to 1945, I was in charge of cigarettes imported by Mitsubishi, which had a trade monopoly on rice and tobacco. The cigarettes were imported from Japan or Thailand. I would open a packet of cigarettes, offer them around to the other staff and smoke a few myself. Then I would come down with a bad sore throat and cough my lungs out for over a week. Invariably, two or three months later I would be tempted to smoke again; and again I would get sick. I developed an extremely bad case of tonsillitis. The end result was that after a year or so I decided it was not worth it. I did not smoke again until the late 1970s when I started to visit Cuba. My Cuban friends would put boxes of Havana cigars in my hotel suite, and I would pretend to be James Bond. I again came down with a sore throat, so cigars too went out the window.

My point is that from bad luck I was saved from worse luck. Cigarettes are nothing but poison.

My favorite protein is fish, and I will eat most seafood, including different types of shellfish. Vegetables and fruits are also the best foods that one can have. My mother became a devout Buddhist and total vegetarian at about the age of 45. She lived until 95 in relatively good health.

I do believe in the modern medical advice that every seven days, one must eat over 20 different kinds of food. In addition, the Chinese through thousands of years of trial and error have found certain foods and ways of cooking which are good for your health.

Healthy values are also crucial. To achieve happiness and live a contented life, I believe there are some important practices every person should adopt and cultivate. Number one is to curb envy and jealousy. Number two is to curb greed.

You need some greed to propel yourself forward; it is the rocket fuel that motivates you. Without greed there is no successful capitalism. But beyond a limit, greed becomes a disease, and is increasingly becoming the curse of mankind.

If you are able to catch 10 fish and are satisfied with six fish, you are always going to be happy; if your ability is limited to catching 10 fish but you desire 20 or 30 fish, then you will never be happy.

Greed can lead to the total destruction of this earth and the people living on it. We must find a balance.

I believe that every person is allotted a quota of good luck and a quota of bad luck. Leading a virtuous life opens the tap of good luck; living an immoral life blocks the flow of good luck.

There is no doubt that some people are born more able than others and with bigger doses of good luck. If you get lucky and then share what you have with people around you, it gives you a sense of happiness that is unmatchable. With happiness and contentment normally comes longevity.

Learn to be humble. Genuine humility must be inner humility, guided by compassion towards your fellow beings. I have found that if a person is truly humble, most people will do anything for him; but if he is a cocky person, out of 20 "friends," barely two will help him.

I would like young people to take stock of what life on earth is really about. Do not confuse material satisfaction with happiness. Money cannot do everything for you. Distinguish between the real and the fanciful. Learn to live simply and, whenever you can, share your wealth with others. You are not alone in this world. There is immense wisdom handed down from ancient sages such as Laozi, who taught that to live a contented life, one should eschew greed and live as simply as possible and in harmony with nature.